THE COMPLETE WORKS OF ROBERT BROWNING, VOLUME XVI

Photograph of Robert Browning, London, 1885.
Courtesy of the Armstrong Browning Library.

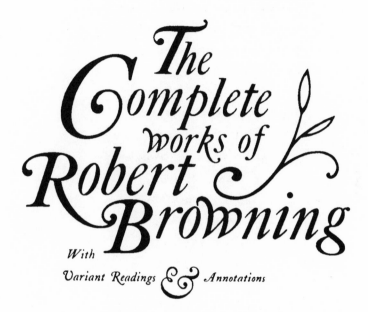

The Complete works of Robert Browning

With Variant Readings & Annotations

Volume XVI

EDITED BY

SUSAN CROWL

ROMA A. KING, JR.

BAYLOR UNIVERSITY

WACO, TEXAS

OHIO UNIVERSITY PRESS

ATHENS, OHIO

1998

THE COMPLETE WORKS OF ROBERT BROWNING

ALLAN C. DOOLEY, Executive Editor

JACK W. HERRING, General Editor

PARK HONAN, Founding Editor

ROMA A. KING, JR. Founding Editor

JOHN C. BERKEY

MICHAEL BRIGHT

ASHBY BLAND CROWDER

SUSAN CROWL

SUSAN E. DOOLEY

DAVID EWBANK

RITA S. PATTESON

PAUL TURNER

Ohio University Press, Athens, Ohio 45701
© 1998 by Ohio University Press and Baylor University
Printed in the United States of America
All rights reserved

03 02 01 00 99 98   5 4 3 2 1

Ohio University Press books are printed on acid-free paper ∞ ™

Library of Congress Cataloging-in-Publication data
(Revised for vol. 16)

Browning, Robert, 1812–1889.
The complete works of Robert Browning, with variant readings & annotations.

Vol. 16 edited by Susan Crowl and Roma A. King, Jr.
Includes bibliographical references and indexes.
I. King, Roma A., 1914–   , ed.
II. Title.
PR4201.K5 1969 821'.8   68-18389
ISBN 0-8214-1251-5 (v. 16)

CONTENTS

	Page Number
PREFACE	vii
TABLES	xxi
ACKNOWLEDGMENTS	xxv
PARELYINGS WITH CERTAIN PEOPLE OF IMPORTANCE IN THEIR DAY	5
Apollo and the Fates—A Prologue	5
With Bernard de Mandeville	20
With Daniel Bartoli	33
With Christopher Smart	48
With George Bubb Dodington	58
With Francis Furini	71
With Gerard de Lairesse	95
With Charles Avison	112
Fust and His Friends—An Epilogue	130
POEMS BY ELIZABETH BARRETT BROWNING (1887)	
Prefatory Note	155
POETICAL WORKS (1888-89)	
Title Page	159
Dedication	163
Contents	165
EDITORIAL NOTES	173

I CONTENTS

This edition of the works of Robert Browning is intended to be complete. It will comprise at least seventeen volumes and will contain:

1. The entire contents of the first editions of Browning's works, arranged in their chronological order of publication. (The poems included in *Dramatic Lyrics, Dramatic Romances and Lyrics,* and *Men and Women,* for example, appear in the order of their first publication rather than in the order in which Browning rearranged them for later publication.)

2. All prefaces and dedications which Browning is known to have written for his own works and for those of Elizabeth Barrett Browning.

3. The two prose essays that Browning is known to have published: the review of a book on Tasso, generally referred to as the "Essay on Chatterton," and the preface for a collection of letters supposed to have been written by Percy Bysshe Shelley, generally referred to as the "Essay on Shelley."

4. The front matter and the table of contents of each of the collected editions (1849, 1863, 1865, 1868 [70, 75], 1888-1889) which Browning himself saw through the press.

5. Poems published during Browning's lifetime but not collected by him.

6. Poems not published during Browning's lifetime which have come to light since his death.

7. John Forster's *Thomas Wentworth, Earl of Strafford,* to which Browning contributed significantly, though the precise extent of his contribution has not been determined.

8. Variants appearing in primary and secondary materials as defined in Section II below.

9. Textual emendations.

10. Informational and explanatory notes for each work.

II PRIMARY AND SECONDARY MATERIALS

Aside from a handful of uncollected short works, all of Browning's works but *Asolando* (1889) went through two or more editions during his lifetime. Except for *Pauline* (1833), *Strafford* (1837), and *Sordello*

(1840), all the works published before 1849 were revised and corrected for the 1849 collection. *Strafford* and *Sordello* were revised and corrected for the collection of 1863, as were all the other works in that edition. Though no further poems were added in the collection of 1865, all the works were once again corrected and revised. The 1868 collection added a revised *Pauline* and *Dramatis Personae* (1864) to the other works, which were themselves again revised and corrected. A new edition of this collection in 1870 contained further revisions, and Browning corrected his text again for an 1875 reimpression. The printing of the last edition of the *Poetical Works* over which Browning exercised control began in 1888, and the first eight volumes are dated thus on their title-pages. Volumes 9 through 16 of this first impression are dated 1889, and we have designated them 1889a to distinguish them from the second impression of all 16 volumes, which was begun and completed in 1889. Some of the earlier volumes of the first impression sold out almost immediately, and in preparation for a second impression, Browning revised and corrected the first ten volumes before he left for Italy in late August,1889. The second impression, in which all sixteen volumes bear the date 1889 on their title-pages, consisted of a revised and corrected second impression of volumes 1-10, plus a second impression of volumes 11-16 altered by Browning in one instance. This impression we term 1889 (see section III below).

Existing manuscripts and editions are classified as either primary or secondary material. The primary materials include the following:

1. The manuscript of a work when such is known to exist.

2. Proof sheets, when known to exist, that contain authorial corrections and revisions.

3. The first and subsequent editions of a work that preserve evidence of Browning's intentions and were under his control.

4. The collected editions over which Browning exercised control:

1849—*Poems*. Two Volumes. London: Chapman and Hall.

1863—*The Poetical Works*. Three Volumes. London: Chapman and Hall.

1865—*The Poetical Works*. Three Volumes. London: Chapman and Hall.

1868—*The Poetical Works*. Six Volumes. London: Smith, Elder and Company.

1870—*The Poetical Works*. Six Volumes. London: Smith, Elder and Company. This resetting constituted a new edition, which was stereotyped and reimpressed several times; the 1875 impression contains revisions by Browning.

1888-1889—*The Poetical Works*. Sixteen Volumes. London: Smith,

Elder and Company. Exists in numerous stereotype impressions, of which two are primary material:

1888-1889a—The first impression, in which volumes 1-8 are dated 1888 and volumes 9-16 are dated 1889.

1889—The corrected second impression of volumes 1-10 and a second impression of volumes 11-16 altered by Browning only as stated in section III below; all dated 1889 on the title pages.

5. The corrections in Browning's hand in the Dykes Campbell copy of 1888-1889a, and the manuscript list of corrections to that impression in the Brown University Library (see section III below).

Other materials (including some in the poet's handwriting) that affected the text are secondary. Examples are: the copy of the first edition of *Pauline* which contains annotations by Browning and John Stuart Mill; the copies of the first edition of *Paracelsus* which contain corrections in Browning's hand; a very early manuscript of *A Blot in the 'Scutcheon* which Browning presented to William Macready, but not the one from which the first edition was printed; informal lists of corrections that Browning included in letters to friends, such as the corrections to *Men and Women* he sent to D. G. Rossetti; verbal and punctuational changes Browning essayed in presentation copies of his works or in his own copies, if not used by his printers; Elizabeth Barrett's suggestions for revisions in *A Soul's Tragedy* and certain poems in *Dramatic Romances and Lyrics;* and the edition of *Strafford* by Emily Hickey for which Browning made suggestions.

The text and variant readings of this edition derive from collation of primary materials as defined above. Secondary materials are occasionally discussed in the notes and sometimes play a part when emendation is required.

III COPY-TEXT

The copy-text for this edition is Browning's final text: the first ten volumes of 1889 and the last six volumes of 1888-1889a, as described above. For this choice we offer the following explanation.

Manuscripts used as printer's copy for twenty of Browning's thirty-four book publications are known to exist; others may yet become available. These manuscripts, or, in their absence, the first editions of the works, might be considered as the most desirable copy-text. And this would be the case for an author who exercised little control over his text after the manuscript or first edition stage, or whose text clearly became corrupted in a succession of editions. To preserve the intention of such an author, one would have to choose an early text and emend it as evidence and judgment demanded.

With Browning, however, the situation is different, and our copy-text choice results from that difference. Throughout his life Browning continually revised his poetry. He did more than correct printer's errors and clarify previously intended meanings; his texts themselves remained fluid, subject to continuous alteration. As the manuscript which he submitted to his publisher was no doubt already a product of revision, so each subsequent edition under his control reflects the results of an ongoing process of creating, revising, and correcting. If we were to choose the manuscript (where extant) or first edition as copy-text, preserving Browning's intention would require extensive emendation to capture the additions, revisions, and alterations which Browning demonstrably made in later editions. By selecting Browning's final corrected text as our copy-text, emending it only to eliminate errors and the consequences of changing house-styling, we present his works in the form closest to that which he intended after years of revision and polishing.

But this is true only if Browning in fact exercised extensive control over the printing of his various editions. That he intended and attempted to do so is apparent in his comments and his practice. In 1855, demanding accuracy from the printers, he pointed out to his publisher Chapman, "I attach importance to the mere stops . . ." (DeVane and Knickerbocker, p. 83). There is evidence of his desire to control the details of his text as early as 1835, in the case of *Paracelsus*. The *Paracelsus* manuscript, now in the Forster and Dyce collection in the Victoria and Albert Museum Library, demonstrates a highly unconventional system of punctuation. Of particular note is Browning's unrestrained use of dashes, often in strings of two or three, instead of more precise or orthodox punctuation marks. It appears that this was done for its rhetorical effect. One sheet of Part 1 of the manuscript and all but the first and last sheets of Part 3 have had punctuation revised in pencil by someone other than Browning, perhaps J. Riggs, whose name appears three times in the margins of Part 3. In addition to these revisions, there are analogous punctuation revisions (in both pencil and ink) which appear to be in Browning's hand, and a few verbal alterations obviously in the poet's script.

A collation of the first edition (1835) with the manuscript reveals that a major restyling of punctuation was carried out before *Paracelsus* was published. However, the revisions incorporated into the first edition by no means slavishly follow the example set by the pencilled revisions of Parts 1 and 3 of the manuscript. Apparently the surviving manuscript was not used as printer's copy for the first edition. Browning may have submitted a second manuscript, or he may have revised extensively in proof. The printers may have carried out the revisions to punctuation, with or without the poet's point by point involvement. With the present evidence, we cannot be conclusive about the extent of Browning's control over the first edition of *Paracelsus*. It can be stated, however, in the light of the incompleteness of the pencilled revisions and the frequent lack or correspondence between the pencilled revisions and the lines as printed in 1835, that Browning himself may have been responsible for the punctuation of the first edition of *Paracelsus*. Certainly he was responsible for the frequent instances in the first and subsequent editions where the punctuation defies conventional rules, as in the following examples:

> What though
> It be so?—if indeed the strong desire
> Eclipse the aim in me—if splendour break
> (Part I, ll. 329-331)

> I surely loved them—that last night, at least,
> When we . . . gone! gone! the better: I am saved
> (Part II, ll. 132-133)

> Of the body, even,)—what God is, what we are,
> (Part V, l. 642, 1849 reading)

The manuscripts of *Colombe's Birthday* (1844) and *Christmas-Eve and Easter-Day* (1850) were followed very carefully in the printing of the first editions. There are slight indications of minor house-styling, such as the spellings *colour* and *honour* for the manuscripts' *color* and *honor*. But the unorthodox punctuation, used to indicate elocutionary and rhetorical subtleties as well as syntactical relationships, is carried over almost unaltered from the manuscripts to the first editions. Similar evidence of Browning's painstaking attention to the smallest details in the printing of his poems can be seen in the manuscript and proof sheets of *The Ring and the Book* (1868-69). These materials reveal an interesting and significant pattern. It appears that Browning wrote swiftly, giving primary attention to wording and less to punctuation, being satisfied to use dashes to indicate almost any break in thought, syntax, or rhythm. Later, in the proof sheets for Books 1-6 of the poem and in the manuscript itself for Books 7-12, he changed the dashes to more specific and purposeful punctuation marks. The revised punctuation is what was printed, for the most part, in the first edition of *The Ring and the Book*; what further revisions there are conform to Browning's practice, though hardly to standard rules. Clearly Browning was in control of nearly every aspect of the published form of his works, even to the "mere stops."

Of still greater importance in our choice of copy-text is the substantial evidence that Browning took similar care with his collected editions. Though he characterized his changes for later editions as trivial and few in number, collations reveal thousands of revisions and corrections in each successive text. *Paracelsus*, for example, was extensively revised for the 1849 *Poems;* it was again reworked for the *Poetical Works* of 1863. *Sordello*, omitted in 1849, reappeared in 1863 with 181 new lines and short marginal glosses; Browning admitted only that it was "corrected *throughout*" (DeVane and Knickerbocker, p. 157). The poems of *Men and Women* (1855) were altered in numerous small but meaningful ways for both the 1863 and 1865 editions of the *Poetical Works* (See Allan C. Dooley, "The Textual Significance of Robert Browning's 1865 *Poetical Works*," *PBSA* 71 [1977], 212-18). Michael Hancher cites evidence of the poet's close supervision of the 1868 collected edition ("Browning and the *Poetical Works* of 1888-1889," *Browning Newsletter,* Spring, 1971, 25-27), and Michael Meredith has traced Browning's attentions to his text in the 1870 edition and an 1875 reimpression of it ("Learning's Crabbed Text," *SBHC* 13 [1985], 97-107); another perspective is offered in Allan C. Dooley's *Author and Printer in Victorian England* (1992), Ch. 4-5. Mrs. Orr, writing of the same period in Browning's life, reports his resentment of those who garbled his text by misplacing his stops (*Life,* pp. 357-58).

There is plentiful and irrefutable evidence that Browning controlled, in the same meticulous way, the text of his last collected edition, that which we term 1888-1889. Hancher has summarized the relevant information:

> The evidence is clear that Browning undertook the 1888-1889 edition of his *Poetical Works* intent on controlling even the smallest minutiae of the text. Though he at one time considered supplying biographical and explanatory notes to the poems, he finally decided against such a scheme, concluding, in his letter to Smith of 12 November 1887, "I am correcting them carefully, and *that* must suffice." On 13 January 1888, he wrote, regarding the six-volume edition of his collected works published in 1868 which was to serve as the printer's copy for the final edition: "I have thoroughly corrected the six volumes of the Works, and can let you have them at once." . . . Browning evidently kept a sharp eye on the production of all sixteen of the volumes, including those later volumes. . . . Browning returned proof for Volume 3 on 6 May 1888, commenting, "I have had, as usual, to congratulate myself on

the scrupulous accuracy of the Printers"; on 31 December he returned proofs of Volume 11, "corrected carefully"; and he returned "the corrected Proofs of Vol. XV" on 1 May 1889.

Throughout his long career, then, Browning continuously revised and corrected his works. Furthermore, his publishers took care to follow his directions exactly, accepting his changes and incorporating them into each successive edition. This is not to say that no one else had any effect whatsoever on Browning's text: Elizabeth Barrett made suggestions for revisions to *A Soul's Tragedy* and *Dramatic Romances and Lyrics*. Browning accepted some suggestions and rejected others, and those which he accepted we regard as his own. Mrs. Orr reports that Browning sent proof sheets to Joseph Milsand, a friend in France, for corrections (*Life*, p. 183), and that Browning accepted suggestions from friends and readers for the corrections of errors in his printed works. In some of the editions, there are slight evidences of minor house-styling in capitalization and the indication of quotations. But the evidence of Browning's own careful attention to revisions and corrections in both his manuscripts and proof sheets assures us that other persons played only a very minor role in the development of his text. We conclude that the vast majority of the alterations in the texts listed above as Primary Materials are Browning's own, and that only Browning's final corrected text, the result of years of careful work by the poet himself, reflects his full intentions.

The first impression of Browning's final collected edition (i.e., 1888-1889a) is not in and of itself the poet's final corrected text. By the spring of 1889 some of the early volumes of the first impression were already sold out, and by mid-August it was evident that a new one would be required. About this time James Dykes Campbell, Honorary Secretary of the London Browning Society, was informed by Browning that he was making further corrections to be incorporated into the new impression. According to Dykes Campbell, Browning had corrected the first ten volumes and offered to transcribe the corrections into Dykes Campbell's copy of 1888-1889a before leaving for Italy. The volumes altered in Browning's hand are now in the British Library and contain on the flyleaf of Volume I Dykes Campbell's note explaining precisely what happened. Of course, Dykes Campbell's copy was not the one used by the printer for the second impression. Nevertheless, these changes are indisputably Browning's and are those which, according to his own statement, he proposed to make in the new impression. This set of corrections carries, therefore, great authority.

Equally authoritative is a second set of corrections, also in Browning's hand, for part of 1888-1889a. In the poet's possession at the time of his death, this handwritten list was included in lot 179 of Sotheby, Wilkinson, and Hodge's auction of Browning materials in 1913; it is today located in the Brown University Library. The list contains corrections only to Volumes 4-10 of 1888-1889a. We know that Browning, on 26 July 1889, had completed and sent to Smith "the corrections for Vol. III in readiness for whenever you need them." By the latter part of August, according to Dykes Campbell, the poet had finished corrections for Volumes 1-10. Browning left for Italy on 29 August. The condition of the Brown University list does not indicate that it was ever used by the printer. Thus we surmise that the Brown list (completing the corrections through volume 10) may be the poet's copy of another list sent to his publisher. Whatever the case, the actual documents used by the printers—a set of marked volumes or handwritten lists—are not known to exist. A possible exception is a marked copy of *Red Cotton Night-Cap Country* (now in the Berg Collection of the New York Public Library) which seems to have been used by printers. Further materials used in preparing Browning's final edition may yet appear.

The matter is complicated further because neither set of corrections of 1888-1889a corresponds exactly to each other nor to the 1889 second impression. Each set contains corrections the other omits, and in a few cases the sets present alternative corrections of the same error. Our study of the Dykes Campbell copy of 1888-1889a reveals fifteen discrepancies between its corrections and the 1889 second impression. The Brown University list, which contains far fewer corrections, varies from the second impression in thirteen instances. Though neither of these sets of corrections was used by the printers, both are authoritative; we consider them legitimate textual variants, and record them as such. The lists are, of course, useful when emendation of the copy-text is required.

The value of the Dykes Campbell copy of 1888-1889a and the Brown University list is not that they render Browning's text perfect. The corrections to 1888-1889a must have existed in at least one other, still more authoritative form: the documents which Browning sent to his publisher. That this is so is indicated by the presence of required corrections in the second impression which neither the Dykes Campbell copy nor the Brown University list calls for. The significance of the existing sets of corrections is that they clearly indicate two important points: Browning's direct and active interest in the preparation of a corrected second impression of his final collected edition; and, given the high degree of correspondence between the two sets of corrections and the affected lines of the second impression, the concern of the printers to follow the poet's directives.

The second impression of 1888-1889 incorporated most of Browning's corrections to the first ten volumes of the first impression. There is no evidence whatever that any corrections beyond those which Browning sent to his publisher in the summer of 1889 were ever made. We choose, therefore, the 1889 corrected second impression of volumes 1-10 as copy-text for the works in those volumes. Corrections to the first impression were achieved by cutting the affected letters or punctuation out of the stereotype plates and pressing or soldering in the correct pieces of type. The corrected plates were then used for many copies, without changing the date on the title pages (except, of course, in volumes 17 [*Asolando*] and 18 [*New Poems*], added to the set by the publishers in 1894 and 1914 respectively). External evidence from publishers' catalogues and the advertisements bound into some volumes of 1889 indicate that copies of this impression were produced as late as 1913, although the dates on the title pages of volumes 1-16 remained 1889. Extensive plate deterioration is characteristic of the later copies, and use of the Hinman collator on early and late examples of 1889 reveals that the inserted corrections were somewhat fragile, some of them having decayed or disappeared entirely as the plates aged. (See Allan C. Dooley, "Browning's *Poetical Works* of 1888-1889," *SBHC* 7:1 [1978], 43-69.)

We do not use as copy-text volumes 11-16 of 1889, because there is a no present evidence indicating that Browning exercised substantial control over this part of the second impression of 1888-1889. We do know that he made one correction, which he requested in a letter to Smith quoted by Hancher:

> I have just had pointed out to [me] that an error, I supposed corrected, still is to be found in the 13th Volume—(Aristophanes' Apology) page 143, line 9, where the word should be Opora—without an i. I should like it altered, if that may be possible.

This correction was indeed made in the second impression. Our collations of copies of volumes 11-16 of 1889a and 1889 show no other intentional changes. The later copies do show, however, extensive type batter, numerous scratches, and irregular inking. Therefore our copy-text for the works in the last six volumes of 1888-1889 is volumes 11-16 of 1888-1889a.

IV VARIANTS

In this edition we record, with a very few exceptions discussed below, all variants from the copy-text appearing in the manuscripts and in the editions under Browning's control. Our purpose in doing this is two-fold.

1. We enable the reader to reconstruct the text of a work as it stood at the various stages of its development.

2. We provide the materials necessary to an understanding of how Browning's growth and development as an artist are reflected in his successive revisions to his works.

As a consequence of this policy our variant listings inevitably contain some variants that were not created by Browning; printer's errors and readings that may result from house-styling will appear occasionally. But the evidence that Browning assumed responsibility for what was printed, and that he considered and used unorthodox punctuation as part of his meaning, is so persuasive that we must record even the smallest and oddest variants. The following examples, characteristic of Browning's revisions, illustrate the point:

> *Pauline,* l. 700:
>> 1833: I am prepared—I have made life my own—
>> 1868: I am prepared: I have made life my own.
> "Evelyn Hope," l. 41:
>> 1855: I have lived, I shall say, so much since then,
>> 1865: I have lived (I shall say) so much since then,
> "Bishop Blougram's Apology," l. 267:
>> 1855: That's the first cabin-comfort I secure—
>> 1865: That's the first-cabin comfort I secure:
> *The Ring and the Book,* Book 11 ("Guido"), l. 1064:
>> 1869: What if you give up boys' and girls' fools'-play
>> 1872: What if you give up boy and girl fools'-play
>> 1889a: What if you give up boy-and-girl-fools' play

We have concluded that Browning himself is nearly always responsible for such changes. But even if he only accepted these changes (rather than originating them), their effect on syntax, rhythm, and meaning is so significant that they must be recorded in our variant listings.

The only variants we do not record are those which strongly appear to result from systematic house-styling. For example, Browning nowhere indicated that he wished to use typography to influence meaning, and our inference is that any changes in line-spacing, depth of paragraph indentation, and the like, were the responsibility of the printers of the various editions, not the poet himself. House-styling was also very probably the cause of certain variants in the apparatus of Browning's plays, including variants in stage directions which involve a change only in manner of statement, such as *Enter Hampden* instead of

Hampden enters; variants in the printing of stage directions, such as *Aside* instead of *aside,* or [*Aside.*] instead of [*Aside*], or [*Strafford.*] instead of [*Strafford*]; variants in character designations, such as *Lady Carlisle* instead of *Car* or *Carlisle.* Browning also accepted current convention for indicating quotations (see section V below). Neither do we list changes in type face (except when used for emphasis), nor the presence or absence of a period at the end of the title of a work.

V ALTERATIONS TO THE COPY-TEXT

We have rearranged the sequence of works in the copy-text, so that they appear in the order of their first publication. This process involves the restoration to the original order of the poems included in *Dramatic Lyrics, Dramatic Romances and Lyrics,* and *Men and Women.* We realize, of course, that Browning himself was responsible for the rearrangement of these poems in the various collected editions; in his prefatory note for the 1888-1889 edition, however, he indicates that he desired a chronological presentation:

> The poems that follow are again, as before, printed in chronological order; but only so far as proves compatible with the prescribed size of each volume, which necessitates an occasional change in the distribution of its contents.

We would like both to indicate Browning's stated intentions about the placement of his poems and to present the poems in the order which suggests Browning's development as a poet. We have chosen, therefore, to present the poems in order of their first publication, with an indication in the notes as to their respective subsequent placement. We also include the tables of contents of the editions listed as Primary Materials above.

We have regularized or modernized the copy-text in the following minor ways:

1. We do not place a period at the end of the title of a work, though the copy-text does.

2. In some of Browning's editions, including the copy-text, the first word of each work is printed in capital letters. We have used the modern practice of capitalizing only the first letter.

3. The inconsistent use of both an ampersand and the word *and* has been regularized to the use of *and.*

4. We have eliminated the space between the two parts of a contraction; thus the copy-text's *it 's* is printed as *it's,* for example.

5. We uniformly place periods and commas within closing quotation marks.

6. We have employed throughout the modern practice of indicating quoted passages with quotation marks only at the beginning and end of the quotation. Throughout Browning's career, no matter which publisher or printer was handling his works, this matter was treated very inconsistently. In some of the poet's manuscripts and in most of his first editions, quotations are indicated by quotation marks only at the beginning and end. In the collected editions of 1863 and 1865, issued by Chapman and Hall, some quoted passages have quotation marks at the beginning of each line of the quotation, while others follow modern practice. In Smith, Elder's collected editions of 1868 and 1888-1889, quotation marks usually appear at the beginning of each line of a quotation. We have regularized and modernized what seems a matter of house-styling in both copy-text and variants.

The remaining way in which the copy-text is altered is by emendation. Our policy is to emend the copy-text to eliminate apparent errors of either Browning or his printers. It is evident that Browning did make errors and overlook mistakes, as shown by the following example from "One Word More," the last poem in *Men and Women*. Stanza sixteen of the copy-text opens with the following lines:

> What, there's nothing in the moon noteworthy?
> Nay: for if that moon could love a mortal,
> Use, to charm him (so to fit a fancy,
> All her magic ('tis the old sweet mythos)
> She . . .

Clearly the end punctuation in the third line is incorrect. A study of the various texts is illuminating. Following are the readings of the line in each of the editions for which Browning was responsible:

MS:	fancy)	1855:	fancy)	1865:	fancy)	1888:	fancy
P:	fancy)	1863:	fancy)	1868:	fancy)	1889:	fancy,

The omission of one parenthesis in 1888 was almost certainly a printer's error. Browning, in the Dykes Campbell copy corrections to 1888-1889a, missed or ignored the error. However, in the Brown University list of corrections, he indicated that *fancy* should be followed by a comma. This is the way the line appears in the corrected second impression of Volume 4, but the correction at best satisfies the demands of syntax only partially. Browning might have written the line:

> Use, to charm him, so to fit a fancy,

or, to maintain parallelism between the third and fourth lines:

> Use, to charm him (so to fit a fancy),

or he might simply have restored the earlier reading. Oversights of this nature demand emendation, and our choice would be to restore the punctuation of the manuscript through 1868. All of our emendations will be based, as far as possible, on the historical collation of the passage involved, the grammatical demands of the passage in context, and the poet's treatment of other similar passages. Fortunately, the multiple editions of most of the works provide the editor with ample textual evidence to make an informed and useful emendation.

All emendations to the copy-text are listed at the beginning of the Editorial Notes for each work. The variant listings for the copy-text also incorporate the emendations, which are preceded and followed there by the symbol indicating an editor's note.

VI APPARATUS

1. *Variants.* In presenting the variants from the copy-text, we list at the bottom of each page readings from the known manuscripts, proof sheets of the editions when we have located them, and the first and subsequent editions.

A variant is generally preceded and followed by a pickup and a drop word (example a). No note terminates with a punctuation mark unless the punctuation mark comes at the end of the line; if a variant drops or adds a punctuation mark, the next word is added (example b). If the normal pickup word has appeared previously in the same line, the note begins with the word preceding it. If the normal drop word appears subsequently in the line, the next word is added (example c). It a capitalized pickup word occurs within the line, it is accompanied by the preceding word (example d). No pickup or drop words, however, are used for any variant consisting of an internal change, for example a hyphen in a compounded word, an apostrophe, a tense change or a spelling change (example e). A change in capitalization within a line of poetry will be preceded by a pickup word, for which, within an entry containing other variants, the < > is suitable (example f). No drop word is used when the variant comes at the end of a line (example g). Examples):

a. $^{611}|$ *1840:*but that appeared   *1863:*but this appeared

b. variant at end of line: $^{109}|$ *1840:*intrigue:"   *1863:*intrigue.

    variant within line: $^{82}|$ *1840:*forests like   *1863:*forests, like

c. $^{132}|$ *1840:*too sleeps; but   *1863:*too sleeps: but $^{77}|$ *1840:*that night

    by   *1863:*that, night by night,   *1888:*by night

d. $^{295}|$ *1840:*at Padua to repulse the   *1863:*at Padua who repulsed the

e. $^{284}|$ *1840:*are   *1863:*were

    $^{344}|$ *1840:*dying-day,   *1863:*dying day,

f. capitalization change with no other variants: $^{741}|$ *1840:*

    retaining Will,   *1863:*will,

    with other variants: $^{843}|$ *1840:*Was < > Him back! Why   *1863:*Is

    < > back!" Why   *1865:*him

g. $^{427}|$ *1840:*dregs: *1863:*dregs.

Each recorded variant will be assumed to be incorporated in the next edition if there is no indication otherwise. This rule applies even in cases where the only change occurs in 1888-1889, although it means that the variant note duplicates the copy-text. A variant listing, then, traces the history of a line and brings it forward to the point where it matches the copy-text.

With regard to manuscript readings, our emphasis is on the textual development and sequence of revisions; visual details of the manuscripts are kept to a minimum. For economy of space, we use formulae such as §crossed out and replaced above by§, but these often cannot report fine details such as whether, when two words were crossed out, the accompanying punctuation was precisely cancelled also. Our MS entries provide enough information to reconstruct with reasonable accuracy B's initial and revised manuscript readings, but they cannot substitute for direct scrutiny of the documents themselves.

It should be noted that we omit drop words in manuscript entries where the final reading is identical to the printed editons—thus

MS:Silence, and all that ghastly §crossed out and replaced above by§ tinted pageant, base

Printed editions: Silence, and all that tinted pageant, base

is entered as

MS:that ghastly §crossed out and replaced above by§ tinted

in our variant listings.

An editor's note always refers to the single word or mark of punctuation immediately preceding or following the comment, unless otherwise specified.

In Browning's plays, all character designations which happen to occur in variant listings are standardized to the copy-text reading. In listing variants in the plays, we ignore character designations unless the designation comes within a numbered line. In such a case, the character designation is treated as any other word, and can be used as a pickup or drop word. When a character designation is used as a pickup word, however, the rule excluding capitalized pickup words (except at the beginning of a line) does not apply, and we do not revert to the next earliest uncapitalized pickup word.

2. *Line numbers.* Poetic lines are numbered in the traditional manner, taking one complete poetic line as one unit of counting. In prose passages the unit of counting is the type line of this edition.

3. *Table of signs in variant listings.* We have avoided all symbols and signs used by Browning himself. The following is a table of the signs used in the variant notes:

§ . . . §	Editor's note
< >	Words omitted
/	Line break
/ / , / / / , . . .	Line break plus one or more lines without internal variants

4 *Annotations.* In general principle, we have annotated proper names, phrases that function as proper names, and words or groups of words the full meaning of which requires factual, historical, or literary background. Thus we have attempted to hold interpretation to a minimum, although we realize that the act of selection itself is to some extent interpretive.

Notes, particularly on historical figures and events, tend to fullness and even to the tangential and unessential. As a result, some of the information provided may seem unnecessary to the scholar. On the other hand, it is not possible to assume that all who use this edition are fully equipped to assimilate unaided all of Browning's copious literary, historical, and mythological allusions. Thus we have directed our efforts toward a diverse audience.

TABLES

1. *Manuscripts.* We have located manuscripts for the following of Browning's works; the list is chronological.

Paracelsus
      Forster and Dyce Collection,
      Victoria and Albert Museum, London
Colombe's Birthday
      New York Public Library
Christmas-Eve and Easter-Day
      Forster and Dyce Collection,
      Victoria and Albert Museum, London
"Love Among the Ruins"
      Lowell Collection,
      Houghton Library, Harvard University
"The Twins"
      Pierpont Morgan Library, New York
"One Word More"
      Pierpont Morgan Library, New York
"James Lee's Wife," ll. 244-69
      Armstrong Browning Library, Baylor University
"May and Death"
      Armstrong Browning Library, Baylor University
"A Face"
      Armstrong Browning Library, Baylor University
Dramatis Personae
      Pierpont Morgan Library, New York
The Ring and the Book
      British Library, London
Balaustion's Adventure
      Balliol College Library, Oxford
Prince Hohenstiel-Schwangau
      Balliol College Library, Oxford
Fifine at the Fair
      Balliol College Library, Oxford
Red Cotton Night-Cap Country
      Balliol College Library, Oxford
Aristophanes' Apology
      Balliol College Library, Oxford
The Inn Album
      Balliol College Library, Oxford
Of Pacchiarotto, and How He Worked in Distemper
      Balliol College Library, Oxford
"Hervé Riel"
      Pierpont Morgan Library, New York

The Agamemnon of Aeschylus
    Balliol College Library, Oxford
La Saisiaz and The Two Poets of Croisic
    Balliol College Library, Oxford
Dramatic Idylls
    Balliol College Library, Oxford
Dramatic Idylls, Second Series
    Balliol College Library, Oxford
Jocoseria
    Balliol College Library, Oxford
Ferishtah's Fancies
    Balliol College Library, Oxford
Parleyings With Certain People of Importance in Their Day
    Balliol College Library, Oxford
Asolando
    Pierpont Morgan Library, New York

We have been unable to locate manuscripts for the following works, and request that persons with information about any of them communicate with us.

Pauline	*The Return of the Druses*
Strafford	*A Blot in the 'Scutcheon*
Sordello	*Dramatic Romances and Lyrics*
Pippa Passes	*Luria*
King Victor and King Charles	*A Soul's Tragedy*
"Essay on Chatterton"	"Essay on Shelley"
Dramatic Lyrics	*Men and Women*

2. *Editions referred to in Volume XVI.* The following editions have been used in preparing the text and variants presented in this volume. The dates given below are used as symbols in the variant listings at the bottom of each page.

    1887   *Parleyings With Certain People of Importance in Their Day.*
            London: Smith, Elder, and Company.

    1889a *The Poetical Works.*
            Volumes 9-16. London: Smith, Elder, and Company.

3. *Short titles and abbreviations.* The following short forms of reference have been used in notes for this edition:

ABL	Armstrong Browning Library
B	Browning
B's Parleyings	W.C. DeVane. *Browning's Parleyings: The Auto-biography of a Mind.* New York, 1964.
B's Trumpeter	*Browning's Trumpeter: The Correspondence of Robert Browning and Frederick J. Furnivall, 1872-1889,* ed. W.S. Peterson. Washington, D.C., 1979.
B's Youth	John Maynard. *Browning's Youth.* Cambridge, MA, 1977.
Correspondence	*The Brownings' Correspondence,* ed. P. Kelley, R. Hudson, and S. Lewis. Winfield, KS, 1984-.
DeVane, *Hbk.*	W.C. DeVane. *A Browning Handbook,* 2nd ed. New York, 1955.
DeVane and Knickerbocker	New Letters of Robert Browning, ed. W.C. DeVane and K.L. Knickerbocker. New Haven, CT, 1950.
EBB	Elizabeth Barrett Browning
Hood	*Letters of Robert Browning Collected by Thomas J. Wise,* ed. T. L. Hood. New Haven, CT, 1933.
Irvine and Honan	W. Irvine and P. Honan. *The Book, the Ring, and the Poet.* New York, 1974.
Kintner	*The Letters of Robert Browning and Elizabeth Barrett Barrett, 1845-46,* ed. E. Kintner. Cambridge, MA, 1969.
Letters of EBB	*The Letters of Elizabeth Barrett Browning,* ed. F.G. Kenyon. New York, 1897.
Landis and Freeman	*Letters of the Brownings to George Barrett,* ed. P. Landis and R.E. Freeman. Urbana, IL, 1958.
OED	*The Oxford English Dictionary,* 2nd ed. Oxford, 1989.
Orr	Mrs. Sutherland Orr. *A Handbook to the Works of Robert Browning,* 6th ed. London, 1892.
P-C	*The Works of Robert Browning,* ed. C. Porter and H.A. Clarke. New York, 1910, 1912.
Reconstruction	*The Browning Collections, a Reconstruction, with Other Memorabilia,* comp. P. Kelley and B.A. Coley. Waco, TX; New York; Winfield, KS; and London, 1984.
Ryals	Clyde de L. Ryals. *The Life of Robert Browning: A Critical Biography.* Oxford; Cambridge, MA, 1993.

Vasari   Giorgio Vasari. *Lives of the Painters. Sculptors and Architects,* ed. and tr. A.B. Hinds. London, 1963.

Citations and quotations from the Bible refer to the King James Version.

Citations and quotations from Shakespeare refer to T*he Riverside Shakespeare,* ed. G.B. Evans, et al. Boston, 1998.

ACKNOWLEDGMENTS

For providing services and money which have made it possible for us to prepare this volume, the following institutions have our gratitude: the Ohio University Press, the Ohio University Library, the Ohio University English Department, the Baker Fund Awards Committee of Ohio University; Baylor University and the Armstrong Browning Library of Baylor University; Kent State University's University Library, Institute for Bibliography and Editing, and English Department; King's College, London.

For making available to us materials under their care we thank the Armstrong Browning Library; the Balliol College Library, Oxford; the British Library; the John Hay Library, Brown University; Philip Kelley; the Ohio University Library; the Wellesley College Library; Yaddo.

Of the many scholars who have assisted the editors of the presnt volume, the following deserve our special gratitude: Mairi Calcraft, Betty Coley Fredeman, Dwight St. John, Philip Kelley, Scott Lewis, William Owens.

The frontispiece is reproduced by permission of the Armstrong Browning Library.

PARLEYINGS WITH CERTAIN PEOPLE OF

IMPORTANCE IN THEIR DAY

Edited by Susan Crowl and Roma A. King, Jr.

PARLEYINGS WITH CERTAIN PEOPLE OF
IMPORTANCE IN THEIR DAY:

TO WIT: BERNARD DE MANDEVILLE,
         DANIEL BARTOLI,
         CHRISTOPHER SMART,
         GEORGE BUBB DODINGTON,
         FRANCIS FURINI,
         GERARD DE LAIRESSE,
   AND   CHARLES AVISON.

INTRODUCED BY

A DIALOGUE BETWEEN APOLLO AND THE FATES;

CONCLUDED BY

ANOTHER BETWEEN JOHN FUST AND HIS FRIENDS.

IN MEMORIAM

J. MILSAND

OBIIT IV. SEPT. MDCCCLXXXVI.

Absens absentem auditque videtque.

PARLEYINGS WITH CERTAIN PEOPLE
1887

APOLLO AND THE FATES

A PROLOGUE

(Hymn. in Mercurium, v. 559. Eumenides, vv. 693-4, 697-8.
Alcestis. vv. 12, 33.)

APOLLO *[From above.*

Flame at my footfall, Parnassus! Apollo,
  Breaking a-blaze on thy topmost peak,
Burns thence, down to the depths—dread hollow—
  Haunt of the Dire Ones. Haste! They wreak
5 Wrath on Admetus whose respite I seek.

THE FATES *[Below. Darkness.*

Dragonwise couched in the womb of our Mother,
  Coiled at thy nourishing heart's core, Night!
Dominant Dreads, we, one by the other,
  Deal to each mortal his dole of light
10 On earth—the upper, the glad, the bright.

CLOTHO

Even so: thus from my loaded spindle
  Plucking a pinch of the fleece, lo, "Birth"

PARLEYINGS WITH CERTAIN PEOPLE OF IMPORTANCE IN THEIR DAY §MS in Balliol
College Library. For description of MS see Editorial Notes. Ed. 1887, 1889a§
Title| MS:Parleyings < > To-wit < > Dodington, *1887:*to wit *1889a:* < > Dodington.
§emended to§ Dodington, §see Editorial Notes§ *Dedication|* MS:M.DLXXXVI.
§marginal note that *CCC* to be inserted after *D*§ *1887:*MDLXXXVI *1889a:*MDCCCLXXXVI
APOLLO AND THE FATES *Title|* MS:Eumenides, v. 164 §crossed out and replaced
above by§ vv.693-4 697-8. Alcestis, vv. 12.33.) §see Editorial Notes§ [12]| MS:pinch from

Brays from my bronze lip: life I kindle:
    Look, 'tis a man! go, measure on earth
15 The minute thy portion, whatever its worth!

LACHESIS

Woe-purfled, weal-prankt,—if it speed, if it linger,—
    Life's substance and show are determined by me,
Who, meting out, mixing with sure thumb and finger,
    Lead life the due length: is all smoothness and glee,
20 All tangle and grief? Take the lot, my decree!

ATROPOS

—Which I make an end of: the smooth as the tangled
    My shears cut asunder: each snap shrieks "One more
Mortal makes sport for us Moirai who dangled
    The puppet grotesquely till earth's solid floor
25 Proved film he fell through, lost in Nought as before."

CLOTHO

I spin thee a thread. Live, Admetus! Produce him!

LACHESIS

Go,—brave, wise, good, happy! Now chequer the thread!
He is slaved for, yet loved by a god. I unloose him
    A goddess-sent plague. He has conquered, is wed,
30 Men crown him, he stands at the height,—

ATROPOS

He is . . .

APOLLO   *[Entering: Light.*

"Dead?"

---

the *1887:* pinch of the   18| MS:meting and mixing   *1887:*meting out, mixing
19| MS:Lead lock the   *1889a:*Lead life the   23| MS:Of mortals *1887:*Mortal
25| MS:before. *1887:*before."   30| MS:is . . *1889a:*is . . .

Nay, swart spinsters! So I surprise you
    Making and marring the fortunes of Man?
Huddling—no marvel, your enemy eyes you—
    Head by head bat-like, blots under the ban
35 Of daylight earth's blessing since time began!

THE FATES

Back to thy blest earth, prying Apollo!
    Shaft upon shaft transpierce with thy beams
Earth to the centre,—spare but this hollow
    Hewn out of Night's heart, where our mystery seems
40 Mewed from day's malice: wake earth from her dreams!

APOLLO

Crones, 'tis your dusk selves I startle from slumber:
    Day's god deposes you—queens Night-crowned!
—Plying your trade in a world ye encumber,
    Fashioning Man's web of life—spun, wound,
45 Left the length ye allot till a clip strews the ground!

Behold I bid truce to your doleful amusement—
    Annulled by a sunbeam!

THE FATES

Boy, are not we peers?

APOLLO

You with the spindle grant birth: whose inducement
    But yours—with the niggardly digits—endears
50 To mankind chance and change, good and evil? Your shears . . .

ATROPOS

Ay, mine end the conflict: so much is no fable.

35| MS:began. *1887:*began! 39| MS:Out of Night's heart hewn, where mystery
*1887:*Hewn out of Night's heart, where *1889a:*where our mystery 42| MS:queens
night-crowned! *1889a:*queens Night-crowned! 50| MS:shears . . *1889a:*shears . . .

We spin, draw to length, cut asunder: what then?
So it was, and so is, and so shall be: art able
To alter life's law for ephemeral men?

APOLLO

55 Nor able nor willing. To threescore and ten

Extend but the years of Admetus! Disaster
O'ertook me, and, banished by Zeus, I became
A servant to one who forbore me though master:
True lovers were we. Discontinue your game,
60 Let him live whom I loved, then hate on, all the same!

THE FATES

And what if we granted—law-flouter, use-trampler—
His life at the suit of an upstart? Judge, thou—
Of joy were it fuller, of span because ampler?
For love's sake, not hate's, end Admetus—ay, now—
65 Not a gray hair on head, nor a wrinkle on brow!

For, boy, 'tis illusion: from thee comes a glimmer
Transforming to beauty life blank at the best.
Withdraw—and how looks life at worst, when to shimmer
Succeeds the sure shade, and Man's lot frowns—confessed
70 Mere blackness chance-brightened? Whereof shall attest

The truth this same mortal, the darling thou stylest,
Whom love would advantage,—eke out, day by day,
A life which 'tis solely thyself reconcilest
Thy friend to endure,—life with hope: take away
75 Hope's gleam from Admetus, he spurns it. For, say—

What's infancy? Ignorance, idleness, mischief:
Youth ripens to arrogance, foolishness, greed:

55| MS:nor wishful. To *1887:* not willing. To
65| MS:head, not *1887:*head, nor a 71| MS:stylest *1887:*stylest,

Age—impotence, churlishness, rancour: call *this* chief
Of boons for thy loved one? Much rather bid speed
80 Our function, let live whom thou hatest indeed!

Persuade thee, bright boy-thing! Our eld be instructive!

APOLLO

And certes youth owns the experience of age.
Ye hold then, grave seniors, my beams are productive
—They—solely of good that's mere semblance, engage
85 Man's eye—gilding evil, Man's true heritage?

THE FATES

So, even so! From without,—at due distance
If viewed,—set a-sparkle, reflecting thy rays,—
Life mimics the sun: but withdraw such assistance,
The counterfeit goes, the reality stays—
90 An ice-ball disguised as a fire-orb.

APOLLO

What craze

Possesses the fool then whose fancy conceits him
As happy?

THE FATES

Man happy?

APOLLO

If otherwise—solve
This doubt which besets me! What friend ever greets him
Except with "Live long as the seasons revolve,"
95 Not "Death to thee straightway"? Your doctrines absolve

88| MS:but, withold such   *1887*:but, withdraw such   *1889a*:but withdraw

9

Such hailing from hatred: yet Man should know best.
 He talks it, and glibly, as life were a load
Man fain would be rid of: when put to the test,
 He whines "Let it lie, leave me trudging the road
100 That is rugged so far, but methinks . . ."

THE FATES

Ay, 'tis owed

To that glamour of thine, he bethinks him "Once past
 The stony, some patch, nay, a smoothness of sward
Awaits my tired foot: life turns easy at last"—
 Thy largess so lures him, he looks for reward
105 Of the labour and sorrow.

APOLLO

It seems, then—debarred

Of illusion—(I needs must acknowledge the plea)
 Man desponds and despairs. Yet,—still further to draw
Due profit from counsel,—suppose there should be
 Some power in himself, some compensative law
110 By virtue of which, independently . . .

THE FATES

Faugh!

Strength hid in the weakling!
What bowl-shape hast there,
 Thus laughingly proffered? A gift to our shrine?
Thanks—worsted in argument! Not so? Declare
 Its purpose!

98| MS:of *1887*:of *1889a*:off §emended to§ of §see Editorial Notes§
100| MS:methinks . . *1887*:methinks . ." *1889a*:methinks . . ."
110| MS:independently . . *1889a*:independently . . . 111| MS:weakness *1887*:weakling

APOLLO

I proffer earth's product, not mine.
₁₁₅ Taste, try, and approve Man's invention of—WINE!

THE FATES

We feeding suck honeycombs.

APOLLO

Sustenance meagre!
Such fare breeds the fumes that show all things amiss.
Quaff wine,—how the spirits rise nimble and eager,
Unscale the dim eyes! To Man's cup grant one kiss
₁₂₀ Of your lip, then allow—no enchantment like this!

CLOTHO

Unhook wings, unhood brows! Dost hearken?

LACHESIS

I listen:
I see—smell the food these fond mortals prefer
To our feast, the bee's bounty!

ATROPOS

The thing leaps! But—glisten
Its best, I withstand it—unless all concur
₁₂₅ In adventure so novel.

APOLLO

Ye drink?

THE FATES

We demur.

---

¹²³| MS:feast—the *1887*:feast, the   ¹²⁶| MS:Sweet trine *1887*:Sweet Trine

APOLLO

Sweet Trine, be indulgent nor scout the contrivance
    Of Man—Bacchus-prompted! The juice, I uphold,
Illuminates gloom without sunny connivance,
    Turns fear into hope and makes cowardice bold,—
130   Touching all that is leadlike in life turns it gold!

THE FATES

Faith foolish as false!

APOLLO

            But essay it, soft sisters!
    Then mock as ye may. Lift the chalice to lip!
Good: thou next—and thou! Seems the web, to you twisters
    Of life's yarn, so worthless?

CLOTHO

                Who guessed that one sip
135   Would impart such a lightness of limb?

LACHESIS

                    I could skip

In a trice from the pied to the plain in my woof!
    What parts each from either? A hair's breadth, no inch.
Once learn the right method of stepping aloof,
    Though on black next foot falls, firm I fix it, nor flinch,
140   —Such my trust white succeeds!

ATROPOS

                One could live—at a pinch!

127| MS:Of Man—Bacchus prompted   *1887:*Of Man—Bacchus-prompted
128| MS:connivence   *1887:*connivance

APOLLO

What, beldames? Earth's yield, by Man's skill, can effect
    Such a cure of sick sense that ye spy the relation
Of evil to good? But drink deeper, correct
    Blear sight more convincingly still! Take your station
145 Beside me, drain dregs! Now for edification!

Whose gift have ye gulped? Thank not me but my brother,
    Blithe Bacchus, our youngest of godships. 'Twas he
Found all boons to all men, by one god or other
    Already conceded, so judged there must be
150 New guerdon to grace the new advent, you see!

Else how would a claim to Man's homage arise?
    The plan lay arranged of his mixed woe and weal,
So disposed—such Zeus' will—with design to make wise
    The witless—that false things were mingled with real,
155 Good with bad: such the lot whereto law set the seal.

Now, human of instinct—since Semele's son,
    Yet minded divinely—since fathered by Zeus,
With nought Bacchus tampered, undid not things done,
    Owned wisdom anterior, would spare wont and use,
160 Yet change—wthout shock to old rule—introduce.

Regard how your cavern from crag-tip to base
    Frowns sheer, height and depth adamantine, one death!
I rouse with a beam the whole rampart, displace
    No splinter—yet see how my flambeau, beneath
165 And above, bids this gem wink, that crystal unsheath!

Withdraw beam—disclosure once more Night forbids you
    Of spangle and sparkle—Day's chance-gift, surmised

141| MS:What, beldames < > by man's   *1887:*by Man's   *1889a:*What beldames §emended to§
What, beldames §see Editorial Notes§   146| MS:have you gulped   *1887:*have ye gulped
148| MS:to mankind, by   *1887:*to all men, by   165| MS:unsheathe!   *1889a:*unsheath!

Rock's permanent birthright: my potency rids you
    No longer of darkness, yet light—recognized—
170 Proves darkness a mask: day lives on though disguised.

If Bacchus by wine's aid avail so to fluster
    Your sense, that life's fact grows from adverse and thwart
To helpful and kindly by means of a cluster—
    Mere hand-squeeze, earth's nature sublimed by Man's art—
175 Shall Bacchus claim thanks wherein Zeus has no part?

Zeus—wisdom anterior? No, maids, be admonished!
    If morn's touch at base worked such wonders, much more
Had noontide in absolute glory astonished
    Your den, filled a-top to o'erflowing. I pour
180 No such mad confusion. 'Tis Man's to explore

Up and down, inch by inch, with the taper his reason:
    No torch, it suffices—held deftly and straight.
Eyes, purblind at first, feel their way in due season,
    Accept good with bad, till unseemly debate
185 Turns concord—despair, acquiescence in fate.

Who works this but Zeus? Are not instinct and impulse,
    Not concept and incept his work through Man's soul
On Man's sense? Just as wine ere it reach brain must brim pulse,
    Zeus' flash stings the mind that speeds body to goal,
190 Bids pause at no part but press on, reach the whole.

For petty and poor is the part ye envisage
    When—(quaff away, cummers!)—ye view, last and first,
As evil Man's earthly existence. Come! *Is* age,
    Is infancy—manhood—so uninterspersed
195 With good—some faint sprinkle?

CLOTHO

I'd speak if I durst.

193| MS:age *1887:*age,   194| MS:manhood so *1887:*manhood—so

APOLLO

Draughts dregward loose tongue-tie.

LACHESIS

I'd see, did no web
Set eyes somehow winking.

APOLLO

Drains-deep lies their purge
—True collyrium!

ATROPOS

Words, surging at high-tide, soon ebb
From starved ears.

APOLLO

Drink but down to the source, they resurge.
200   Join hands! Yours and yours too! A dance or a dirge?

CHORUS

Quashed be our quarrel! Sourly and smilingly,
    Bare and gowned, bleached limbs and browned,
Drive we a dance, three and one, reconcilingly,
    Thanks to the cup where dissension is drowned,
205   Defeat proves triumphant and slavery crowned.

Infancy? What if the rose-streak of morning
    Pale and depart in a passion of tears?
Once to have hoped is no matter for scorning!
    Love once—e'en love's disappointment endears!
210   A minute's success pays the failure of years.

204| MS:dissention   *1887*:dissension   205| *1887*:crowned   *1889a*:crowned.

Manhood—the actual? Nay, praise the potential!
    (Bound upon bound, foot it around!)
What *is*? No, what *may* be—sing! that's Man's essential!
    (Ramp, tramp, stamp and compound
215 Fancy with fact—the lost secret is found!)

Age? Why, fear ends there: the contest concluded,
    Man *did* live his life, *did* escape from the fray:
Not scratchless but unscathed, he somehow eluded
    Each blow fortune dealt him, and conquers to-day:
220 To-morrow—new chance and fresh strength,—might we say?

Laud then Man's life—no defeat but a triumph!
                             [*Explosion from the earth's centre.*

CLOTHO

Ha, loose hands!

LACHESIS

I reel in a swound.

ATROPOS

Horror yawns under me, while from on high—humph!
    Lightnings astound, thunders resound,
225 Vault-roof reverberates, groans the ground!   [*Silence.*

APOLLO

I acknowledge.

THE FATES

Hence, trickster! Straight sobered are we!
The portent assures 'twas our tongue spoke the truth,
Not thine. While the vapour encompassed us three
We conceived and bore knowledge—a bantling uncouth,

212| MS:around)   *1887*:around!)   217| MS:life, did escape   *1887*:life, *did* escape
226| MS:we.   *1887*:we!   229| MS:uncouth   *1887*:uncouth,

230 Old brains shudder back from: so—take it, rash youth!

Lick the lump into shape till a cry comes!

APOLLO

I hear.

THE FATES

Dumb music, dead eloquence! Say it, or sing!
What was quickened in us and thee also?

APOLLO

I fear.

THE FATES

Half female, half male—go, ambiguous thing!
235 While we speak—perchance sputter—pick up what we fling!

Known yet ignored, nor divined nor unguessed,
Such is Man's law of life. Do we strive to declare
What is ill, what is good in our spinning? Worst, best,
Change hues of a sudden: now here and now there
240 Flits the sign which decides: all about yet nowhere.

'Tis willed so,—that Man's life be lived, first to last,
Up and down, through and through,—not in portions, forsooth,
To pick and to choose from. Our shuttles fly fast,
Weave living, not life sole and whole: as age—youth,
245 So death completes living, shows life in its truth.

Man learningly lives: till death helps him—no lore!
It is doom and must be. Dost submit?

231| MS:hear! *1887*:hear.   233| MS:fear! *1887*:fear.   238| MS:best *1887*:best,
240| MS:decides—all < > no-where. *1887*:decides: all *1889a*:nowhere.

17

APOLLO

I assent—
Concede but Admetus! So much if no more
Of my prayer grant as peace-pledge! Be gracious though, blent,
250 Good and ill, love and hate streak your life-gift!

THE FATES

Content!

Such boon we accord in due measure. Life's term
We lengthen should any be moved for love's sake
To forego life's fulfilment, renounce in the germ
Fruit mature—bliss or woe—either infinite. Take
255 Or leave thy friend's lot: on his head be the stake!

APOLLO

On mine, griesly gammers! Admetus, I know thee!
Thou prizest the right these unwittingly give
Thy subjects to rush, pay obedience they owe thee!
Importunate one with another they strive
260 For the glory to die that their king may survive.

Friends rush: and who first in all Pheræ appears
But thy father to serve as thy substitute?

CLOTHO

Bah!

APOLLO

Ye wince? Then his mother, well-stricken in years,
Advances her claim—or his wife—

---

²⁴⁹| MS:gracious, though *1889a:*gracious though ²⁵⁹| MS:another all strive
*1887:*another they strive ²⁶¹| MS:Friends flock, but who *1887:*Friends rush: and who
²⁶³| *1887:*years *1889a:*years,

LACHESIS

Tra-la-la!

APOLLO

265 But he spurns the exchange, rather dies!

ATROPOS

Ha, ha, ha !
[*Apollo ascends. Darkness.*

WITH BERNARD DE MANDEVILLE

I

I

Ay, this same midnight, by this chair of mine,
Come and review thy counsels: art thou still
Staunch to their teaching?—not as fools opine
Its purport might be, but as subtler skill
5   Could, through turbidity, the loaded line
Of logic casting, sound deep, deeper, till
It touched a quietude and reached a shrine
And recognized harmoniously combine
Evil with good, and hailed truth's triumph—thine,
10   Sage dead long since, Bernard de Mandeville!

II

Only, 'tis no fresh knowledge that I crave,
Fuller truth yet, new gainings from the grave;
Here we alive must needs deal fairly, turn
To what account Man may Man's portion, learn
15   Man's proper play with truth in part, before
Entrusted with the whole. I ask no more
Than smiling witness that I do my best
With doubtful doctrine: afterward the rest!
So, silent face me while I think and speak!
20   A full disclosure? Such would outrage law.
Law deals the same with soul and body: seek
Full truth my soul may, when some babe, I saw
A new-born weakling, starts up strong—not weak—
Man every whit, absolved from earning awe,
25   Pride, rapture, when the soul attains to wreak
Its will on flesh, at last can thrust, lift, draw,

WITH BERNARD DE MANDEVILLE   *Title*| MS:I/With Bernard de Mandeville.
1889a:§numeral deleted§   4| MS:purport may be   *1887:*purport might be
17| MS:that I do §crossed out and replaced above by word scraped out§   *1887:*do
18| MS:afterwards *1889a:*afterward   20| MS:law; *1887:*law.   22| MS:may—when
*1887:*may, when   25| MS:rapture, when the *1887:*rapture, if the
*1889a:*rapture, if the §emended to§ rapture, when the §see Editorial Notes§

As mind bids muscle—mind which long has striven,
Painfully urging body's impotence
To effort whereby—once law's barrier riven,
Life's rule abolished—body might dispense
With infancy's probation, straight be given
—Not by foiled darings, fond attempts back-driven,
Fine faults of growth, brave sins which saint when shriven—
To stand full-statured in magnificence.

III

No: as with body so deals law with soul
That's stung to strength through weakness, strives for good
Through evil,—earth its race-ground, heaven its goal,
Presumably: so far I understood
Thy teaching long ago. But what means this
—Objected by a mouth which yesterday
Was magisterial in antithesis
To half the truths we hold, or trust we may,
Though tremblingly the while? "No sign"—groaned he—
"No stirring of God's finger to denote
He wills that right should have supremacy
On earth, not wrong! How helpful could we quote
But one poor instance when he interposed
Promptly and surely and beyond mistake
Between oppression and its victim, closed
Accounts with sin for once, and bade us wake
From our long dream that justice bears no sword,
Or else forgets whereto its sharpness serves!
So might we safely mock at what unnerves
Faith now, be spared the sapping fear's increase
That haply evil's strife with good shall cease
Never on earth. Nay, after earth, comes peace
Born out of life-long battle? Man's lip curves

28| MS:Painfully urged the §last two words crossed out and replaced above by§ urging body's
39| MS:long. ago. §paragraph indication and section number crossed out§ But   *1887*:long
ago. But   47| MS:A single §two words crossed out and replaced above by three words§
But one poor instance < > He   *1889a*:he   56| MS:earth; nay   *1887*:earth. Nay

With scorn: there, also, what if justice swerves
From dealing doom, sets free by no swift stroke
60 Right fettered here by wrong, but leaves life's yoke—
Death should loose man from—fresh laid, past release?"

IV

Bernard de Mandeville, confute for me
This parlous friend who captured or set free
Thunderbolts at his pleasure, yet would draw
65 Back, panic-stricken by some puny straw
Thy gold-rimmed amber-headed cane had whisked
Out of his pathway if the object risked
Encounter, 'scaped thy kick from buckled shoe!
As when folk heard thee in old days pooh-pooh
70 Addison's tye-wig preachment, grant this friend—
(Whose groan I hear, with guffaw at the end
Disposing of mock-melancholy)—grant
His bilious mood one potion, ministrant
Of homely wisdom, healthy wit! For, hear!
75 "With power and will, let preference appear
By intervention ever and aye, help good
When evil's mastery is understood
In some plain outrage, and triumphant wrong
Tramples weak right to nothingness: nay, long
80 Ere such sad consummation brings despair

---

[58] MS:scorn: "There also—what *1887*:scorn: there, also, what [60] MS:yoke,—
1887:yoke— [61] MS:Which §crossed out§ Death <> loose Man §inserted above§ from
<> release'?" *1887*:loose man <> release?" [63] MS:this later §crossed out and
replaced above by§ parlous [65] MS:Back, planet-stricken by *1887*:Back, panic-stricken
by [67] MS:of the §crossed out and replaced above by§ his <> the upstart risked
1887:the object risked [68] MS:Encounter, and is §last two words crossed out§ <> thy
kick from §last two words inserted above line§ *1887*:Encounter, 'scaped thy
[69] MS:folks *1889a*:folk [70] MS:preachments §altered to§ preachment
[71] MS:hear yet §crossed out§ with the §crossed out§ guf §inserted above§ laugh §altered to§
faugh at its §inserted above§ end *1887*:hear, with guffaugh at the end *1889a*:guffaw
[73] MS:His §next word illegibly crossed out§ bilious mood §last two words inserted above§
one §next two words illegibly crossed out§ potion §inserted above§ [75] MS:§first word
illegibly crossed out and replaced by another illegibly crossed out word§ "With §inserted
above§ <> and §followed by illegible erasure§ will §inserted above§ [78] MS:By
§crossed out and replaced above by§ In [80] MS:bring *1889a*:brings

To right's adherents, ah, what help it were
If wrong lay strangled in the birth—each head
Of the hatched monster promptly crushed, instead
Of spared to gather venom! We require
85   No great experience that the inch-long worm,
Free of our heel, would grow to vomit fire,
And one day plague the world in dragon form.
So should wrong merely peep abroad to meet
Wrong's due quietus, leave our world's way safe
90   For honest walking."

V

          Sage, once more repeat
Instruction! 'Tis a sore to soothe not chafe.
Ah, Fabulist, what luck, could I contrive
To coax from thee another "Grumbling Hive"!
My friend himself wrote fables short and sweet:
95   Ask him—"Suppose the Gardener of Man's ground
Plants for a purpose, side by side with good,
Evil—(and that he does so—look around!
What does the field show?)—were it understood
That purposely the noxious plant was found
100   Vexing the virtuous, poison close to food,
If, at first stealing-forth of life in stalk
And leaflet-promise, quick his spud should baulk
Evil from budding foliage, bearing fruit?
Such timely treatment of the offending root

---

⁸³| MS:monster forthwith §crossed out and replaced above by§ promptly
⁸⁴| MS:gather poison §crossed out and replaced above by§ venom   ⁸⁵| MS:Nowise
experience < > worm   *1887*:No great experience < > worm,   ⁸⁶| MS:Beneath §crossed
out and replaced above by two words§ Free of   ⁸⁷| MS:dragon-form.   *1887*:dragon
form.   ⁹⁰| MS:honest walking."§altered to§ walkers."   *1887*:honest walking."
⁹³| MS:thee §next word illegibly crossed out§ another §inserted above§   ⁹⁵| MS:the
gardener §altered to§ Gardener of §next word illegibly crossed out§ Man's §inserted above§
⁹⁷| *1887*:that He   *1889a*:he   ⁹⁹| MS:How came it §last three words crossed out§
happened §inserted above and crossed out§ That purposely §inserted above§
¹⁰¹| MS:first peeping-forth §*peeping-* crossed out and replaced above by§ stealing-
¹⁰²| MS:leafet promise, quick his §altered to§ His   *1887*:leaflet-promise   *1889a*:his

105 Might strike the simple as wise husbandry,
But swift sure extirpation scarce would suit
Shrewder observers. Seed once sown thrives: why
Frustrate its product, miss the quality
Which sower binds himself to count upon?
110 Had seed fulfilled the destined purpose, gone
Unhindered up to harvest—what know I
But proof were gained that every growth of good
Sprang consequent on evil's neighbourhood?"
So said your shrewdness: true—so did not say
115 That other sort of theorists who held
Mere unintelligence prepared the way
For either seed's upsprouting: you repelled
Their notion that both kinds could sow themselves.
True! but admit 'tis understanding delves
120 And drops each germ, what else but folly thwarts
The doer's settled purpose? Let the sage
Concede a use to evil, though there starts
Full many a burgeon thence, to disengage
With thumb and finger lest it spoil the yield
125 Too much of good's main tribute! But our main
Tough-tendoned mandrake-monster—purge the field
Of him for once and all? It follows plain
Who set him there to grow beholds repealed
His primal law: his ordinance proves vain:
130 And what beseems a king who cannot reign,

105| MS:as §next word, perhaps *care,* illegibly crossed out§ wise §inserted above§
106| MS:But such prompt §last two words crossed out and replaced above by two words§ swift
sure   107| MS:observers: seed §last two words altered to§ observers. Seed
108| MS:Frustrate the §crossed out and replaced above by§ its   109| MS:Who sows §last
two words altered to§ Which sower seed §crossed out§   110| MS:fulfilled its §crossed out
and replaced above by§ the   112| MS:gained that §crossed out and restored§
113| MS:Was §crossed out and replaced above by§ Sprang   118| MS:Their confidence
§crossed out and replaced above by two words§ notion that < > themselves:
1887:themselves.   119| MS:Good §crossed out and replaced above by§ True
125| MS:main product §crossed out and replaced by§ tribute   126| MS:purge §next
word, perhaps *earth's,* crossed out§ the §inserted above§   127| MS:all, it   *1887*:all? It
129| MS:vain,   *1887*:law: His < > vain: *1889a*:law: his   130| MS:reign   *1887*:reign,

But to drop sceptre valid arm should wield?

VI

"Still there's a parable"—retorts my friend—
"Shows agriculture with a difference!
What of the crop and weeds which solely blend
135 Because, once planted, none may pluck them thence?
The Gardener contrived thus? Vain pretence!
An enemy it was who unawares
Ruined the wheat by interspersing tares.
Where's our desiderated forethought? Where's
140 Knowledge, where power and will in evidence?
'Tis Man's-play merely! Craft foils rectitude,
Malignity defeats beneficence.
And grant, at very last of all, the feud
'Twixt good and evil ends, strange thoughts intrude
145 Though good be garnered safely and good's foe
Bundled for burning. Thoughts steal: 'even so—
Why grant tares leave to thus o'ertop, o'ertower
Their field-mate, boast the stalk and flaunt the flower,
Triumph one sunny minute? Knowledge, power
150 And will thus worked?' Man's fancy makes the fault!
Man, with the narrow mind, must cram inside
His finite God's infinitude,—earth's vault
He bids comprise the heavenly far and wide.
Since Man may claim a right to understand

131| MS:But to §crossed out and restored§ drop the §inserted above and crossed out§
132| MS:"Ay, but the §last three words crossed out and replaced above by three words§ "But
there's a §*But* crossed out and replaced above by§ "Still <> Parable!" retorts my friend,
1887:parable"—retorts my friend—   133| MS:"There's §crossed out and replaced above
by§ "Shows   136| MS:The gardener §altered to§ Gardener   139| MS:Alack, for your
§last three words crossed out and replaced above by two words§ What of §last two words
crossed out and replaced by two words§ Where's our   140| MS:evidence? *1889a*:evidence
§emended to§ evidence? §see Editorial Notes§   143| MS:And even §crossed out§ <>
last, §crossed out§ of all, §last two words and comma inserted above§ the   144| MS:ends,
what §crossed out and replaced above by§ strange   146| MS:burning." §quotation marks
crossed out§ <> steal: 'Even   *1887*:steal: "Even   *1889a*:steal: 'even   147| MS:o'er-top
1889a:o'ertop   150| MS:worked?' Man's   *1887*:worked? Man's   *1889a*:worked? Man's
§emended to§ worked?' Man's §see Editorial Notes§   152| MS:finite God's infinity

¹⁵⁵   What passes understanding. So, succinct
    And trimly set in order, to be scanned
    And scrutinized, lo—the divine lies linked
    Fast to the human, free to move as moves
    Its proper match: awhile they keep the grooves,
¹⁶⁰   Discretely side by side together pace,
    Till sudden comes a stumble incident
    Likely enough to Man's weak-footed race,
    And he discovers—wings in rudiment,
    Such as he boasts, which full-grown, free-distent
¹⁶⁵   Would lift him skyward, fail of flight while pent
    Within humanity's restricted space.
    Abjure each fond attempt to represent
    The formless, the illimitable! Trace
    No outline, try no hint of human face
¹⁷⁰   Or form or hand!"

VII

                Friend, here's a tracing meant
    To help a guess at truth you never knew.
    Bend but those eyes now, using mind's eye too,
    And note—sufficient for all purposes—
    The ground-plan—map you long have yearned for—yes,
¹⁷⁵   Made out in markings—more what artist can?—
    Goethe's Estate in Weimar,—just a plan!
    A. is the House, and B. the Garden-gate,
    And C. the Grass-plot—you've the whole estate
    Letter by letter, down to Y. the Pond,
¹⁸⁰   And Z. the Pig-stye. Do you look beyond
    The algebraic signs, and captious say
    "Is A. the House? But where's the Roof to A.,
    Where's Door, where's Window? Needs must House have such!"

---

§altered above to§ infinitude   ¹⁵⁷| *1887*:scrutinised   *1889a*:scrutinized
¹⁵⁹| MS:Its equal §crossed out and replaced by§ proper   ¹⁶⁰| MS: discretely
1887:discreetly   *1889a*:discreetly §emended to§ discretely §see Editorial Notes§
¹⁶⁴| MS:boasts,—which *1887*:boasts, which   ¹⁶⁵| MS:skyward,—fail *1887*:skyward,
fail   ¹⁶⁷| MS:Abjure §next word illegibly crossed out and replaced by§ each
¹⁷⁴| MS:you §next word illegibly crossed out and replaced by§ long   ¹⁸³| MS:must

Ay, that were folly. Why so very much
185　More foolish than our mortal purblind way
Of seeking in the symbol no mere point
To guide our gaze through what were else inane,
But things—their solid selves? "Is, joint by joint,
Orion man-like,—as these dots explain
190　His constellation? Flesh composed of suns—
How can such be?" exclaim the simple ones.
Look through the sign to the thing signified—
Shown nowise, point by point at best descried,
Each an orb's topmost sparkle: all beside
195　Its shine is shadow: turn the orb one jot—
Up flies the new flash to reveal 'twas not
The whole sphere late flamboyant in your ken!

VIII

"What need of symbolizing? Fitlier men
Would take on tongue mere facts—few, faint and far,
200　Still facts not fancies: quite enough they are,
That Power, that Knowledge, and that Will,—add then
Immensity, Eternity: these jar
Nowise with our permitted thought and speech.
Why human attributes?"

　　　　　　　　　　A myth may teach:
205　Only, who better would expound it thus
Must be Euripides not Æschylus.

IX

Boundingly up through Night's wall dense and dark,

House §next word illegibly crossed out and replaced by§ have
189|　MS:as your §crossed out and replaced above by§ these　　194|　MS:sparkle—all
1887:sparkle: all　　195|　MS:shadow—turn <> jot　*1887*:shadow: turn <> jot—
199|　MS:tongue facts—few and faint　*1889a*:tongue mere facts—few, faint
201|　MS:that Will,—what more? §last two words and question mark crossed out and
replaced above by two words§ add then　　203|　MS:with man's §crossed out and replaced
above by§ our　　206-7|　MS:§misnumbered by B as section 8§　*1887*:IX

27

Embattled crags and clouds, outbroke the Sun
Above the conscious earth, and one by one
210   Her heights and depths absorbed to the last spark
His fluid glory, from the far fine ridge
Of mountain-granite which, transformed to gold,
Laughed first the thanks back, to the vale's dusk fold
On fold of vapour-swathing, like a bridge
215   Shattered beneath some giant's stamp. Night wist
Her work done and betook herself in mist
To marsh and hollow there to bide her time
Blindly in acquiescence. Everywhere
Did earth acknowledge Sun's embrace sublime
220   Thrilling her to the heart of things: since there
No ore ran liquid, no spar branched anew,
No arrowy crystal gleamed, but straightway grew
Glad through the inrush—glad nor more nor less
Than, 'neath his gaze, forest and wilderness,
225   Hill, dale, land, sea, the whole vast stretch and spread,
The universal world of creatures bred
By Sun's munificence, alike gave praise—
All creatures but one only: gaze for gaze,
Joyless and thankless, who scowls, all he can,
230   Protests against the innumerous praises? Man,
Sullen and silent.

        Stand thou forth then, state
Thy wrong, thou sole aggrieved—disconsolate—
While every beast, bird, reptile, insect, gay
And glad acknowledges the bounteous day!

208| MS:the sun §altered to§ Sun   *1887:*out-broke   *1889a:*outbroke
215| MS:beneath a §crossed out and replaced above by§ some <> whist   *1887:*wist
220| MS:things—since   *1887:*things: since   224| MS:Than 'neath his gaze forest and
wilderness   *1887:*Than, 'neath his gaze, forest and wilderness,   225| MS:the whole
§inserted above§ vast of §crossed out§   227| MS:By sun's §altered to§ Sun's
229| MS:thankless—who scowls, §last word crossed out§ all he §crossed out§ scowling
§inserted above§ can,   *1887:*thankless, who—all scowling can—   *1889a:*who—all scowling
can— §emended to§ who scowls, all he can, §see Editorial Notes§   230| MS:innumerous
praising §altered to§ praises   231| MS:silent. <> forth and §crossed out and replaced
above by word and comma§ then, state   232| MS:wrong, tho §altered to§ thou

X

²³⁵ Man speaks now: "What avails Sun's earth-felt thrill
To me? Sun penetrates the ore, the plant—
They feel and grow: perchance with subtler skill
He interfuses fly, worm, brute, until
Each favoured object pays life's ministrant
²⁴⁰ By pressing, in obedience to his will,
Up to completion of the task prescribed,
So stands and stays a type. Myself imbibed
Such influence also, stood and stand complete—
The perfect Man,—head, body, hands and feet,
²⁴⁵ True to the pattern: but does that suffice?
How of my superadded mind which needs
—Not to be, simply, but to do, and pleads
For—more than knowledge that by some device
Sun quickens matter: mind is nobly fain
²⁵⁰ To realize the marvel, make—for sense
As mind—the unseen visible, condense
—Myself—Sun's all-pervading influence
So as to serve the needs of mind, explain
What now perplexes. Let the oak increase
²⁵⁵ His corrugated strength on strength, the palm
Lift joint by joint her fan-fruit, ball and balm,—
Let the coiled serpent bask in bloated peace,—
The eagle, like some skyey derelict,
Drift in the blue, suspended, glorying,—
²⁶⁰ The lion lord it by the desert-spring,—
What know or care they of the power which pricked
Nothingness to perfection? I, instead,
When all-developed still am found a thing
All-incomplete: for what though flesh had force

---

^{235|}   MS:now. "What avails sun's §altered to§ Sun's   *1887*:now: "What
^{239|}   MS:pays its §crossed out and replaced above by§ life's   ^{240|}   MS:to plain
§crossed out and replaced above by§ his   ^{243|}   MS:also, §next word illegibly
crossed out and replaced above by§ stood   ^{249|}   MS:is rather §crossed out and
replaced above by§ nobly   ^{252|}   MS:—Myself §dash in margin§ —sun's
§altered to§ Sun's   ^{258|}   MS:derelict   *1887*:derelict,
^{263|}   MS:all-developed still am §last two words transposed and original order restored§

265 Transcending theirs—hands able to unring
The tightened snake's coil, eyes that could outcourse
The eagle's soaring, voice whereat the king
Of carnage couched discrowned? Mind seeks to see,
Touch, understand, by mind inside of me,
270 The outside mind—whose quickening I attain
To recognize—I only. All in vain
Would mind address itself to render plain
The nature of the essence. Drag what lurks
Behind the operation—that which works
275 Latently everywhere by outward proof—
Drag that mind forth to face mine? No! aloof
I solely crave that one of all the beams
Which do Sun's work in darkness, at my will
Should operate—myself for once have skill
280 To realize the energy which streams
Flooding the universe. Above, around,
Beneath—why mocks that mind my own thus found
Simply of service, when the world grows dark,
To half-surmise—were Sun's use understood,
285 I might demonstrate him supplying food,
Warmth, life, no less the while? To grant one spark
Myself may deal with—make it thaw my blood
And prompt my steps, were truer to the mark
Of mind's requirement than a half-surmise

270| MS:mind— §next word illegibly crossed out and replaced above by§ whose
272| MS:Would §over perhaps *Should*§   273| MS:essence. Drag §over perhaps *drag*§
275| MS:everywhere §next three words illegibly crossed out and replaced above by two words§ by
outward   276| MS:to §next two words illegibly crossed out and replaced by§ face mine?
No!— §last word, exclamation point and dash inserted above§ aloof   *1887*:mine? No! aloof
277| MS:§first two words illegibly crossed out§ I solely §inserted above§
278| MS:do sun's §altered to§ Sun's   279| MS:operate—for once myself §last three words
transposed to§ myself for once   280| MS:To imagine fresh §last two words crossed out and
replaced above by§ realize   283| MS:§first word illegibly crossed out and replaced above
by§ Simply   284| MS:half-surmise 'were sun's §altered to§ Sun's   *1887*:half-surmise—were
285| MS:might §next word illegibly crossed out and replaced above by§ demonstrate him still
§crossed out§   286| MS:life, §next four words illegibly crossed out and replaced above by
four words§ no less the while? §next word illegibly crossed out and replaced by two words§ To
grant   288| MS:And lead my steps; §next word illegibly crossed out and replaced above by
word crossed out and replaced by§ were   *1887*:And prompt my steps, were

290   That somehow secretly is operant
       A power all matter feels, mind only tries
       To comprehend! Once more—no idle vaunt
       'Man comprehends the Sun's self!' Mysteries
       At source why probe into? Enough: display,
295   Make demonstrable, how, by night as day,
       Earth's centre and sky's outspan, all's informed
       Equally by Sun's efflux!—source from whence
       If just one spark I drew, full evidence
       Were mine of fire ineffably enthroned—
300   Sun's self made palpable to Man!"

XI

Thus moaned

       Man till Prometheus helped him,—as we learn,—
       Offered an artifice whereby he drew
       Sun's rays into a focus,—plain and true,
       The very Sun in little: made fire burn
305   And henceforth do Man service—glass-conglobed
       Though to a pin-point circle—all the same
       Comprising the Sun's self, but Sun disrobed
       Of that else-unconceived essential flame
       Borne by no naked sight. Shall mind's eye strive
310   Achingly to companion as it may
       The supersubtle effluence, and contrive
       To follow beam and beam upon their way
       Hand-breadth by hand-breadth, till sense faint—confessed
       Frustrate, eluded by unknown unguessed

293| MS:the sun's §altered to§ Sun's   294| MS:into? Enough—my play   *1887*:into?
Enough: display,   295| MS:Makes demonstrable how   *1887*:Make demonstrable, how
296| MS:and heaven's outstretch §last two words altered to§ sky's outspan   297| MS:by
sun's §altered to§ Sun's efflux—source   *1887*:by Sun's efflux!—source   298| MS:If this
§crossed out and replaced above by§ just < > drew, what evidence   *1887*:drew, full evidence
300| MS:to Mind §word crossed out and replaced above by§ man!" §¶§ So moaned   *1887*:to
Man! §¶§ Thus moaned   302| MS:Came with an   *1887*:Offered an   303| MS:The
§crossed out and replaced above by§ Sun's < > true.   *1887*:true,   304| MS:very sun in
little—made   *1887*:very Sun in little: made   307| MS:the sun's < > sun   *1887*:the Sun's
< > Sun   308| MS:else unconceived   *1887*:else-unconceived   313| MS:Handbreadth
by handbreadth, till it faint   *1887*:Hand-breadth by hand-breadth, till sense faint

315   Infinitude of action? Idle quest!
       Rather ask aid from optics. Sense, descry
       The spectrum—mind, infer immensity!
       Little? In little, light, warmth, life are blessed—
       Which, in the large, who sees to bless? Not I
320   More than yourself: so, good my friend, keep still
       Trustful with—me? with thee, sage Mandeville!

316| MS:Rather get help from   *1887*:Rather ask aid from   320| MS:my Sage, keep
1887:my friend, keep   321| MS:me?—thee, sager Mandeville!   *1887*:me? with thee, sage
Mandeville!

WITH DANIEL BARTOLI*

I

Don, the divinest women that have walked
Our world were scarce those saints of whom we talked.
My saint, for instance—worship if you will!
'Tis pity poets need historians' skill:
5   What legendary's worth a chronicle?

II

Come, now! A great lord once upon a time
Visited—oh a king, of kings the prime,
To sign a treaty such as never was:
For the king's minister had brought to pass
10   That this same duke—so style him—must engage
Two of his dukedoms as an heritage
After his death to this exorbitant
Craver of kingship. "Let who lacks go scant,
Who owns much, give the more to!" Why rebuke?
15   So bids the devil, so obeys the duke.

III

Now, as it happened, at his sister's house

---

*A learned and ingenious writer. "Fu Gesuita e Storico della Compagnia; onde
scrisse lunghissime storie, le quali sarebbero lette se non fossero ripiene traboccanti
di tutte le superstizioni . . . Egli vi ha ficcati dentro tanti miracoloni, che diviene una
noia insopportabile a chiunque voglia leggere quelle storie: e anche a me, non mi
5   bastò l'animo di proseguire molto avanti."—ANGELO CERUTTI.

WITH DANIEL BARTOLI   *Title*| MS:III §altered to§ II./With §original name illegibly
erased and replaced below by§ Daniel Bartoli.   *1889a:*§numeral deleted§
Footnote [1]| MS:and excellent writer   *1887:*and ingenious writer   [2]| MS:storie le
*1887:*storie, le   [5]| MS:l'animo   *1889a:*l animo §emended to§ l'animo §see Editorial
Notes§   [1]| MS:Sir, §word and comma crossed out and replaced above by word and
comma§ Don,   [3]| MS:will: *1887:*will!   [4]| MS:poets lack §crossed out and
replaced above by§ need   [7]| MS:Visited—oh §word and dash inserted above§ a great
§crossed out§   [10]| MS:this poor §crossed out and replaced above by§ same   [11]|
MS:dukedoms go §crossed out§ as an §inserted above§   [13]| MS:lacks be scant §last two

—Duchess herself—indeed the very spouse
Of the king's uncle,—while the deed of gift
Whereby our duke should cut his rights adrift
20　　Was drawing, getting ripe to sign and seal—
What does the frozen heart but uncongeal
And, shaming his transcendent kin and kith,
Whom do the duke's eyes make acquaintance with?
A girl. "What, sister, may this wonder be?"
25　　"Nobody! Good as beautiful is she,
With gifts that match her goodness, no faint flaw
I' the white: she were the pearl you think you saw,
But that she is—what corresponds to white?
Some other stone, the true pearl's opposite,
30　　As cheap as pearls are costly. She's—now, guess
Her parentage! Once—twice—thrice? Foiled, confess!
Drugs, duke, her father deals in—faugh, the scents!—
Manna and senna—such medicaments
For payment he compounds you. Stay—stay—stay!
35　　I'll have no rude speech wrong her! Whither away,
The hot-head? Ah, the scapegrace! She deserves
Respect—compassion, rather! Right it serves
My folly, trusting secrets to a fool!
Already at it, is he? She keeps cool—
40　　Helped by her fan's spread. Well, our state atones
For thus much license, and words break no bones!"
(Hearts, though, sometimes.)

---

words crossed out and replaced above by two words§ go scant,　　²²| MS:his ancestral
§crossed out and replaced above by§ transcendent　　²⁵| MS:"Nobody! good §altered to§
Good　*1887:*"Nobody　　²⁷| MS:white which were the pearl's you　*1887:*white: she were
the pearl you　　³⁰| MS:pearls are §over perhaps *were*§　　³²| MS:Drugs— §altered to§ ,
drugs §crossed out and replaced above by word and comma§ duke,　　³³| MS:Rhubarb
§crossed out and replaced above by§ Manna　　³⁴| MS:For asking he　*1887:*For payment
he　　³⁷| MS:the 'scape-grace　*1889a:*the scapegrace　　³⁷| MS:compassion. §altered
to§ , rather! §word and exclamation point inserted above§ Properly §crossed out and replaced
above by§ Right　　³⁸| MS:folly, that §crossed out§ trusts §altered to§ trusting
⁴¹| MS:For some slight §two words crossed out and replaced by two words§ thus much < >
bones."　*1887:*Bones!"　　⁴²| MS:Next day §crossed out and replaced above by§ morn

IV

Next morn 'twas "Reason, rate,
Rave, sister, on till doomsday! Sure as fate,
I wed that woman—what a woman is
⁴⁵ Now that I know, who never knew till this!"
So swore the duke. "I wed her: once again—
Rave, rate, and reason—spend your breath in vain!"

V

At once was made a contract firm and fast,
Published the banns were, only marriage, last,
⁵⁰ Required completion when the Church's rite
Should bless and bid depart, make happy quite
The coupled man and wife for evermore:
Which rite was soon to follow. Just before—
All things at all but end—the folk o' the bride
⁵⁵ Flocked to a summons. Pomp the duke defied:
"Of ceremony—so much as empowers,
Nought that exceeds, suits best a tie like ours—"
He smiled—"all else were mere futility.
We vow, God hears us: God and you and I—
⁶⁰ Let the world keep at distance! This is why
We choose the simplest forms that serve to bind
Lover and lover of the human kind,
No care of what degree—of kings or clowns—
Come blood and breeding. Courtly smiles and frowns
⁶⁵ Miss of their mark, would idly soothe or strike

---

⁴³| MS:doomsday! sure §altered to§ Sure   ⁴⁵| MS:this:" *1887*:this!"
⁴⁷| MS:spend your §crossed out§ breath all §inserted above§ in vain!" *1887*:spend your
breath in   *1889a*:vain! §emended to§ vain!" §see Editorial Notes§   ⁵⁰| MS:completion
by §crossed out and replaced above by§ when   ⁵¹| MS:To §crossed out and replaced by§
Should <> depart, be §crossed out and replaced above by§ make   ⁵²| MS:couple
§altered to§ coupled   ⁵³| MS:And this §last two words crossed out and replaced above
by§ Which rite   ⁵⁴| MS:things arranged, §last word and comma crossed out and
replaced above by four words§ at all but end—the kins §crossed out§ folk of §altered to§ o'
⁵⁷| MS:ours," *1887*:ours—"   ⁵⁸| MS:The duke §last two words crossed out and
replaced above by§ He <> else proves §crossed out and replaced above by two words§ were
mere   ⁶²| MS:humankind *1887*:human kind   ⁶³| MS:Whatever their §last two
words crossed out and replaced above by four words§ No care of what <> clowns
1887:clowns—   ⁶⁵| MS:mark, here, §last word and comma crossed out and replaced

My style and yours—in one style merged alike—
God's man and woman merely. Long ago
'Twas rounded in my ears 'Duke, wherefore slow
To use a privilege? Needs must one who reigns
70 Pay reigning's due: since statecraft so ordains—
Wed for the commonweal's sake! law prescribes
One wife: but to submission license bribes
Unruly nature: mistresses accept
—Well, at discretion!' Prove I so inept
75 A scholar, thus instructed? Dearest, be
Wife and all mistresses in one to me,
Now, henceforth, and forever!" So smiled he.

VI

Good: but the minister, the crafty one,
Got ear of what was doing—all but done—
80 Not sooner, though, than the king's very self,
Warned by the sister on how sheer a shelf
Royalty's ship was like to split. "I bar
The abomination! Mix with muck my star?
Shall earth behold prodigiously enorbed
85 An upstart marsh-born meteor sun-absorbed?
Nuptial me no such nuptials!" "Past dispute,
Majesty speaks with wisdom absolute,"
Admired the minister: "yet, all the same,
I would we may not—while we play his game,
90 The ducal meteor's—also lose our own,
The solar monarch's: we relieve your throne

---

above by§ would   66| MS:alike   *1887:*alike—   68| MS:Was §crossed out and
replaced above by§ Friends rounded <> "Duke   *1887:*'Twas rounded <> 'Duke
69| MS:must one §inserted above§   70| MS:Pay the §crossed out and replaced above by§
reigning's due, price §crossed out§ since   *1887:*due: since   71| MS:sake: law   *1887:*sake!
law   72| MS:but licence to submission §last three words transposed to§ to submission
licence   *1889a:*license   74| MS:discretion!" Am §crossed out and replaced by§ Prove
*1887:*discretion! Prove   77-78| MS:forever!" So said §crossed out and replaced above by§
smiled he./"Now!" That same §last two words crossed out and replaced above by two words§
But the   *1887:*he./Good: but   89| MS:game—   *1887:*game,   90| MS:own—
*1887:*own,   91| MS:relieve the §crossed out and replaced above by§ your

36

Of an ungracious presence, like enough:
Baulked of his project he departs in huff,
And so cuts short—dare I remind the king?—
95   Our not so unsuccessful bargaining.
The contract for eventual heritage
Happens to *pari passu* reach the stage
Attained by just this other contract,—each
Unfixed by signature though fast in speech.
100   Off goes the duke in dudgeon—off withal
Go with him his two dukedoms past recall.
You save a fool from tasting folly's fruit,
Obtain small thanks thereby, and lose to boot
Sagacity's reward. The jest is grim:
105   The man will mulct you—for amercing him?
Nay, for . . . permit a poor similitude!
A witless wight in some fantastic mood
Would drown himself: you plunge into the wave,
Pluck forth the undeserving: he, you save,
110   Pulls you clean under also for your pains.
Sire, little need that I should tax my brains
To help your inspiration!" "Let him sink!
Always contriving"—hints the royal wink—
"To keep ourselves dry while we claim his clothes."

VII

115   Next day, the appointed day for plighting troths
At eve,—so little time to lose, you see,
Before the Church should weld indissolubly
Bond into bond, wed these who, side by side,
Sit each by other, bold groom, blushing bride,—
120   At the preliminary banquet, graced
By all the lady's kinsfolk come in haste

---

⁹²| MS:enough,— *1887*:enough: ⁹³| MS:huff *1887*:huff,   ⁹⁴| MS:king?
1887: king?—   ¹⁰⁶| MS:for . . permit *1887*:for . . . permit   ¹⁰⁷| MS:in mere
§crossed out and replaced by§ some   ¹⁰⁹| MS:undesering,—he *1887*:undeserving: he
¹¹¹| MS:need that §crossed out and replaced above by§ weak *1887*:need that I
¹¹⁴| MS:dry and to §last two words crossed out and replaced by two words§ while we
¹¹⁵| MS:day,—the *1887*:day, the   ¹¹⁶| MS:eve, so—little *1887*:eve,—so little
¹¹⁹| MS:Sat each <> bride, *1887*:Sit each <> bride,—

To share her triumph,—lo, a thunderclap!
"Who importunes now?" "Such is my mishap—
In the king's name! No need that any stir
125 Except this lady!" bids the minister:
"With her I claim a word apart, no more:
For who gainsays—a guard is at the door.
Hold, duke! Submit you, lady, as I bow
To him whose mouthpiece speaks his pleasure now!
130 It well may happen I no whit arrest
Your marriage: be it so,—we hope the best!
By your leave, gentles! Lady, pray you, hence!
Duke, with my soul and body's deference!"

VIII

Doors shut, mouth opens and persuasion flows
135 Copiously forth. "What flesh shall dare oppose
The king's command? The matter in debate
—How plain it is! Yourself shall arbitrate,
Determine. Since the duke affects to rate
His prize in you beyond all goods of earth,
140 Accounts as nought old gains of rank and birth,
Ancestral obligation, recent fame,
(We know his feats)—nay, ventures to disclaim
Our will and pleasure almost—by report—
Waives in your favour dukeliness, in short,—
145 We—('tis the king speaks)—who might forthwith stay
Such suicidal purpose, brush away

125| MS:lady!—" bids the minister— *1887*:lady!" bids the minister: 126| MS:word,—
§comma and dash crossed out§ apart, alone §crossed out and replaced above by two words
and colon§ no more: 127| MS:door." *1887*:door. 128| MS:Alone: §word and
colon crossed out and replaced above by two words and exclamation point§ Hold, duke!
"Submit §quotation marks crossed out§ 129| MS:now. *1887*:now!
131| MS:so—, and §crossed out and replaced by§ we 135-36| MS:forth. "The king's
command oppose/ What flesh shall dare? The *1887*:forth. "What flesh shall dare oppose/
The King's command? The 137| MS:—How §dash in margin§ 140| MS:nought
the §crossed out and replaced by§ old 142| MS:feats)—is tempted §last two words
crossed out and replaced by two words§ nay, ventures 144| MS:favor *1889a*:favour
145| MS:speaks) who at once §last two words crossed out§ might forthwith §inserted above§
1887:speaks)—who 146| MS:purpose, bid §crossed out and replaced above by§ breathe
§crossed out and original reading restored§ away *1887*:purpose, brush away

38

A bad example shame would else record,—
Lean to indulgence rather. At his word
We take the duke: allow him to complete
150 The cession of his dukedoms, leave our feet
Their footstool when his own head, safe in vault,
Sleeps sound. Nay, would the duke repair his fault
Handsomely, and our forfeited esteem
Recover,—what if wisely he redeem
155 The past,—in earnest of good faith, at once
Give us such jurisdiction for the nonce
As may suffice—prevent occasion slip—
And constitute our actual ownership?
Concede this—straightway be the marriage blessed
160 By warrant of this paper! Things at rest,
This paper duly signed, down drops the bar,
To-morrow you become—from what you are,
The druggist's daughter—not the duke's mere spouse,
But the king's own adopted: heart and house
165 Open to you—the idol of a court
'Which heaven might copy'—sing our poet-sort.
In this emergency, on you depends
The issue: plead what bliss the king intends!
Should the duke frown, should arguments and prayers
170 Nay, tears if need be, prove in vain,—who cares?
We leave the duke to his obduracy,
Companionless,—you, madam, follow me
Without, where divers of the body-guard

147| MS:The §crossed out and replaced above by§ A   149| MS:duke: bid §crossed out
and replaced above by§ allow him forthwith §crossed out§ to §inserted above§
150| MS:dukedoms, give §crossed out and replaced above by§ leave   151| MS:Such
§crossed out and replaced above by§ Their   152| MS:Sleeps soundly. Nay, would he
repair   *1887*:Sleeps sound. Nay, would the duke repair   157| MS:slip   *1887*:slip—
159| MS:this—straight §altered to§ straightway shall §crossed out§   165| MS:of his
§crossed out and replaced above by§ a   166| MS:Which <> copy,—sing the §crossed out
and replaced above by§ our   *1887*:'Which <> copy'—sing   167-68| §added and separated
by a solidus§   *1887*: emergency, on   169| MS:If the refuse, if §last two words
crossed out and replaced above by three words§ duke frowns, should   *1887*:Should the duke
frown, should   171| MS:Leave §in margin§ The dull §inserted above§ duke is left §last
two words crossed out§ to   *1887*:We leave the duke to   172| MS:Companionless,—
because §crossed out§ you, madam, §last word and comma inserted above§

Wait signal to enforce the king's award
175 Of strict seclusion: over you at least
Vibratingly the sceptre threats increased
Precipitation! How avert its crash?"

IX

"Re-enter, sir! A hand that's calm, not rash,
Averts it!" quietly the lady said.
180 "Yourself shall witness."

At the table's head
Where, mid the hushed guests, still the duke sat glued
In blank bewilderment, his spouse pursued
Her speech to end—syllabled quietude.

X

"Duke, I, your duchess of a day, could take
185 The hand you proffered me for love's sole sake,
Conscious my love matched yours; as you, myself
Would waive, when need were, all but love—from pelf
To potency. What fortune brings about
Haply in some far future, finds me out,
190 Faces me on a sudden here and now.
The better! Read—if beating heart allow—
Read this, and bid me rend to rags the shame!
I and your conscience—hear and grant our claim!
Never dare alienate God's gift you hold

174| MS:Await now §inserted above§ to carry out §last two words crossed out and replaced
above by§ enforce   *1887:*Wait signal to   176| MS:The sceptre hangs vibratingly: §last
four words transposed to§ Vibratingly the sceptre hangs: increased   *1887:*sceptre threats
increased   178| MS:—"Re-enter, §dash in margin§ with me: §last two words and colon
crossed out and replaced above by two words§ Sir! a <> calm not rash   *1887:*"Re-enter sir! A
<> calm, not rash,   181| MS:mid his hushed ones, still   *1887:*mid the hushed guests,
still   184| MS:of an hour §last two words crossed out and replaced above by two words§ a
day   187| MS:waive, when §crossed out and replaced above by§ if §crossed out§ need
<> all beside §crossed out and replaced above by two words§ but love   *1887:*waive, when
need   190| MS:on the §crossed out and replaced above by§ a   191| MS:better!
Read this §crossed out and replaced above by§ —if your §crossed out and replaced above by§
beating   192| MS:read and §crossed out and replaced above by§ this—then bid

195 Simply in trust for him! Choose muck for gold?
Could you so stumble in your choice, cajoled
By what I count my least of worthiness
—The youth, the beauty,—you renounce them—yes,
With all that's most too: love as well you lose,
200 Slain by what slays in you the honour! Choose!
Dear—yet my husband—dare I love you yet?"

XI

How the duke's wrath o'erboiled,—words, words and yet
More words,—I spare you such fool's fever-fret.
They were not of one sort at all, one size,
205 As souls go—he and she. 'Tis said, the eyes
Of all the lookers-on let tears fall fast.
The minister was mollified at last:
"Take a day,—two days even, ere through pride
You perish,—two days' counsel—then decide!"

XII

210 —"If I shall save his honour and my soul?
Husband,—this one last time,—you tear the scroll?
Farewell, duke! Sir, I follow in your train!"

XIII

So she went forth: they never met again,
The duke and she. The world paid compliment
215 (Is it worth noting?) when, next day, she sent
Certain gifts back—"jewelry fit to deck

---

*1887:*this, and bid   195| MS:for Him   *1889a:*for him   198| MS:—The §dash in
margin§   199| MS:With §in margin§ All <> most—my §last word and dash crossed out and
replaced above by word and colon§ too: *1887:*With all   200| MS:honor   *1889a:*honour
201| MS:Duke—late §crossed out and replaced above by§ still my husband—may §crossed out
and replaced above by§ dare   *1887:*Dear—yet my   202| MS:o'erboiled, in §crossed out and
replaced above by§ —words,   203| MS:you a §crossed out and replaced above by§ such
206| MS:fast: *1887:*fast.   210| MS:honor   *1887:*"If   *1889a:*—"If <> honour
211| MS:one sole §crossed out and replaced above by§ last time,—I §crossed out and replaced
above by§ you   213| MS:again,   *1889a:*again §emended to§ again, §see Editorial Notes§

Whom you call wife." I know not round what neck
They took to sparkling, in good time—weeks thence.

XIV

Of all which was the pleasant consequence,
220 So much and no more—that a fervid youth,
Big-hearted boy,—but ten years old, in truth,—
Laid this to heart and loved, as boyhood can,
The unduchessed lady: boy and lad grew man:
He loved as man perchance may: did meanwhile
225 Good soldier-service, managed to beguile
The years, no few, until he found a chance:
Then, as at trumpet-summons to advance,
Outbroke the love that stood at arms so long,
Brooked no withstanding longer. They were wed.
230 Whereon from camp and court alike he fled,
Renounced the sun-king, dropped off into night,
Evermore lost, a ruined satellite:
And, oh, the exquisite deliciousness
That lapped him in obscurity! You guess
235 Such joy is fugitive: she died full soon.
He did his best to die—as sun, so moon
Left him, turned dusk to darkness absolute.
Failing of death—why, saintship seemed to suit:
Yes, your sort, Don! He trembled on the verge
240 Of monkhood: trick of cowl and taste of scourge
He tried: then, kicked not at the pricks perverse,
But took again, for better or for worse,

---

²¹⁸| MS:time—months §crossed out and replaced above by§ weeks   ²¹⁹| MS:was a pleasant
*1889a:*was the pleasant   ²²⁰| MS:youth *1887:*youth,   ²²¹| MS:boy,—ten years of age,
in *1887:*boy,—but ten years old, in   ²²²| MS:loved as < > can *1887:*loved, as < > can,
²²⁴| MS:man perchance §inserted above§   ²²⁵| MS:soldier service *1887:*soldier-service
²²⁶| MS:chance, *1887:*chance: ²²⁷|MS:trumpet summons *1887:*trumpet-summons
²³⁰| MS:fled *1887:*fled,   ²³¹| MS:night *1887:*night,   ²³²| MS:Lost evermore, a
luckless §crossed out and replaced above by§ ruined satellite— *1887:*satellite:
*1889a:*Evermore lost, a   ²³⁷| MS:Leaving turned < > absolute: *1887:*Left him, turned < >
absolute.   ²³⁸| MS:death,—why *1887:*death—why   ²³⁹⁻⁴⁰| MS:§in right margin§
²³⁹| MS:sort, Doctor §crossed out and replaced above by word and exclamation point§ Daniel!—
trembled *1887:*sort, Don! He trembled   ²⁴⁰| MS:monkhood—trick
*1887:*monkhood: trick   ²⁴²| MS:Took up again *1887:*But took again

The old way in the world, and, much the same
Man o' the outside, fairly played life's game.

XV

245 "Now, Saint Scholastica, what time she fared
In Paynimrie, behold, a lion glared
Right in her path! Her waist she promptly strips
Of girdle, binds his teeth within his lips,
And, leashed all lamblike, to the Soldan's court
250 Leads him." Ay, many a legend of the sort
Do you praiseworthily authenticate:
Spare me the rest. This much of no debate
Admits: my lady flourished in grand days
When to be duchess was to dance the hays
255 Up, down, across the heaven amid its host:
While to be hailed the sun's own self almost—
So close the kinship—was—was—

       Saint, for this,
Be yours the feet I stoop to—kneel and kiss!
So human? Then the mouth too, if you will!
260 Thanks to no legend but a chronicle.

XVI

One leans to like the duke, too: up we'll patch
Some sort of saintship for him—not to match
Hers—but man's best and woman's worst amount

---

²⁴³| MS:old life §crossed out and replaced above by§ way in the sunshine, much *1887:*the world, and, much ²⁴⁴| MS:played §next word illegibly crossed out and replaced above by§ life's ²⁴⁵| MS:"Now, Saint Scholastica §compressed into space left for shorter word§ ²⁴⁶| MS:In paynimrie, behold a *1887:*In Paynimrie, behold, a ²⁴⁷| MS:path! and off §last two words crossed out and replaced above by two words§ Her waist ²⁴⁸| MS:With §crossed out and replaced above by§ Of < > binds §over illegible word§ ²⁴⁹| MS:And, leads him captive §last three words crossed out and replaced above by three words§ leashed all lamblike < > court, §comma crossed out§ ²⁵⁰| MS:him . . Ay, many a story §crossed out and replaced above by§ legend *1887:*him." Ay ²⁵⁵| MS:heaven its host amid: §last four words transposed to§ heaven amid its host: ²⁵⁷| MS:close a kinship—was—was—Saint, §last word crossed out and restored§ *1887:*close the kinship < > this, ²⁵⁸| MS:kiss: *1887:*kiss! ²⁶¹| MS:And yet §last two words crossed out§ one §altered to§ like < > too: can §crossed out and replaced above by§ up ²⁶³| MS:The

So nearly to the same thing, that we count
265 In man a miracle of faithfulness
If, while unfaithful somewhat, he lay stress
On the main fact that love, when love indeed,
Is wholly solely love from first to last—
Truth—all the rest a lie. Too likely, fast
270 Enough that necklace went to grace the throat
—Let's say, of such a dancer as makes doat
The senses when the soul is satisfied—
Trogalia, say the Greeks—a sweetmeat tried
Approvingly by sated tongue and teeth,
275 Once body's proper meal consigned beneath
Such unconsidered munching.

XVII

Fancy's flight

Makes me a listener when, some sleepless night,
The duke reviewed his memories, and aghast
Found that the Present intercepts the Past
280 With such effect as when a cloud enwraps
The moon and, moon-suffused, plays moon perhaps
To who walks under, till comes, late or soon,
A stumble: up he looks, and lo, the moon
Calm, clear, convincingly herself once more!
285 How could he 'scape the cloud that thrust between

---

lady's §last two words crossed out and replaced above by word and dash§ Hers—
264| MS:thing,—that §inserted above§ we should §crossed out and replaced above by§ may
§crossed out§ *1887:*thing, that   266| MS:If, all the §last two words crossed out§ < >
unfaithful, he lays §altered to§ lay handsome §inserted above then altered to§ some stress
*1887:*unfaithful somewhat, he lay stress   267| MS:love, if love *1887:*love when love
268| MS:wholly and §crossed out§ solely the §crossed out§   269| MS:And §crossed out
and replaced above by word and dash§ Truth— < > a make-believe. If §last two words crossed
out and replaced above by four words§ lie. Put care that fast *1887:*lie. Too likely, fast
270| MS:Enough §in margin§ < > went full soon §last two words crossed out§
271| MS:—Suppose §crossed out and replaced above by two words and comma§ Let's say, of
273| MS:*Trogmalia,* say the Greeks,—the §crossed out and replaced above by§ a sweetmeats
§altered to§ sweetmeat *1887:Trogalia,* say the Greeks—a   274| MS:teeth *1887:*teeth,
282| MS:under, until §altered to§ till comes, §last word and comma inserted above§
283| MS:—A stumble—up *1887:*A stumble: up   285| MS:How might §crossed out and
replaced above by§ could he spurn the < > thrust before §altered to§ between *1887:*he

Him and effulgence? Speak, fool—duke, I mean!

XVIII

"Who bade you come, brisk-marching bold she-shape,
    A terror with those black-balled worlds of eyes,
    That black hair bristling solid-built from nape
290   To crown it coils about? O dread surmise!
Take, tread on, trample under past escape
    Your capture, spoil and trophy! Do—devise
Insults for one who, fallen once, ne'er shall rise!

"Mock on, triumphant o'er the prostrate shame!
295   Laugh 'Here lies he among the false to Love—
Love's loyal liegeman once: the very same
    Who, scorning his weak fellows, towered above
Inconstancy: yet why his faith defame?
    Our eagle's victor was at least no dove,
300   No dwarfish knight picked up our giant's glove—

" 'When, putting prowess to the proof, faith urged
    Her champion to the challenge: had it chanced
That merely virtue, wisdom, beauty—merged
    All in one woman—merely these advanced
305   Their claim to conquest,—hardly had he purged
    His mind of memories, dearnesses enhanced
Rather than harmed by death, nor, disentranced,

" 'Promptly had he abjured the old pretence
    To prove his kind's superior—first to last

'scape the   286| MS:His true §last two words crossed out and replaced above by two words§ Him and effulgence? Fancy to the §last three words crossed out and replaced above by two words and dash§ Speak, fool— <> mean.   *1887:*mean!   287| MS:brisk marching <> she-shape   *1887:*brisk-marching <> she-shape,   288| MS:worlds in eyes,   *1887:*worlds of eyes,   293| MS:fallen once, §last word and comma inserted above§   295| MS:Laugh," §altered to§ '   299| MS:The eagle's   *1887:*Our eagle's
304| MS:woman—these alone advanced   *1887:*woman—merely these advanced
305| MS:A claim   *1887:*Their claim   307| MS:Not harmed by death at all, nor
*1887:*Rather than harmed by death, nor   308| MS:" 'Promptly abjured the old and vain pretence   *1887:*" 'Promptly had he abjured the old pretence

45

310   Display erect on his heart's eminence
       An altar to the never-dying Past.
    For such feat faith might boast fit play of fence
       And easily disarm the iconoclast
    Called virtue, wisdom, beauty: impudence

315   " 'Fought in their stead, and how could faith but fall?
       There came a bold she-shape brisk-marching, bent
    No inch of her imperious stature, tall
       As some war-engine from whose top was sent
    One shattering volley out of eye's black ball,
320   And prone lay faith's defender!' Mockery spent?
    Malice discharged in full? In that event,

    "My queenly impudence, I cover close,
       I wrap me round with love of your black hair,
    Black eyes, black every wicked inch of those
325   Limbs' war-tower tallness: so much truth lives there
    'Neath the dead heap of lies. And yet—who knows?
       What if such things are? No less, such things were.
    Then was the man your match whom now you dare

    "Treat as existent still. A second truth!
330   They held—this heap of lies you rightly scorn—
    A man who had approved himself in youth
       More than a match for—you? for sea-foam-born
    Venus herself: you conquer him forsooth?
       'Tis me his ghost: he died since left and lorn,

---

³¹⁰| MS:Keeping erect   *1887*:Display erect   ³¹³| MS:iconoclast: *1887*:iconoclast
³¹⁴| MS:Mere §crossed out and replaced above by§ Not virtue <> beauty,—impudence
1887:Called virtue <> beauty: impudence   ³¹⁵| MS:" 'Came in   *1887*:" 'Fought in
³¹⁶| MS:brisk marching   *1887*:brisk-marching   ³¹⁷| MS:stature tall   *1887*:stature, tall
³¹⁹| MS:One shattering §over perhaps *battering*§ <> ball   *1887*:ball,
³²⁰| MS:defender!' Mocking spent—   *1887*:defender!' Mockery spent?
³²²| MS:close   *1887*:close,   ³²³| MS:hair   *1887*:hair,   ³²⁶| *1887*:Neath
1889a:'Neath   ³²⁷| MS:were—   *1887*:were.   ³²⁹| MS:truth—   *1887*:truth!
³³¹| MS:A love which had approved itself in   *1887*:A man who had approved himself in
³³⁴| MS:died when §crossed out and replaced above by§ since

335   As needs must Samson when his hair is shorn.

"Some day, and soon, be sure himself will rise,
    Called into life by her who long ago
Left his soul whiling time in flesh-disguise.
    Ghosts tired of waiting can play tricks, you know!
340   Tread, trample me—such sport we ghosts devise,
    Waiting the morn-star's re-appearance—though
You think we vanish scared by the cock's crow."

335| MS:must Sampson   *1887*:must Samson   336| MS:rise   *1887*:rise,
338| MS:Left his §inserted above§ soul to while the §last three words altered to§ whiling

WITH CHRISTOPHER SMART

I

It seems as if . . . or did the actual chance
Startle me and perplex? Let truth be said!
How might this happen? Dreaming, blindfold led
By visionary hand, did soul's advance
5   Precede my body's, gain inheritance
Of fact by fancy—so that when I read
At length with waking eyes your Song, instead
Of mere bewilderment, with me first glance
Was but full recognition that in trance
10   Or merely thought's adventure some old day
Of dim and done-with boyishness, or—well,
Why might it not have been, the miracle
Broke on me as I took my sober way
Through veritable regions of our earth
15   And made discovery, many a wondrous one?

II

Anyhow, fact or fancy, such its birth:
I was exploring some huge house, had gone
Through room and room complacently, no dearth
Anywhere of the signs of decent taste,
20   Adequate culture: wealth had run to waste
Nowise, nor penury was proved by stint:
All showed the Golden Mean without a hint
Of brave extravagance that breaks the rule.
The master of the mansion was no fool
25   Assuredly, no genius just as sure!
Safe mediocrity had scorned the lure
Of now too much and now too little cost,
And satisfied me sight was never lost

WITH CHRISTOPHER SMART   *Title*| MS:IV. §numeral crossed out and replaced by numeral and period§ III./With   *1889a*:§numeral deleted§   ¹| MS:if . . or *1889a*:if . . . or   ¹⁹| MS:taste,— *1887*:taste,   ²⁵| MS:sure: *1887*:sure!

Of moderate design's accomplishment
30   In calm completeness. On and on I went,
With no more hope than fear of what came next,
Till lo, I push a door, sudden uplift
A hanging, enter, chance upon a shift
Indeed of scene! So—thus it is thou deck'st,
35   High heaven, our low earth's brick-and-mortar work?

III

It was the Chapel. That a star, from murk
Which hid, should flashingly emerge at last,
Were small surprise: but from broad day I passed
Into a presence that turned shine to shade.
40   There fronted me the Rafael Mother-Maid,
Never to whom knelt votarist in shrine
By Nature's bounty helped, by Art's divine
More varied—beauty with magnificence—
Than this: from floor to roof one evidence
45   Of how far earth may rival heaven. No niche
Where glory was not prisoned to enrich
Man's gaze with gold and gems, no space but glowed
With colour, gleamed with carving—hues which owed
Their outburst to a brush the painter fed
50   With rainbow-substance—rare shapes never wed
To actual flesh and blood, which, brain-born once,
Became the sculptor's dowry, Art's response
To earth's despair. And all seemed old yet new:
Youth,—in the marble's curve, the canvas' hue,
55   Apparent,—wanted not the crowning thrill

---

[31]   MS:of what §inserted above§   [32]   MS:When lo   *1887*:Till lo
[33]   MS:enter, §next word illegibly crossed out and replaced above by§ chance
[34]   MS:scene: so—thus it is §last two words inserted above§   *1887*:scene! So
[35]   MS:heaven, this §crossed out and replaced above by§ our <> work!   *1887*:work?
[39]   MS:presence that §inserted above§   [40]   MS:the Rafael Mother-Maid   *1887*:the
Rafael Mother-Maid,   [42]   MS:By nature's <> helped by   *1887*:By Nature's <>
helped, by   [50]   MS:rainbow-substance—shapes were never   *1887*:rainbow-substance—
rare shapes never   [51]   MS:blood, but, brain-born   *1887*:blood, which, brain-born
[53]   MS:despair: and <> new—   *1887*:despair. And <> new:

Of age the consecrator. Hands long still
Had worked here—could it be, what lent them skill
Retained a power to supervise, protect,
Enforce new lessons with the old, connect
60   Our life with theirs? No merely modern touch
Told me that here the artist, doing much,
Elsewhere did more, perchance does better, lives—
So needs must learn.

IV

Well, these provocatives
Having fulfilled their office, forth I went
65   Big with anticipation—well-nigh fear—
Of what next room and next for startled eyes
Might have in store, surprise beyond surprise.
Next room and next and next—what followed here?
Why, nothing! not one object to arrest
70   My passage—everywhere too manifest
The previous decent null and void of best
And worst, mere ordinary right and fit,
Calm commonplace which neither missed, nor hit
Inch-high, inch-low, the placid mark proposed.

V

75   Armed with this instance, have I diagnosed
Your case, my Christopher? The man was sound
And sane at starting: all at once the ground
Gave way beneath his step, a certain smoke
Curled up and caught him, or perhaps down broke
80   A fireball wrapping flesh and spirit both
In conflagration. Then—as heaven were loth
To linger—let earth understand too well
How heaven at need can operate—off fell

---

⁶¹| MS:artist did so much,   *1887:*artist, doing much,   ⁶²| MS:Elsewhere does more—
perchance < > lives   *1887:*Elsewhere did more, perchance < > lives—   ⁶⁵| MS:well
nigh   *1889a:*well-nigh   ⁷³| MS:Our commonplace   *1887:*Calm commonplace

The flame-robe, and the untransfigured man
85 Resumed sobriety,—as he began,
So did he end nor alter pace, not he!

VI

Now, what I fain would know is—could it be
That he—whoe'er he was that furnished forth
The Chapel, making thus, from South to North,
90 Rafael touch Leighton, Michelagnolo
Join Watts, was found but once combining so
The elder and the younger, taking stand
On Art's supreme,—or that yourself who sang
A Song where flute-breath silvers trumpet-clang,
95 And stations you for once on either hand
With Milton and with Keats, empowered to claim
Affinity on just one point—(or blame
Or praise my judgment, thus it fronts you full)—
How came it you resume the void and null,
100 Subside to insignificance,—live, die
—Proved plainly two mere mortals who drew nigh
One moment—that, to Art's best hierarchy,
This, to the superhuman poet-pair?
What if, in one point only, then and there
105 The otherwise all-unapproachable
Allowed impingement? Does the sphere pretend
To span the cube's breadth, cover end to end
The plane with its embrace? No, surely! Still,
Contact is contact, sphere's touch no whit less

84| MS:The fire-robe and   *1887:*The flame-robe, and   86| MS:So ended §crossed out
and replaced above by§ did he nor ended §last two words crossed out and replaced above by
two words§ end nor   88| MS:That whoso'er he   *1887:*That he—whoe'er he
89| MS:The Chapel, as he made from <> North   *1887:*The Chapel, making thus, from <>
North,   91| MS:Join Watts, could boast of once   *1887:*Join Watts, was found but once
93| MS:supreme of altar-steps,—or sang   *1887:*supreme,—or that yourself who sang
94| MS:Your Song   *1887:*A Song   95| MS:And found you stationed thus on   *1887:*And
stations you for once on   96| MS:with Keats, of right §last two words crossed out and
replaced above by§ empowered   99| MS:Could either man resume   *1887:*How came it
you resume   101| MS:—Each §crossed out and replaced above by§ Proved plainly each
§inserted above§ a mere §crossed out§ mortal who was nigh   *1887:*plainly two mere mortals
who drew nigh   108| MS:embrace? No question! Still,   *1887:*embrace? No, surely! Still,

110   Than cube's superimposure. Such success
       Befell Smart only out of throngs between
       Milton and Keats that donned the singing-dress—
       Smart, solely of such songmen, pierced the screen
       'Twixt thing and word, lit language straight from soul,—
115   Left no fine film-flake on the naked coal
       Live from the censer—shapely or uncouth,
       Fire-suffused through and through, one blaze of truth
       Undeadened by a lie,—(you have my mind)—
       For, think! this blaze outleapt with black behind
120   And blank before, when Hayley and the rest . . .
       But let the dead successors worst and best
       Bury their dead: with life be my concern—
       Yours with the fire-flame: what I fain would learn
       Is just—(suppose me haply ignorant
125   Down to the common knowledge, doctors vaunt)
       Just this—why only once the fire-flame was:
       No matter if the marvel came to pass
       The way folk judged—if power too long suppressed
       Broke loose and maddened, as the vulgar guessed,
130   Or simply brain-disorder (doctors said)
       A turmoil of the particles disturbed
       Brain's workaday performance in your head,
       Spurred spirit to wild action health had curbed:
       And so verse issued in a cataract
135   Whence prose, before and after, unperturbed
       Was wont to wend its way. Concede the fact
       That here a poet was who always could—
       Never before did—never after would—
       Achieve the feat: how were such fact explained?

---

[111] MS:Befell you only   *1887*:Befell Smart only   [112] MS:and Keats who §crossed out and replaced above by§ that   [113] MS:You, solely of the §crossed out and replaced above by§ such   *1887*:Smart, solely   [116] MS:censer,—shapely   *1887*:censer—shapely   [118] MS:mind)   *1887*:mind)—   [119] MS:To think this   *1887*:For, think! this   [121] MS:let your dead   *1887*:let the dead   [128] MS:way men thought—if   *1887*:way folks judged—if   *1889a*:folk   [130] MS:Or brain-disorder merely (doctors   *1887*:Or simply brain-disorder (doctors   [132] MS:workyday   *1887*:workaday   [133] MS:curbed,   *1889a*:curbed:

VII

¹⁴⁰ Was it that when, by rarest chance, there fell
    Disguise from Nature, so that Truth remained
    Naked, and whoso saw for once could tell
    Us others of her majesty and might
    In large, her lovelinesses infinite
¹⁴⁵ In little,—straight you used the power wherewith
    Sense, penetrating as through rind to pith
    Each object, thoroughly revealed might view
    And comprehend the old things thus made new,
    So that while eye saw, soul to tongue could trust
¹⁵⁰ Thing which struck word out, and once more adjust
    Real vision to right language, till heaven's vault
    Pompous with sunset, storm-stirred sea's assault
    On the swilled rock-ridge, earth's embosomed brood
    Of tree and flower and weed, with all the life
¹⁵⁵ That flies or swims or crawls, in peace or strife,
    Above, below,—each had its note and name
    For Man to know by,—Man who, now—the same
    As erst in Eden, needs that all he sees
    Be named him ere he note by what degrees
¹⁶⁰ Of strength and beauty to its end Design
    Ever thus operates—(your thought and mine,
    No matter for the many dissident)—
    So did you sing your Song, so truth found vent
    In words for once with you?

---

^{141|} MS:from Nature so   *1887*:from Nature, so   ^{142|} MS:Naked for once and <> saw
might §crossed out and replaced above by§ could   *1887*:Naked, and <> saw for once could
^{143|} MS:Us §altered to§ As truly of the §crossed out and replaced above by§ her   *1887*:Us
others of her   ^{144|} MS:large, and §crossed out and replaced above by§ her
^{145|} MS:little—so we others say wherewith   *1887*:little,—straight you used the power wherewith
^{147|} MS:object thoroughly   *1887*:object, thoroughly   ^{148|} MS:comprehend the §inserted
above§ <> anew   *1887*:new,   ^{157|} MS:For man <> by,—man who, all §crossed out and
replaced above by word and dash§ now—   *1887*:For Man <> by,—Man   ^{162|} MS:the
others §crossed out and replaced above by§ many dissident.)   *1887*:dissident)—   ^{163|}
MS:§new section begins§ <> your Song, thus §crossed out and replaced above by§ so
1887:§no new section§   ^{164|} MS:you: when—back   *1887*:you? §new section§ Then—back

VIII

Then—back was furled
165 The robe thus thrown aside, and straight the world
Darkened into the old oft-catalogued
Repository of things that sky, wave, land,
Or show or hide, clear late, accretion-clogged
Now, just as long ago, by tellings and
170 Re-tellings to satiety, which strike
Muffled upon the ear's drum. Very like
None was so startled as yourself when friends
Came, hailed your fast-returning wits: "Health mends
Importantly, for—to be plain with you—
175 This scribble on the wall was done—in lieu
Of pen and paper—with—ha, ha!—your key
Denting it on the wainscot! Do you see
How wise our caution was? Thus much we stopped
Of babble that had else grown print: and lopped
180 From your trim bay-tree this unsightly bough—
Smart's who translated Horace! Write us now" . . .
Why, what Smart did write—never afterward
One line to show that he, who paced the sward,
Had reached the zenith from his madhouse cell.

IX

185 Was it because you judged (I know full well
You never had the fancy)—judged—as some—
That who makes poetry must reproduce
Thus ever and thus only, as they come,
Each strength, each beauty, everywhere diffuse

165| MS:robe for once §last two words crossed out and replaced above by§ thus thrown wide
§altered to§ aside   167| MS:things that §inserted above§ sky, and §crossed out§ wave, and
§crossed out§   169| MS:Now as so long ago by   *1887:*Now, just as long ago, by
170| MS:Retellings   *1889a:*Re-tellings   173| MS:hailing §altered to§ hailed your fast
§inserted above§   *1887:*fast-returning   178| MS:much was §crossed out and replaced above
by§ we   179| MS:print: we §crossed out and replaced above by§ and   181| *1887:*now"
. . *1889a:*now" . . .   183| MS:he who §next word inserted above and illegibly crossed out§
< > sward   *1887:*he, who < > sward,   184| MS:Soared to §last two words crossed out and
replaced above by two words§ Had reached the zenith in §crossed out and replaced above by§
from   189| MS:strength and §crossed out and replaced by§ each   *1887:*strength, each

190   Throughout creation, so that eye and ear,
        Seeing and hearing, straight shall recognize,
        At touch of just a trait, the strength appear,—
        Suggested by a line's lapse see arise
        All evident the beauty,—fresh surprise
195   Startling at fresh achievement? "So, indeed,
        Wallows the whale's bulk in the waste of brine,
        Nor otherwise its feather-tufts make fine
        Wild Virgin's Bower when stars faint off to seed!"
        (My prose—your poetry I dare not give,
200   Purpling too much my mere grey argument.)
        —Was it because you judged—when fugitive
        Was glory found, and wholly gone and spent
        Such power of startling up deaf ear, blind eye,
        At truth's appearance,—that you humbly bent
205   The head and, bidding vivid work good-bye,
        Doffed lyric dress and trod the world once more
        A drab-clothed decent proseman as before?
        Strengths, beauties, by one word's flash thus laid bare
        —That was effectual service: made aware
210   Of strengths and beauties, Man but hears the text,
        Awaits your teaching. Nature? What comes next?
        Why all the strength and beauty?—to be shown
        Thus in one word's flash, thenceforth let alone
        By Man who needs must deal with aught that's known
215   Never so lately and so little? Friend,

191| MS:straight should §altered to§ shall recognize   *1887*:recognize,
192| MS:trait the   *1887*:trait, the   194| MS:An evidence §last two words altered to§ All evident the beauty,—still §crossed out and replaced above by§ fresh
195| MS:at such §crossed out and replaced above by§ fresh achievement: "So *1887*:achievement? "So   198| MS:faint off §inserted above§   200| MS:Purpling thereby §crossed out§ my mere §last two words crossed out, replaced above by two words, and restored§ too much §last two words crossed out and restored; line altered to read§ Purpling too much my mere grey argument   *1887*:argument.)   201| MS:—Was §dash in margin§
204| MS:appearance,—straight you   *1887*:appearance,—that you   205| MS:goodbye, *1889a*:good-bye,   207| MS:decent classic as   *1887*:decent proseman as
210| MS:beauties, man has heard the   *1887*:beauties, Man but hears for the teaching. Nature! What   *1887*:Awaits your teaching. Nature? What   211| MS:Waits   212| MS:Why all §inserted above§ this same §crossed out§ strength   *1887*:all the strength
213| MS:Thus by §crossed out and replaced above by§ in

First give us knowledge, then appoint its use!
Strength, beauty are the means: ignore their end?
As well you stopped at proving how profuse
Stones, sticks, nay stubble lie to left and right
220 Ready to help the builder,—careless quite
If he should take, or leave the same to strew
Earth idly,—as by word's flash bring in view
Strength, beauty, then bid who beholds the same
Go on beholding. Why gains unemployed?
225 Nature was made to be by Man enjoyed
First; followed duly by enjoyment's fruit,
Instruction—haply leaving joy behind:
And you, the instructor, would you slack pursuit
Of the main prize, as poet help mankind
230 Just to enjoy, there leave them? Play the fool,
Abjuring a superior privilege?
Please simply when your function is to rule—
By thought incite to deed? From edge to edge
Of earth's round, strength and beauty everywhere
235 Pullulate—and must you particularize
All, each and every apparition? Spare
Yourself and us the trouble! Ears and eyes
Want so much strength and beauty, and no less
Nor more, to learn life's lesson by. Oh, yes—
240 The other method's favoured in our day!
The end ere the beginning: as you may,
Master the heavens before you study earth,
Make you familiar with the meteor's birth
Ere you descend to scrutinize the rose!

216| MS:knowledge then   *1887*:knowledge, then   217| MS:means—ignore
1887:means: ignore   220| MS:builder, careless   *1887*:builder,—careless
221| MS:take or   *1887*:take, or   223| MS:beauty, and bid   *1887*:beauty, then bid
224| MS:beholding, leave §crossed out§ gains all-unemployed.   *1887*:beholding. Why gains
unemployed?   230| MS:fool   *1887*:fool,   231| MS:Abjuring the instructor's
privilege—   *1887*:Abjuring a superior privilege?   235| MS:and shall you particularise
1887:and must you particularize   236| MS:all—each   *1887*:All, each
237| MS:trouble: ears   *1887*:trouble! Ears   238| MS:beauty and   *1887*:beauty, and
239| MS:more to   *1887*:more, to   244| MS:Before §crossed out and replaced above by§
Ere <> scrutize §altered to§ scrutinize the rose: *1887*:rose!

245 I say, o'erstep no least one of the rows
That lead man from the bottom where he plants
Foot first of all, to life's last ladder-top:
Arrived there, vain enough will seem the vaunts
Of those who say—"We scale the skies, then drop
250 To earth—to find, how all things there are loth
To answer heavenly law: we understand
The meteor's course, and lo, the rose's growth—
How other than should be by law's command!"
Would not you tell such—"Friends, beware lest fume
255 Offuscate sense: learn earth first ere presume
To teach heaven legislation. Law must be
Active in earth or nowhere: earth you see,—
Or there or not at all, Will, Power and Love
Admit discovery,—as below, above
260 Seek next law's confirmation! But reverse
The order, where's the wonder things grow worse
Than, by the law your fancy formulates,
They should be? Cease from anger at the fates
Which thwart themselves so madly. Live and learn,
265 Not first learn and then live, is our concern."

245| MS:no least §inserted above§ one of all §crossed out§   246| MS:where his foot §last
two words crossed out and replaced above by two words§ he plants   247| MS:Is planted
§last two words crossed out and replaced above by§ Foot < > to very §crossed out and replaced
above by two words§ life's last   248| MS:Of life: §last two words and colon crossed out§
arrived §altered to§ Arrived < > vain enough §inserted above§   250| MS:find, also §word
and comma crossed out§   251| MS:law,—we   1887:law: we   254| MS:such "Friends
1887:such—"Friends   255| MS:sense,—learn   1887:sense: learn   256| MS:legislation:
law   1887:legislation. Law   257| MS:see,   1887:see,—   258| MS:all Love, Power
and Will §last four words transposed to§ all Will, Power and Love   1887:all, Will
259| MS:Await discovery   1887:Admit discovery   260| MS:Look for law's confirmation,—but
1887:Seek next law's confirmation! But   261| MS:order, wonder not if things
1887:order, where's the wonder things   262| MS:laws   1887:law   263| MS:be:
hence much anger   1887:be? Cease from anger   264| MS:learn   1887:learn,
265| MS:Not learn and live, is thus our sole concern—   1887:Not first learn and then live, is
our concern.   1889a:concern. §emended to§ concern." §see Editorial Notes§

WITH GEORGE BUBB DODINGTON

I

Ah, George Bubb Dodington Lord Melcombe,—no,
Yours was the wrong way!—always understand,
Supposing that permissibly you planned
How statesmanship—your trade—in outward show
5   Might figure as inspired by simple zeal
For serving country, king, and commonweal,
(Though service tire to death the body, tease
The soul from out an o'ertasked patriot-drudge)
And yet should prove zeal's outward show agrees
10   In all respects—right reason being judge—
With inward care that, while the statesman spends
Body and soul thus freely for the sake
Of public good, his private welfare take
No harm by such devotedness. Intends
15   Scripture aught else—let captious folk inquire—
Which teaches "Labourers deserve their hire,
And who neglects his household bears the bell
Away of sinning from an infidel"?
Wiselier would fools that carp bestow a thought
20   How birds build nests; at outside, roughly wrought,
Twig knots with twig, loam plasters up each chink,
Leaving the inmate rudely lodged—you think?
Peep but inside! That specious rude-and-rough
Covers a domicile where downy fluff
25   Embeds the ease-deserving architect,
Who toiled and moiled not merely to effect
'Twixt sprig and spray a stop-gap in the teeth
Of wind and weather, guard what swung beneath

WITH GEORGE BUBB DODINGTON   *Title*| MS:VI §crossed out and replaced by§ IV.
1889a:§numeral deleted§   6| MS:king and *1889a*:king, and   7| MS:teaze
1889a:tease   11| MS:that while *1887*:that, while   15| MS:enquire *1889a*:inquire
16| MS:Which tells us §last two words crossed out and replaced above by§ teaches
18| MS:infidel?" *1887*:infidel"?   19| MS:would whoso §crossed out and replaced above
by two words§ fools that carps §altered to§ carp   25| MS:architect *1887*:architect,

From upset only, but contrived himself
30   A snug interior, warm and soft and sleek.
Of what material? Oh, for that, you seek
How nature prompts each volatile! Thus—pelf
Smoothens the human mudlark's lodging, power
Demands some hardier wrappage to embrace
35   Robuster heart-beats: rock, not tree nor tower,
Contents the building eagle: rook shoves close
To brother rook on branch, while crow morose
Apart keeps balance perched on topmost bough.
No sort of bird but suits his taste somehow:
40   Nay, Darwin tells of such as love the bower—
His bower-birds opportunely yield us yet
The lacking instance when at loss to get
A feathered parallel to what we find
The secret motor of some mighty mind
45   That worked such wonders—all for vanity!
Worked them to haply figure in the eye
Of intimates as first of—doers' kind?
Actors', that work in earnest sportively,
Paid by a sourish smile. How says the Sage?
50   Birds born to strut prepare a platform-stage
With sparkling stones and speckled shells, all sorts
Of shiny rubbish, odds and ends and orts,
Whereon to pose and posture and engage
The priceless female simper.

II

I have gone

55   Thus into detail, George Bubb Dodington,
Lest, when I take you presently to task
For the wrong way of working, you should ask

30| MS:sleek: §altered to§ sleek.   38| MS:bough: §altered to§ bough.
39| MS:somehow—   *1887*:somehow: *1889a*:somehow §emended to§ somehow: §see Editorial Notes§   41| MS:bower-bird §altered to§ bower-birds <> yields §altered to§ yield
48| MS:sportively   *1887*:Actors,' <> sportively,   *1889a*:Actors', that   52| MS:Of shiny rubbish   *1887*:Of slimy rubbish   *1889a*:Of slimy §emended to§ shiny §see Editorial Notes§

"What fool conjectures that profession means
Performance? that who goes behind the scenes
60   Finds,—acting over,—still the soot-stuff screens
Othello's visage, still the self-same cloak's
Bugle-bright-blackness half reveals half chokes
Hamlet's emotion, as ten minutes since?
No, each resumes his garb, stands—Moor or prince—
65   Decently draped: just so with statesmanship!"
All outside show, in short, is sham—why wince?
Concede me—while our parley lasts! You trip
Afterwards—lay but this to heart! (there lurks
Somewhere in all of us a lump which irks
70   Somewhat the sprightliest-scheming brain that's bent
On brave adventure, would but heart consent!)
—Here trip you, that—your aim allowed as right—
Your means thereto were wrong. Come, we, this night,
Profess one purpose, hold one principle,
75   Are at odds only as to—not the will
But way of winning solace for ourselves
—No matter if the ore for which zeal delves
Be gold or coprolite, while zeal's pretence
Is—we do good to men at—whose expense
80   But ours? who tire the body, tease the soul,
Simply that, running, we may reach fame's goal
And wreathe at last our brows with bay—the State's
Disinterested slaves, nay—please the Fates—
Saviours and nothing less: such lot has been!
85   Statesmanship triumphs pedestalled, serene,—
O happy consummation!—brought about
By managing with skill the rabble-rout
For which we labour (never mind the name—

---

[63]   MS:since?   *1889a*:since?" §emended to§ since? §see Editorial Notes§
[65]   MS:statesmanship!   *1889a*:statesmanship §emended to§ statesmanship!" §see Editorial
Notes§   [70]   MS:spriteliest-scheming   *1889a*:sprightliest-scheming
[80]   MS:ours who < > teaze   *1887*:ours? who   *1889a*:tease   [81]   MS:running hard, we
reach   *1887*:running, we may reach   [83]   MS:Disinterested servants—please the Fates,
1887:Disinterested slaves, nay—please the Fates—   [85]   MS:serene,   *1887*:serene,—

People or populace), for praise or blame
90 Making them understand—their heaven, their hell,
Their every hope and fear is ours as well.
Man's cause—what other can we have at heart?
Whence follows that the necessary part
High o'er Man's head we play,—and freelier breathe
95 Just that the multitude which gasps beneath
May reach the level where unstifled stand
Ourselves at vantage to put forth a hand,
Assist the prostrate public. 'Tis by right
Merely of such pretence, we reach the height
100 Where storms abound, to brave—nay, court their stress,
Though all too well aware—of pomp the less,
Of peace the more! But who are we, to spurn
For peace' sake, duty's pointing? Up, then—earn
Albeit no prize we may but martyrdom!
105 Now, such fit height to launch salvation from,
How get and gain? Since help must needs be craved
By would-be saviours of the else-unsaved,
How coax them to co-operate, lend a lift,
Kneel down and let us mount?

III

You say "Make shift
110 By sham—the harsh word: preach and teach, persuade
Somehow the Public—not despising aid
Of salutary artifice—we seek
Solely their good: our strength would raise the weak,
Our cultivated knowledge supplement

89| MS:populace) for <> blame *1887*:populace, for <> blame) *1889a*:populace, for <>
blame) §emended to§ populace), for <> blame §see Editorial Notes§   91| MS:well—
1887:well.   94| MS:play, and §crossed out and replaced above by dash and word§ —to
freelier *1887*:play,—and freelier   97| MS:vantage to §last two words altered to§ vantage,
who put *1887*:vantage to put   99| MS:we claim the *1887*:we reach the   100| MS:to
bear—nay *1887*:to brave—nay   102| MS:more! but <> we to *1887*:more! But <> we, to
104| MS:prize may we §transposed to§ prize we may   107| MS:else unsaved, *1887*:else-
unsaved,   108| MS:them lend co-operant a *1887*:them to co-operate, lend lift,
1889a:lend a lift,   109| MS:say: "Make *1887*:say "Make   113| MS:weak *1887*:weak,

¹¹⁵ Their rudeness, rawness: why to us were lent
Ability except to come in use?
Who loves his kind must by all means induce
That kind to let his love play freely, press
In Man's behalf to full performance!"

IV

Yes—

¹²⁰ Yes, George, we know!—whereat they hear, believe,
And bend the knee, and on the neck receive
Who fawned and cringed to purpose? Not so, George!
Try simple falsehood on shrewd folk who forge
Lies of superior fashion day by day
¹²⁵ And hour by hour? With craftsmen versed as they
What chance of competition when the tools
Only a novice wields? Are knaves such fools?
Disinterested patriots, spare your tongue
The tones thrice-silvery, cheek save smiles it flung
¹³⁰ Pearl-like profuse to swine—a herd, whereof
No unit needs be taught, his neighbour's trough
Scarce holds for who but grunts and whines the husks
Due to a wrinkled snout that shows sharp tusks.
No animal—much less our lordly Man—
¹³⁵ Obeys its like: with strength all rule began,
The stoutest awes the pasture. Soon succeeds
Discrimination,—nicer power Man needs
To rule him than is bred of bone and thew:
Intelligence must move strength's self. This too
¹⁴⁰ Lasts but its time: the multitude at length
Looks inside for intelligence and strength

---

^{115|} MS:The §altered to§ Their   ^{118|} MS:let that love   *1889a:*let his love
^{119|} MS:In man's   *1887:*In Man's   ^{123|} MS:folks   *1889a:*folk
^{128|} MS:patriot   *1889a:*patriots   ^{129|} MS:Its tones thrice-silvery, save the smiles you
flung   *1887:*The tones thrice-silvery, cheek save smiles it flung   ^{131|} MS:What §crossed
out and replaced above by§ No <> taught his   *1887:*taught, his   ^{132|} MS:Scarce
§inserted above§ Holds §altered to§ holds not §crossed out§ for him who grunts <> husks,
*1887:*for who but grunts <> husks   ^{133|} MS:to the §crossed out and replaced above
by§ a   ^{137|} MS:power man §altered to§ Man   ^{138|} MS:thew,—   *1887:*thew:

And finds them here and there to pick and choose:
"All at your service, mine, see!" Ay, but who's
My George, at this late day, to make his boast
145 "In strength, intelligence, I rule the roast,
Beat, all and some, the ungraced who crowd your ranks?"
"Oh, but I love, would lead you, gain your thanks
By unexampled yearning for Man's sake—
Passion that solely waits your help to take
150 Effect in action!" George, which one of us
But holds with his own heart communion thus:
"I am, if not of men the first and best,
Still—to receive enjoyment—properest:
Which since by force I cannot, nor by wit
155 Most likely—craft must serve in place of it.
Flatter, cajole! If so I bring within
My net the gains which wit and force should win,
What hinders?" 'Tis a trick we know of old:
Try, George, some other of tricks manifold!
160 The multitude means mass and mixture—right!
Are mixtures simple, pray, or composite?
Dive into Man, your medley: see the waste!
Sloth-stifled genius, energy disgraced
By ignorance, high aims with sorry skill,
165 Will without means and means in want of will
—Sure we might fish, from out the mothers' sons
That welter thus, a dozen Dodingtons!
Why call up Dodington, and none beside,

145| MS:intelligence, he §crossed out and replaced above by§ I rules §altered to§ rule
146| MS:Beats §altered to§ Beat all and some the <> our §altered to§ your ranks? *1887*:Beat,
all and some, the <> ranks?" 147| MS:but he §crossed out and replaced above by§ I loves
§altered to§ love <> you, claims §altered to§ claim our §altered to§ your *1887*:you, gain your
149| MS:solely craves your *1887*:solely waits your 154| MS:Which get §crossed out§ by
mere §inserted above§ force I cannot, and §crossed out and replaced above by§ nor
1887:Which since by force 155| MS:Scarce §crossed out and replaced above by§ Much
likelier: craft *1887*:Most likely—craft 157| MS:force might §crossed out and replaced
above by§ should 160| MS:right! *1887*:right! *1889a*:right §emended to§ right! §see
Editorial Notes§ 162| MS:medley—see the waste— *1887*:medley: see the waste!
166|MS:fish from *1887*:fish, from 167| MS:thus a *1887*:thus, a 168| MS:up
§crossed out§ Dodington and <> beside *1887*:up Dodington, and <> beside,

To take his seat upon our backs and ride
170 As statesman conquering and to conquer? Well,
The last expedient, which must needs excel
Those old ones—this it is,—at any rate
To-day's conception thus I formulate:
As simple force has been replaced, just so
175 Must simple wit be: men have got to know
Such wit as what you boast is nowise held
The wonder once it was, but, paralleled
Too plentifully, counts not,—puts to shame
Modest possessors like yourself who claim,
180 By virtue of it merely, power and place
—Which means the sweets of office. Since our race
Teems with the like of you, some special gift,
Your very own, must coax our hands to lift,
And backs to bear you: is it just and right
185 To privilege your nature?

V

"State things quite
Other than so"—make answer! "I pretend
No such community with men. Perpend
My key to domination! Who would use
Man for his pleasure needs must introduce
190 The element that awes Man. Once for all,
His nature owns a Supernatural
In fact as well as phrase—which found must be
—Where, in this doubting age? Old mystery

169| MS:back   *1887*:backs   170| MS:Our §crossed out and replaced above by§ As
173| MS:The new §last two words crossed out and replaced above by§ To-day's
176| MS:as that you   *1887*:as what you   178| MS:plentifully, mere wit puts
1887:plentifully, counts not,—puts   180| MS:of possession §crossed out and replaced
above by two words and comma§ it merely, power   181| MS:office. Since
the §crossed out and replaced above by§ our   182| MS:gift—   *1887*:gift,
184| MS:Our backs <> it natural §crossed out§   *1887*:And backs
185| MS:nature? §¶§ "Not at all §last three words crossed out and replaced by three words§
"State things quite   188| MS:The key   *1887*:My key   190| MS:awes Man: Once
1887:awes Man. Once   191| MS:a supernatural   *1887*:a Supernatural

Has served its turn—seen through and sent adrift
¹⁹⁵ To nothingness: new wizard-craft makes shift
Nowadays shorn of help by robe and book,—
Otherwise, elsewhere, for success must look
Than chalked-ring, incantation-gibberish.
Somebody comes to conjure: that's he? Pish!
²⁰⁰ He's like the roomful of rapt gazers,—there's
No sort of difference in the garb he wears
From ordinary dressing,—gesture, speech,
Deportment, just like those of all and each
That eye their master of the minute. Stay!
²⁰⁵ What of the something—call it how you may—
Uncanny in the—quack? That's easy said!
Notice how the Professor turns no head
And yet takes cognizance of who accepts,
Denies, is puzzled as to the adept's
²¹⁰ Supremacy, yields up or lies in wait
To trap the trickster! Doubtless, out of date
Are dealings with the devil: yet, the stir
Of mouth, its smile half smug half sinister,
Mock-modest boldness masked in diffidence,—
²¹⁵ What if the man have—who knows how or whence?—
Confederate potency unguessed by us—
Prove no such cheat as he pretends ?"

VI

Ay, thus
Had but my George played statesmanship's new card
That carries all! "Since we"—avers the Bard—
²²⁰ "All of us have one human heart"—as good
As say—by all of us is understood
Right and wrong, true and false—in rough, at least,

---

¹⁹⁷| MS:Quite §crossed out§ Otherwise, elsewhere for   *1887:*elsewhere, for   ²⁰⁴| MS:minute.
Stay—   *1887:*minute. Stay!   ²⁰⁸| MS:accepts   *1887:*accepts,   ²⁰⁹| MS:is doubtful
§crossed out and replaced above by§ puzzled   ²¹²| MS:devil,—yet   *1887:*devil: yet
²¹⁷| MS:Is no < > pretends?   *1887:*Prove no   *1889a:*pretends?"   ²²⁰| MS:All   *1887:*"All

We own a common conscience. God, man, beast—
How should we qualify the statesman-shape
225   I fancy standing with our world agape?
Disguise, flee, fight against with tooth and nail
The outrageous designation! "Quack" men quail
Before? You see, a little year ago
They heard him thunder at the thing which, lo,
230   To-day he vaunts for unscathed, while what erst
Heaven-high he lauded, lies hell-low, accursed!
And yet where's change? Who, awe-struck, cares to point
Critical finger at a dubious joint
In armour, true *æs triplex,* breast and back
235   Binding about, defiant of attack,
An imperturbability that's—well,
Or innocence or impudence—how tell
One from the other? Could ourselves broach lies,
Yet brave mankind with those unaltered eyes,
240   Those lips that keep the quietude of truth?
Dare we attempt the like? What quick uncouth
Disturbance of thy smug economy,
O coward visage! Straight would all descry
Back on the man's brow the boy's blush once more!
245   No: he goes deeper—could our sense explore—
Finds conscience beneath conscience such as ours.
Genius is not so rare,—prodigious powers—
Well, others boast such,—but a power like this
Mendacious intrepidity—*quid vis?*

223| MS:Own to a   *1887:*We own a   224| MS:How do we <> statesman shape
*1887:*How should we <> statesman-shape   225| MS:a-gape   *1887:*agape?
227| MS:designation! Him §crossed out and replaced above by§ "Quack"   228| MS:Before
—§altered to§ ? how else? §last two words and question mark crossed out and replaced above by
two words and comma§ You see, A little   *1887:*see, a little   230| MS:To day   *1887:*To-day
238| MS:lies   *1887:*lies,   239| MS:brave the world §last two words crossed out and
replaced above by§ mankind   241| MS:Do we   *1887:*Dare we   242| MS:thy whole
§crossed out and replaced above by§ smug   243| MS:visage, so that §last two words and
comma crossed out and replaced by§ ! Forthwith all   *1887:*visage! Straight would all
245| MS:No: there's found §last two words crossed out and replaced above by two words§ he goes
246| MS:Thus §crossed out and replaced above by§ So conscience <> ours: *1887:*Finds
conscience <> ours.   248| MS:others have §crossed out and replaced above by§ boast

250 Besides, imposture plays another game,
Admits of no diversion from its aim
Of captivating hearts, sets zeal a-flare
In every shape at every turn,—nowhere
Allows subsidence into ash. By stress
255 Of what does guile succeed but earnestness,
Earnest word, look and gesture? Touched with aught
But earnestness, the levity were fraught
With ruin to guile's film-work. Grave is guile;
Here no act wants its qualifying smile,
260 Its covert pleasantry to neutralize
The outward ardour. Can our chief despise
Even while most he seems to adulate?
As who should say "What though it be my fate
To deal with fools? Among the crowd must lurk
265 Some few with faculty to judge my work
Spite of its way which suits, they understand,
The crass majority:—the Sacred Band,
No duping them forsooth!" So tells a touch
Of subintelligential nod and wink—
270 Turning foes friends. Coarse flattery moves the gorge:
Mine were the mode to awe the many, George!
They guess you half despise them while most bent
On demonstrating that your sole intent
Strives for their service. Sneer at them? Yourself
275 'Tis you disparage,—tricksy as an elf,
Scorning what most you strain to bring to pass,
Laughingly careless,—triply cased in brass,—
While pushing strenuous to the end in view.
What follows? Why, you formulate within

258| MS:guile: *1887*:guile;   261| MS:ardour: does our *1887*:ardour. Can our
264| MS:fools?—among *1887*:fools? Among   269| MS:Of friendly §crossed out and
replaced above by§ subintelligential   270| MS:foes to §crossed out§
271| MS:Now for the §three words crossed out and replaced above by two words§ Receive my
mode *1887*:Mine were the mode   273| MS:Demonstrating your whole sole *1887*:On
demonstrating that your sole   274| MS:service: sneer *1887*:service. Sneer

280   The vulgar headpiece this conception: "Win
       A master-mind to serve us needs we must,
       One who, from motives we but take on trust,
       Acts strangelier—haply wiselier than we know—
       Stronglier, for certain. Did he say 'I throw
285   Aside my good for yours, in all I do
       Care nothing for myself and all for you'—
       We should both understand and disbelieve:
       Said he 'Your good I laugh at in my sleeve,
       My own it is I solely labour at,
290   Pretending yours the while'—that, even that,
       We, understanding well, give credence to,
       And so will none of it. But here 'tis through
       Our recognition of his service, wage
       Well earned by work, he mounts to such a stage
295   Above competitors as all save Bubb
       Would agonize to keep. Yet,—here's the rub—
       So slightly does he hold by our esteem
       Which solely fixed him fast there, that we seem
       Mocked every minute to our face, by gibe
300   And jest—scorn insuppressive: what ascribe
       The rashness to? Our pay and praise to boot—
       Do these avail him to tread underfoot
       Something inside us all and each, that stands
       Somehow instead of somewhat which commands
305   'Lie not'? Folk fear to jeopardize their soul,
       Stumble at times, walk straight upon the whole,—
       That's nature's simple instinct: what may be

280| MS:conception: "Win   *1887*:conception "Win   *1889a*:conception "Win §emended to§
conception: "Win §see Editorial Notes§   281| MS:§first word illegibly crossed out§ A
282| MS:Who, from a motive we   *1887*:One who, from motives we   290| MS:even that
1887:even that,   *1889a*:even that §emended to§ even that, §see Editorial Notes§
295| MS:as no George §last two words crossed out and replaced above by two words§ all save
296| MS:Needs §crossed out and replaced above by§ Would <> to reach §crossed out and
replaced above by§ keep. Yet—here's   *1889a*:keep. Yet,—here's   298| MS:Which solely
§inserted above§ fixed and keeps §last two words crossed out§   302| MS:Can §crossed out
and replaced above by§ Do   305| MS:not!" Folks   *1887*:not'? Folks   *1889a*:not'? Folk
306| MS:times, but §crossed out§ <> straight on §altered to§ upon the whole,   *1887*:whole,—

The portent here, the influence such as we
Are strangers to?"—

VII

Exact the thing I call
³¹⁰ Man's despot, just the Supernatural
Which, George, was wholly out of—far beyond
Your theory and practice. You had conned
But to reject the precept "To succeed
In gratifying selfishness and greed,
³¹⁵ Asseverate such qualities exist
Nowise within yourself! then make acquist
By all means, with no sort of fear!" Alack,
That well-worn lie is obsolete! Fall back
On still a working pretext—"Hearth and Home,
³²⁰ The Altar, love of England, hate of Rome"—
That's serviceable lying—that perchance
Had screened you decently: but 'ware advance
By one step more in perspicacity
Of these our dupes! At length they get to see
³²⁵ As through the earlier, this the latter plea—
And find the greed and selfishness at source!
Ventum est ad triarios: last resource
Should be to what but—exquisite disguise
Disguise-abjuring, truth that looks like lies,
³³⁰ Frankness so sure to meet with unbelief?
Say—you hold in contempt—not them in chief—
But first and foremost your own self! No use
In men but to make sport for you, induce

---

³¹⁰| MS:the Supernatural, *1887:*the Supernatural   ³¹³| MS:The elemental precept—
'to §altered to§ To   *1887:*But to reject the precept "To   ³¹⁶| MS:yourself, then
*1887:*yourself! then   ³¹⁷| MS:fear!' Alack,   *1887:*fear!" Alack,
³¹⁹| MS:pretext—'Hearth   *1887:*pretext—"Hearth   ³²⁰| MS:of Rome,'   *1887:*of
Rome"—   ³²²| MS:'ware the §inserted above§ advance   *1887:*'ware advance
³²⁶| MS:And plain lie greed   *1887:*And find the greed   ³³⁰| MS:unbelief!—
*1887:*unbelief?   ³³¹| MS:You hold in due contempt <> chief   *1887:*Say—you hold in
contempt <> chief—   ³³²| MS:self: no   *1887:*self! No

The puppets now to dance, now stand stock-still,
335　Now knock their heads together, at your will
For will's sake only—while each plays his part
Submissive: why? through terror at the heart:
"Can it be—this bold man, whose hand we saw
Openly pull the wires, obeys some law
340　Quite above Man's—nay, God's?" On face fall they.
This was the secret missed, again I say,
Out of your power to grasp conception of,
Much less employ to purpose. Hence the scoff
That greets your very name: folk see but one
345　Fool more, as well as knave, in Dodington.

---

³³⁶| MS:while they play their parts　*1887:*while each plays his part　³³⁷| MS:at men's
hearts:　*1887:*at the heart:　³³⁸| MS:be this < > hand they §crossed out and replaced
above by§ we　*1887:*be—this　³⁴¹| MS:say,—　*1887:*say,　³⁴⁴| MS:folks
*1889a:*folk

I

Nay, *that,* Furini, never I at least
Mean to believe! What man you were I know,
While you walked Tuscan earth, a painter-priest,
Something about two hundred years ago.
5   Priest—you did duty punctual as the sun
That rose and set above Saint Sano's church,
Blessing Mugello: of your flock not one
But showed a whiter fleece because of smirch,
Your kind hands wiped it clear from: were they poor?
10   Bounty broke bread apace,—did marriage lag
For just the want of moneys that ensure
Fit hearth-and-home provision?—straight your bag
Unplumped itself,—reached hearts by way of palms
Goodwill's shake had but tickled. All about
15   Mugello valley, felt some parish qualms
At worship offered in bare walls without
The comfort of a picture?—prompt such need
Our painter would supply, and throngs to see
Witnessed that goodness—no unholy greed
20   Of gain—had coaxed from Don Furini—he
Whom princes might in vain implore to toil
For worldly profit—such a masterpiece.
Brief—priest, you poured profuse God's wine and oil
Praiseworthily, I know: shall praising cease
25   When, priestly vesture put aside, mere man,
You stand for judgment? Rather—what acclaim

WITH FRANCIS FURINI   *Title*| MS:III §altered to§ IV §crossed out and replaced by§ V.
1889a:§numeral deleted§   6| MS:church   *1887:*church,   8| MS:smirch
*1887:*smirch,   11| MS:monies   *1889a:*moneys   13| MS:itself, §next word altered to§
reached   *1887:*itself,—reached   14| MS:Good-will's shake merely tickled
*1887:*Goodwill's shake had but tickled   15| MS:valley, had some   *1887:*valley, felt some
17| MS:picture? prompt such want §crossed out and replaced above by§ need   *1887:*picture?—
prompt   19| MS:Applauded §crossed out and replaced above by§ Attested shrewdness—
no   *1887:*Witnessed that goodness—no   24| MS:know: shall §crossed out and replaced
above by do, do crossed out and *shall* restored§ praising §illegibly altered and restored§

—"Good son, good brother, friend in whom we scan
No fault nor flaw"—salutes Furini's name,
The loving as the liberal! Enough:
30   Only to ope a lily, though for sake
Of setting free its scent, disturbs the rough
Loose gold about its anther. I shall take
No blame in one more blazon, last of all—
Good painter were you: if in very deed
35   I styled you great—what modern art dares call
My word in question? Let who will take heed
Of what he seeks and misses in your brain
To balance that precision of the brush
Your hand could ply so deftly: all in vain
40   Strives poet's power for outlet when the push
Is lost upon a barred and bolted gate
Of painter's impotency. Agnolo—
Thine were alike the head and hand, by fate
Doubly endowed! Who boasts head only—woe
45   To hand's presumption should brush emulate
Fancy's free passage by the pen, and show
Thought wrecked and ruined where the inexpert
Foolhardy fingers half grasped, half let go
Film-wings the poet's pen arrests unhurt!
50   No—painter such as that miraculous
Michael, who deems you? But the ample gift
Of gracing walls else blank of this our house
Of life with imagery, one bright drift
Poured forth by pencil,—man and woman mere,
55   Glorified till half owned for gods,—the dear
Fleshly perfection of the human shape,—

27| MS:brother—friend   *1887:*brother, friend   31| MS:scent disturbs   *1887:*scent, disturbs
32| MS:its petals §crossed out and replaced above by§ anther   35| MS:modern brush
§crossed out and replaced above by§ art   42| MS:impotency. Angelo—   *1889a:*impotency.
Agnolo—   43| MS:were alike §inserted above§   44| MS:boasts one
§crossed out and replaced above by§ head   51| MS:deems thee? but   *1887:*deems you?
But   55| MS:till we own them gods   *1887:*till half owned for gods

This was apportioned you whereby to praise
Heaven and bless earth. Who clumsily essays,
By slighting painter's craft, to prove the ape
Of poet's pen-creation, just betrays
Two-fold ineptitude.

60

II

By such sure ways

Do I return, Furini, to my first
And central confidence—that he I proved
Good priest, good man, good painter, and rehearsed
Praise upon praise to show—not simply loved
For virtue, but for wisdom honoured too
Needs must Furini be,—it follows—who
Shall undertake to breed in me belief
That, on his death-bed, weakness played the thief
With wisdom, folly ousted reason quite?
List to the chronicler! With main and might—
So fame runs—did the poor soul beg his friends
To buy and burn his hand-work, make amends
For having reproduced therein—(Ah me!
Sighs fame—that's friend Filippo)—nudity!
Yes, I assure you: he would paint—not men
Merely—a pardonable fault—but when
He had to deal with—oh, not mother Eve
Alone, permissibly in Paradise
Naked and unashamed,—but dared achieve
Dreadful distinction, at soul-safety's price

65

70

75

80

57| MS:apportioned thee whereby   *1887*:apportioned you whereby
58| MS:earth. §¶§ Who   *1887*:earth. §no ¶§ Who   60| MS:pen-creation, thus §crossed
out and replaced above by§ just   61| MS:ineptitude—by   *1887*:ineptitude.
§¶§ By   62| MS:to that §crossed out and replaced above by§ my
63| MS:confidence: the man §last two words crossed out and replaced above by two words§
that he   *1887*:confidence—that   65| MS:to prove §crossed out and replaced above by
one word and dash§ show—   66| MS:virtue but   *1887*:virtue, but
69| MS:That on his death-bed weakness   *1887*:That, on his death-bed, weakness
74| MS:therein—(ah, me!   *1887*:therein—(Ah, me!   *1889a*:therein—(Ah me!
78| MS:with—Oh   *1889a*:with—oh   81| MS:price,   *1887*:price

By also painting women—(why the need?)
Just as God made them: there, you have the truth!
Yes, rosed from top to toe in flush of youth,
85   One foot upon the moss-fringe, would some Nymph
Try, with its venturous fellow, if the lymph
Were chillier than the slab-stepped fountain-edge;
The while a-heap her garments on its ledge
Of boulder lay within hand's easy reach,
90   —No one least kid-skin cast around her! Speech
Shrinks from enumerating case and case
Of—were it but Diana at the chase,
With tunic tucked discreetly hunting-high!
No, some Queen Venus set our necks awry,
95   Turned faces from the painter's all-too-frank
Triumph of flesh! For—whom had he to thank
—This self-appointed nature-student? Whence
Picked he up practice? By what evidence
Did he unhandsomely become adept
100   In simulating bodies? How except
By actual sight of such? Himself confessed
The enormity: quoth Philip "When I pressed
The painter to acknowledge his abuse
Of artistry else potent—what excuse
105   Made the infatuated man? I give
His very words: 'Did you but know, as I,
—O scruple-splitting sickly-sensitive
Mild-moral-monger, what the agony

82| MS:By . . needs must he paint women—(why the §crossed out and replaced above by§ such need?)   *1887:*By also painting women—(why the need?)   84| MS:from head §crossed out and replaced above by§ top to foot §crossed out and replaced above by§ toe
85| MS:would the §crossed out and replaced above by§ some   86| MS:its venturous §inserted above§   87| MS:slabbed §altered to§ slab-stepped   88| MS:on the §crossed out and replaced above by§ its   93| MS:discretely   *1889a:*discreetly
97| MS:nature-student?—Whence   *1887:*nature-student? Whence   98| MS:practice?— by   *1887:*practice? By   100| MS:bodies—how   *1887:*Bodies? How
102| MS:enormity: "when I (that's §crossed out and replaced above by§ quoth Philip) "pressed   *1887:*enormity: quoth Philip "When I pressed   103| MS:For penitence thereat— confessed §crossed out and replaced above by two words§ bade own abuse   *1887:*The painter to acknowledge his abuse   106| MS:words: 'If §crossed out and replaced above by§ 'Did they but   *1887:*words: 'Did you but   107| MS:—These scruple-splitting   *1887:*—O scruple-splitting   108| MS:Mild-moral-mongers   *1887:*Mild-moral-monger

Of Art is ere Art satisfy herself
110 In imitating Nature—(Man, poor elf,
Striving to match the finger-mark of Him
The immeasurably matchless)—gay or grim,
Pray, would your smile be? Leave mere fools to tax
Art's high-strung brain's intentness as so lax
115 That, in its mid-throe, idle fancy sees
The moment for admittance!' Pleadings these—
Specious, I grant." So adds, and seems to wince
Somewhat, our censor—but shall truth convince
Blockheads like Baldinucci?

III

I resume
120 My incredulity: your other kind
Of soul, Furini, never was so blind,
Even through death-mist, as to grope in gloom
For cheer beside a bonfire piled to turn
Ashes and dust all that your noble life
125 Did homage to life's Lord by,—bid them burn
—These Baldinucci blockheads—pictures rife
With record, in each rendered loveliness,
That one appreciative creature's debt
Of thanks to the Creator, more or less,
130 Was paid according as heart's-will had met
Hand's-power in Art's endeavour to express
Heaven's most consummate of achievements, bless
Earth by a semblance of the seal God set
On woman his supremest work. I trust
135 Rather, Furini, dying breath had vent

109| MS:satisfy itself *1887:*satisfy herself   113| MS:would their smile be, at such fools as
tax *1887:*would your smile be? Leave mere fools to tax   116| MS:Fit moment for
admittance'? Pleadings *1887:*The moment for admittance!' Pleadings   117| MS:grant:"
so *1887:*grant." So   122| MS:Even by death-mist *1889a:*Even through death-mist   124| MS:To §crossed out and replaced above by§ Mere dust and ashes all your *1887:*Ashes
and dust all that your   129| MS:the Creator, more *1889a:*the Creator more §emended
to§ the Creator, more §see Editorial Notes§   133| MS:by some §crossed out and replaced
above by§ a   134| MS:On woman §inserted above§ < > work: I *1887:*work. I

In some fine fervour of thanksgiving just
For this—that soul and body's power you spent—
Agonized to adumbrate, trace in dust
That marvel which we dream the firmament
140 Copies in star-device when fancies stray
Outlining, orb by orb, Andromeda—
God's best of beauteous and magnificent
Revealed to earth—the naked female form.
Nay, I mistake not: wrath that's but lukewarm
145 Would boil indeed were such a critic styled
Himself an artist: artist! Ossa piled
Topping Olympus—the absurd which crowns
The extravagant—whereat one laughs, not frowns.
Paints he? One bids the poor pretender take
150 His sorry self, a trouble and disgrace,
From out the sacred presence, void the place
Artists claim only. What—not merely wake
Our pity that suppressed concupiscence—
A satyr masked as matron—makes pretence
155 To the coarse blue-fly's instinct—can perceive
No better reason why she should exist—
—God's lily-limbed and blush-rose-bosomed Eve—
Than as a hot-bed for the sensualist
To fly-blow with his fancies, make pure stuff
160 Breed him back filth—this were not crime enough?
But further—fly to style itself—nay, more—
To steal among the sacred ones, crouch down
Though but to where their garments sweep the floor—
—Still catching some faint sparkle from the crown
165 Crowning transcendent Michael, Leonard,

---

¹³⁷| MS:power was spent—   *1887*:power you spent—   ¹³⁸| MS:adumbrate—trace
1887:adumbrate, trace   ¹⁴⁸| MS:frowns—   *1887*:frowns.   ¹⁴⁹| MS:Painter himself
forsooth: §first word altered to *Paints* and last two crossed out and replaced above by five
words§ Paints he? One bids the poor   ¹⁵⁰| MS:This §altered to§ His
¹⁵⁴| MS:A §in margin§ satyr disguised §crossed out and replaced above by§ masked
¹⁵⁵| MS:percieve *1887*:perceive   ¹⁵⁶| MS:exist *1887*:exist—
¹⁵⁸| MS:Than §over illegible word§   ¹⁶¹| MS:more *1887*:more—   ¹⁶³| MS:floor
1887:floor—   ¹⁶⁴| MS:—Still reached §altered to§ touched thence by some sparkle from
one §altered to§ the   *1887*:—Still catching some faint sparkle   ¹⁶⁵| MS:Of some
transcendent Michel, Lionard,   *1887*:Crowning transcendent Michael, Leonard,

Rafael,—to sit beside the feet of such,
Unspurned because unnoticed, then reward
Their toleration—mercy overmuch—
By stealing from the throne-step to the fools
170   Curious outside the gateway, all-agape
To learn by what procedure, in the schools
Of Art, a merest man in outward shape
May learn to be Correggio! Old and young,
These learners got their lesson: Art was just
175   A safety-screen—(Art, which Correggio's tongue
Calls "Virtue")—for a skulking vice: mere lust
Inspired the artist when his Night and Morn
Slept and awoke in marble on that edge
Of heaven above our awestruck earth: lust-born
180   His Eve low bending took the privilege
Of life from what our eyes saw—God's own palm
That put the flame forth—to the love and thanks
Of all creation save this recreant!

IV

Calm
Our phrase, Furini! Not the artist-ranks
185   Claim riddance of an interloper: no—
This Baldinucci did but grunt and sniff
Outside Art's pale—ay, grubbed, where pine-trees grow,
For pignuts only.

167| MS:unnoticed—then   *1887*:unnoticed, then   169| MS:stealing to §crossed out and
replaced above by§ from   170| MS:all agape   *1887*:all-agape   171| MS:procedure
in   *1887*:procedure, in   173| MS:be Correggio: these needs must §last three words
crossed out and replaced above by three words and comma§ old and young,   *1887*:be
Correggio! Old   174| MS:These must §crossed out and replaced above by§ learners get
§altered to§ got <> lesson—Art   *1887*:lesson: Art   182| MS:puts   *1887*:put
184| MS:phrase, Furini! Not you §crossed out and replaced above by§ the
186| MS:Good §crossed out and replaced above by§ This
187| MS:pale—but §crossed out and replaced above by word and comma§ ay, grubbed

V

You the Sacred! If
Indeed on you has been bestowed the dower
190   Of Art in fulness, graced with head and hand,
Head—to look up not downwards, hand—of power
To make head's gain the portion of a world
Where else the uninstructed ones too sure
Would take all outside beauty—film that's furled
195   About a star—for the star's self, endure
No guidance to the central glory,—nay,
(Sadder) might apprehend the film was fog,
Or (worst) wish all but vapour well away,
And sky's pure product thickened from earth's bog—
200   Since so, nor seldom, have your worthiest failed
To trust their own souls' insight—why? except
For warning that the head of the adept
May too much prize the hand, work unassailed
By scruple of the better sense that finds
205   An orb within each halo, bids gross flesh
Free the fine spirit-pattern, nor enmesh
More than is meet a marvel custom blinds
Only the vulgar eye to. Now, less fear
That you, the foremost of Art's fellowship,
210   Will oft—will ever so offend! But—hip
And thigh—smite the Philistine! *You*—slunk here—
Connived at, by too easy tolerance,
Not to scrape palette simply or squeeze brush,
But dub your very self an Artist? Tush—
215   You, of the daubings, is it, dare advance

193| MS:uninstruced *1887*:uninstructed   197| MS:fog *1887*:fog,
198| MS:(worse) §altered to§ (worst)   200| MS:worthies *1887*:worthiest
201| MS:souls' *1887*:soul's *1889a*:soul's §emended to§ souls' §see Editorial Notes§
205| MS:The §crossed out and replaced above by§ An orb within the §crossed out and
replaced above by§ each   206| MS:spirit-pattern, custom blinds §last two words crossed
out and replaced above by two words§ nor enmesh   207| MS:meet the marvel, custom
1887:meet a marvel *1889a*:marvel custom   208| MS:to. Little fear *1889a*:to. Now, less
fear   209| MS:The foremost of Art's noble §last five words transposed to§ The noble
foremost of Art's fellowship *1887*:That you, the foremost of Art's fellowship
1889a:fellowship,   210| MS:offend! but §altered to§ But

This doctrine that the Artist-mind must needs
Own to affinity with yours—confess
Provocative acquaintance, more or less,
With each impurely-peevish worm that breeds
220 Inside your brain's receptacle?

VI

Enough.
Who owns "I dare not look on diadems
Without an itch to pick out, purloin gems
Others contentedly leave sparkling"—gruff
Answers the guard of the regalia: "Why—
225 Consciously kleptomaniac—thrust yourself
Where your illicit craving after pelf
Is tempted most—in the King's treasury?
Go elsewhere! Sort with thieves, if thus you feel—
When folk clean-handed simply recognize
230 Treasure whereof the mere sight satisfies—
But straight your fingers are on itch to steal!
Hence with you!"
Pray, Furini!

VII

"Bounteous God,
Deviser and Dispenser of all gifts
To soul through sense,—in Art the soul uplifts
235 Man's best of thanks! What but Thy measuring-rod
Meted forth heaven and earth? more intimate,
Thy very hands were busied with the task
Of making, in this human shape, a mask—

216| MS:the Artist mind   *1887*:the Artist-mind   219| MS:impurely peevish
1887:impurely-peevish   220| MS:§B has misnumbered this section as 5 and the rest of
Furini accordingly§   221| MS:owns I   *1887*:owns "I   223| MS:sparkling,—gruff
1887:sparkling"—gruff   224| MS:regalia: "Why,—   *1887*:regalia: "Why—
225| MS:kleptomaniac,—thrust   *1887*:kleptomaniac—thrust   229| MS:folks   *1889a*:folk
231| MS:That straight   *1887*:But straight   232| MS:you!" §¶§ Here
§crossed out and replaced above by§ Pray   233| MS:Diviser and dispenser
1887:Deviser   *1889a*:and Dispenser   238| MS:mask   *1887*:mask—

A match for that divine. Shall love abate
240 Man's wonder? Nowise! True—true—all too true—
No gift but, in the very plenitude
Of its perfection, goes maimed, misconstrued
By wickedness or weakness: still, some few
Have grace to see Thy purpose, strength to mar
245 Thy work by no admixture of their own,
—Limn truth not falsehood, bid us love alone
The type untampered with, the naked star!"

VIII

And, prayer done, painter—what if you should preach?
Not as of old when playing pulpiteer
250 To simple-witted country folk, but here
In actual London try your powers of speech
On us the cultured, therefore sceptical—
What would you? For, suppose he has his word
In faith's behalf, no matter how absurd,
255 This painter-theologian? One and all
We lend an ear—nay, Science takes thereto—
Encourages the meanest who has racked
Nature until he gains from her some fact,
To state what truth is from his point of view,
260 Mere pin-point though it be: since many such
Conduce to make a whole, she bids our friend
Come forward unabashed and haply lend
His little life-experience to our much
Of modern knowledge. Since she so insists,

---

²³⁹| MS:divine: shall §word and colon altered to§. Shall   ²⁴¹| MS:but in the §over perhaps
its§ *1887:*but, in   ²⁴²| MS:perfection goes unmisconstrued *1887:*perfection, goes
maimed, misconstrued   ²⁴³| MS:still some *1887:*still, some   ²⁴⁴| MS:to aid §crossed
out and replaced above by§ see Thy will and §last two words crossed out and replaced above by§
purpose   ²⁴⁶| MS:—Limn not a faulty likeness, love *1887:*—Limn truth not falsehood,
bid us love   ²⁵³| MS:you? Still, §word and comma crossed out and replaced above by word
and comma§ For,   ²⁵⁵| MS:painter-theologian; §altered to§ ?   ²⁵⁶| MS:science
*1887:*Science   ²⁵⁸| MS:her one fact, *1887:*her some fact,   ²⁵⁹| MS:from his
§crossed out and replaced above by§ such *1887:*from his   ²⁶⁰| MS:Mere §over illegible
word§   ²⁶¹| MS:Go far §last two words crossed out and replaced above by§ Conduce

265   Up stands Furini.

IX

"Evolutionists!
At truth I glimpse from depths, you glance from heights,
Our stations for discovery opposites,—
How should ensue agreement? I explain:
'Tis the tip-top of things to which you strain
270   Your vision, until atoms, protoplasm,
And what and whence and how may be the spasm
Which sets all going, stop you: down perforce
Needs must your observation take its course,
Since there's no moving upwards: link by link
275   You drop to where the atoms somehow think,
Feel, know themselves to be: the world's begun,
Such as we recognize it. Have you done
Descending? Here's ourself,—Man, known to-day,
Duly evolved at last,—so far, you say,
280   The sum and seal of being's progress. Good!
Thus much at least is clearly understood—
Of power does Man possess no particle:
Of knowledge—just so much as shows that still
It ends in ignorance on every side:
285   But righteousness—ah, Man is deified
Thereby, for compensation! Make survey
Of Man's surroundings, try creation—nay,
Try emulation of the minimized
Minuteness fancy may conceive! Surprised
290   Reason becomes by two defeats for one—

---

²⁶⁶| MS:heights,— *1887*:heights,   ²⁷⁴| MS:moving up now: link *1887*:moving
upwards: link   ²⁷⁶| MS:be; the *1887*:be: the   ²⁷⁷| MS:we understand §crossed
out and replaced above by§ recognize it. have §altered to§ Have   ²⁷⁸| MS:Descending?
Here's ourself,—§last word, comma and dash inserted above§ the §crossed out§ man §altered
to§ Man §followed by word illegibly crossed out§   ²⁸²| MS:does man §altered to§ Man
< > particle; *1887*:particle: ²⁸³| MS:shows him §altered to§ that   ²⁸⁴| MS:side;
1887:side: ²⁸⁵| MS:ah, man §altered to§ Man   ²⁸⁶| MS:compensation! Take
1887:compensation! Make   ²⁸⁷| MS:Of man's *1887*:Of Man's
²⁸⁸| MS:minimized minute, §word and comma crossed out§   ²⁸⁹| MS:Minuteness
§over perhaps *Minutened*§ fancy shall §crossed out and replaced above by§ may

Not only power at each phenomenon
Baffled, but knowledge also in default—
Asking what *is* minuteness—yonder vault
Speckled with suns, or this the millionth—thing,
295 How shall I call?—that on some insect's wing
Helps to make out in dyes the mimic star?
Weak, ignorant, accordingly we are:
What then? The worse for Nature! Where began
Righteousness, moral sense except in Man?
300 True, he makes nothing, understands no whit:
Had the initiator-spasm seen fit
Thus doubly to endow him, none the worse
And much the better were the universe.
What does Man see or feel or apprehend
305 Here, there, and everywhere, but faults to mend,
Omissions to supply,—one wide disease
Of things that are, which Man at once would ease
Had will but power and knowledge? failing both—
Things must take will for deed—Man, nowise loth,
310 Accepts pre-eminency: mere blind force—
Mere knowledge undirected in its course
By any care for what is made or marred
In either's operation—*these* award
The crown to? Rather let it deck thy brows,
315 Man, whom alone a righteousness endows
Would cure the wide world's ailing! Who disputes
Thy claim thereto? Had Spasm more attributes

292| MS:Baffled, §word and comma inserted above§   294| MS:suns—or   *1887:*suns, or
295| MS:What §crossed out and replaced above by§ How <> on this §crossed out and replaced
above by§ some   296| MS:out in dyes §last two words inserted above§ the mimic §inserted
above§   298| MS:for nature §altered to§ Nature   299| MS:in man §altered to§ Man
300| MS:nothing—understands no whit—   *1887:*nothing, understands no whit:
302| MS:So further §crossed out and replaced above by§ doubly   *1887:*Thus doubly
303| MS:But §crossed out and replaced above by§ And   304| MS:does man §altered to§
Man   307| MS:that be §crossed out and replaced above by two words§ are, which man
§altered to§ Man §followed by illegible erasure§ will §crossed out§   309| MS:deed—man
*1887:*deed—Man   315| MS:alone a §over word illegibly crossed out§   316| MS:ailing.
Who   *1887:*ailing! Who   317| MS:This §altered to§ Thy <> spasm §altered to§ Spasm

Than power and knowledge in its gift, before
Man came to pass? The higher that we soar,
320 The less of moral sense like Man's we find:
No sign of such before,—what comes behind,
Who guesses? But until there crown our sight
The quite new—not the old mere infinite
Of changings,—some fresh kind of sun and moon,—
325 Then, not before, shall I expect a boon
Of intuition just as strange, which turns
Evil to good, and wrong to right, unlearns
All Man's experience learned since Man was he.
Accept in Man, advanced to this degree,
330 The Prime Mind, therefore! neither wise nor strong—
Whose fault? but were he both, then right, not wrong
As now, throughout the world were paramount
According to his will,—which I account
The qualifying faculty. He stands
335 Confessed supreme—the monarch whose commands
Could he enforce, how bettered were the world!
He's at the height this moment—to be hurled
Next moment to the bottom by rebound
Of his own peal of laughter. All around
340 Ignorance wraps him,—whence and how and why
Things are,—yet cloud breaks and lets blink the sky
Just overhead, not elsewhere! What assures
His optics that the very blue which lures

318| MS:knowledge in its gift, §last three words and comma inserted above§
319| MS:that you §crossed out and replaced above by§ we   320| MS:like Man's you
§crossed out and replaced above by§ we   321| MS:before, leave: §word and colon
crossed out and replaced above by§ —what s §crossed out§ comes §inserted above§ behind,—
§dash crossed out§   322| MS:there comes an §last two words crossed out and replaced
above by two words§ crown our   325| MS:expect the boon   *1887*:expect a boon
328| MS:All man's §altered to§ Man's <> since man §altered to§ Man was he: *1887*:he.
329| MS:in man §altered to§ Man   330| MS:therefore—neither   *1887*:therefore!
neither   331| MS:right not   *1887*:right, not   332| MS:now throughout <>
paramount,   *1887*:now, throughout <> paramount   336| MS:could he enforce, §last
three words and comma inserted above§ How §altered to§ how   340| MS:wraps you
§crossed out and replaced above by§ him   341| MS:lets through §crossed out and
replaced above by§ blink   342| MS:Bright §crossed out and replaced above by§ Just
343| MS:Your §crossed out and replaced above by§ His <> the very §inserted above§

Comes not of black outside it, doubly dense?
345 Ignorance overwraps his moral sense,
Winds him about, relaxing, as it wraps,
So much and no more than lets through perhaps
The murmured knowledge—'Ignorance exists.'

X

"I at the bottom, Evolutionists,
350 Advise beginning, rather. I profess
To know just one fact—my self-consciousness,—
'Twixt ignorance and ignorance enisled,—
Knowledge: before me was my Cause—that's styled
God: after, in due course succeeds the rest,—
355 All that my knowledge comprehends—at best—
At worst, conceives about in mild despair.
Light needs must touch on either darkness: where?
Knowledge so far impinges on the Cause
Before me, that I know—by certain laws
360 Wholly unknown, whate'er I apprehend
Within, without me, had its rise: thus blend
I, and all things perceived, in one Effect.
How far can knowledge any ray project
On what comes after me—the universe?
365 Well, my attempt to make the cloud disperse
Begins—not from above but underneath:
I climb, you soar,—who soars soon loses breath
And sinks, who climbs keeps one foot firm on fact
Ere hazarding the next step: soul's first act
370 (Call consciousness the soul—some name we need)
Getting itself aware, through stuff decreed

---

³⁴⁵| MS:Ignorance overwinds §altered to§ overwraps your §crossed out and replaced above
by§ his <> sense   *1887*:sense,   ³⁴⁶| MS:Closes §crossed out and
replaced above by§ Winds about you §crossed out and replaced above by§ him §last two words
transposed to§ him about, relaxing as it wraps   *1887*:relaxing, as it wraps,
³⁴⁸| MS:murmured knowledge— §word and dash inserted above§ "Ignorance at least §last
two words crossed out§ exists."   *1887*:knowledge—'Ignorance exists.'
³⁵⁴| MS:rest   *1887*:rest,—   ³⁶⁶| MS:underneath—   *1887*:underneath:
³⁷¹| MS:getting §altered to§ Getting <> aware through   *1887*:aware, through

Thereto (so call the body)—who has stept
So far, there let him stand, become adept
In body ere he shift his station thence
375 One single hair's breadth. Do I make pretence
To teach, myself unskilled in learning? Lo,
My life's work! Let my pictures prove I know
Somewhat of what this fleshly frame of ours
Or is or should be, how the soul empowers
380 The body to reveal its every mood
Of love and hate, pour forth its plenitude
Of passion. If my hand attained to give
Thus permanence to truth else fugitive,
Did not I also fix each fleeting grace
385 Of form and feature—save the beauteous face—
Arrest decay in transitory might
Of bone and muscle—cause the world to bless
For ever each transcendent nakedness
Of man and woman? Were such feats achieved
390 By sloth, or strenuous labour unrelieved,
—Yet lavished vainly? Ask that underground
(So may I speak) of all on surface found
Of flesh-perfection! Depths on depths to probe
Of all-inventive artifice, disrobe
395 Marvel at hiding under marvel, pluck
Veil after veil from Nature—were the luck
Ours to surprise the secret men so name,
That still eludes the searcher—all the same,
Repays his search with still fresh proof—'Externe,
400 Not inmost, is the Cause, fool! Look and learn!'
Thus teach my hundred pictures: firm and fast

375| MS:One single §inserted above§ < > breadth. If §crossed out and replaced above by§ Do
376| MS:teach, at all §last two words crossed out and replaced above by§ myself
378| MS:frame of §inserted above§   387| MS:muscle—to §inserted above§ bless cause
§inserted above§ the world §last six words transposed to§ muscle—cause the world to bless
with sight §last two words crossed out§   388| MS:each majestic §crossed out and
replaced above by§ transcendent 391| MS:—Yet §over illegible word, dash in margin§
394| *1887*:all inventive *1889a*:all-inventive   397| MS:name— *1887*:name,
399| MS:proof—Externe, *1887*:proof—'Externe,   400| MS:learn! *1887*:learn!'
401| MS:Thus §over illegible word§ < > pictures! Firm *1887*:pictures: firm

There did I plant my first foot. And the next?
Nowhere! 'Twas put forth and withdrawn, perplexed
At touch of what seemed stable and proved stuff
405   Such as the coloured clouds are: plain enough
There lay the outside universe: try Man—
My most immediate! and the dip began
From safe and solid into that profound
Of ignorance I tell you surges round
410   My rock-spit of self-knowledge. Well and ill,
Evil and good irreconcilable
Above, beneath, about my every side,—
How did this wild confusion far and wide
Tally with my experience when my stamp—
415   So far from stirring—struck out, each a lamp,
Spark after spark of truth from where I stood—
Pedestalled triumph? Evil there was good,
Want was the promise of supply, defect
Ensured completion,—where and when and how?
420   Leave that to the First Cause! Enough that now,
Here where I stand, this moment's me and mine,
Shows me what is, permits me to divine
What shall be. Wherefore? Nay, how otherwise?
Look at my pictures! What so glorifies
425   The body that the permeating soul
Finds there no particle elude control
Direct, or fail of duty,—most obscure
When most subservient? Did that Cause ensure
The soul such raptures as its fancy stings
430   Body to furnish when, uplift by wings
Of passion, here and now, it leaves the earth,
Loses itself above, where bliss has birth—
(Heaven, be the phrase)—did that same Cause contrive

402| MS:Thus §altered to§ There <> first §inserted above§   403| MS:Nowhere; 'twas
1887:Nowhere! 'Twas   406| MS:try man §altered to§ Man—   412| MS:side.
1887:side,—   414| MS:when each §crossed out and replaced above by§ my stamp
1887:stamp—   420| MS:the first Cause   *1889a*:the First Cause   424| MS:at thy
§altered to§ my   428| MS:subservient,—did   *1887*:subservient? Did
433| MS:Heaven—be the phrase,—did   *1887*:(Heaven, be the phrase)—did

Such solace for the body, soul must dive
435   At drop of fancy's pinion, condescend
To bury both alike on earth, our friend
And fellow, where minutely exquisite
Low lie the pleasures, now and here—no herb
But hides its marvel, peace no doubts perturb
440   In each small mystery of insect life—
—Shall the soul's Cause thus gift the soul, yet strife
Continue still of fears with hopes,—for why?
What if the Cause, whereof we now descry
So far the wonder-working, lack at last
445   Will, power, benevolence—a protoplast,
No consummator, sealing up the sum
Of all things,—past and present and to come
Perfection? No, I have no doubt at all!
There's my amount of knowledge—great or small,
450   Sufficient for my needs: for see! advance
Its light now on that depth of ignorance
I shrank before from—yonder where the world
Lies wreck-strewn,—evil towering, prone good—hurled
From pride of place, on every side. For me
455   (Patience, beseech you!) knowledge can but be
Of good by knowledge of good's opposite—
Evil,—since, to distinguish wrong from right,
Both must be known in each extreme, beside—
(Or what means knowledge—to aspire or bide
460   Content with half-attaining? Hardly so!)
Made to know on, know ever, I must know
All to be known at any halting-stage
Of my soul's progress, such as earth, where wage
War, just for soul's instruction, pain with joy,

440| MS:each mild §crossed out and replaced above by§ small   441| MS:—Shall §dash in
margin§   442| MS:Continue there of   *1887*:Continue still of   448| MS:—Perfection?
<> have no §inserted above§   *1887*:Perfection   451| MS:My §crossed out and replaced
above by§ Its   453| MS:towering, §next two words illegibly crossed out and replaced above
by§ prone   456| MS:of its §crossed out and replaced above by§ good's
457| MS:Evil,—since, §word and comma inserted above§   458| MS:known—in   *1887*:known
in   459| MS:Or   *1887*:(Or   460| MS:with its §crossed out and replaced above by word
and hyphen§ half- <> so: *1887*:so!)   464| MS:for its instruction   *1887*:for soul's instruction

465   Folly with wisdom, all that works annoy
      With all that quiets and contents,—in brief,
      Good strives with evil.

                    "Now then for relief,
      Friends, of your patience kindly curbed so long.
      'What?' snarl you, 'Is the fool's conceit thus strong—
470   Must the whole outside world in soul and sense
      Suffer, that he grow sage at its expense?'
      By no means! 'Tis by merest touch of toe
      I try—not trench on—ignorance, just know—
      And so keep steady footing: how you fare,
475   Caught in the whirlpool—that's the Cause's care,
      Strong, wise, good,—this I know at any rate
      In my own self,—but how may operate
      With you—strength, wisdom, goodness—no least blink
      Of knowledge breaks the darkness round me. Think!
480   Could I see plain, be somehow certified
      All was illusion,—evil far and wide
      Was good disguised,—why, out with one huge wipe
      Goes knowledge from me. Type needs antitype:
      As night needs day, as shine needs shade, so good
485   Needs evil: how were pity understood
      Unless by pain? Make evident that pain
      Permissibly masks pleasure—you abstain
      From outstretch of the finger-tip that saves
      A drowning fly. Who proffers help of hand

467| MS:Good's strife with evil. §¶§ "Now   *1887:*Good strives with <> Now   *1889a:*§¶§ Now
§emended to§ "Now §see Editorial Notes§   469| MS:"What?" snarl you 'Is   *1887:*'What'
snarl you 'Is   *1889a:*you, 'Is   470| MS:Does the whole world outside in   *1887:*Must the
whole outside world in   471| MS:expense?"   *1887:*expense?'   472| MS:means,
brother! 'Tis by touch   *1887:*means! 'Tis by merest touch   473| MS:ignorance, and
know—   *1887:*ignorance, just know—   474| MS:So far keep   *1887:*And so keep
476| MS:wise and good,—I   *1887:*wise, good,—this I   477| MS:how these operate
*1887:*how may operate   480| MS:see light, be   *1887:*see plain, be   482| MS:Good
in disguise   *1887:*Was good disguised   483| MS:Knowledge goes out of §last two words
crossed out and replaced above by§ from me—type <> antitype,   *1887:*Goes knowledge from
me. Type <> antitype: 484| MS:as bright needs dusk, so   *1887:*as shine need shade, so
487| MS:Permissibly §inserted above§ <> pleasure merely §crossed out and replaced above
by§ —I abstain   *1887:*pleasure—you abstain   489| MS:fly: who   *1887:*fly. Who

490 To weak Andromeda exposed on strand
At mercy of the monster? Were all true,
Help were not wanting: 'But 'tis false,' cry you,
'Mere fancy-work of paint and brush!' No less,
Were mine the skill, the magic, to impress
495 Beholders with a confidence they saw
Life,—veritable flesh and blood in awe
Of just as true a sea-beast,—would they stare
Simply as now, or cry out, curse and swear,
Or call the gods to help, or catch up stick
500 And stone, according as their hearts were quick
Or sluggish? Well, some old artificer
Could do as much,—at least, so books aver,—
Able to make-believe, while I, poor wight,
Make fancy, nothing more. Though wrong were right,
505 Could we but know—still wrong must needs seem wrong
To do right's service, prove men weak or strong,
Choosers of evil or of good. 'No such
Illusion possible!' Ah, friends, you touch
Just here my solid standing-place amid
510 The wash and welter, whence all doubts are bid
Back to the ledge they break against in foam,
Futility: my soul, and my soul's home
This body,—how each operates on each,
And how things outside, fact or feigning, teach

490| MS:To my Andromeda you see on   *1887*:To weak Andromeda exposed on
491| MS:monster?—were it true,   *1887*:monster? Were all true,   492| MS:wanting—
"This is false," say you,   *1887*:wanting: 'But 'tis false,' cry you,   493| MS:Furini's work of
<> brush!" No   *1887*:'Mere fancy-work of <> brush!' No   494| MS:skill so truly §last
two words crossed out and replaced above by two words§ the magic to   *1887*:skill, the magic, to
498| MS:out—curse and swear—   *1887*:out, curse and swear,   501| MS:sluggish? Well,
those §crossed out and replaced by§ some old artificers §altered to§ artificer
502| MS:much,—there's many §last two words crossed out and replaced above by two words§
at least a §altered to§ the book avers §altered to§ books aver,—   *1887*:least, so books
504| MS:more, Let wrong be right—   *1887*:more. Though wrong were right,
505| MS:know—no less must wrong seem   *1887*:know—still wrong must needs seem
506| MS:right <> prove us weak   *1887*:right's <> prove men weak   507| MS:good.
"Were such   *1887*:good. 'No such   508| MS:possible!" My friends   *1887*:possible!' Ah,
friends   510| MS:doubts I bid   *1887*:doubts are bid   511| MS:foam—   *1887*:foam,

515 What good is and what evil,—just the same,
Be feigning or be fact the teacher,—blame
Diffidence nowise if, from this I judge
My point of vantage, not an inch I budge.
All—for myself—seems ordered wise and well
520 Inside it,—what reigns outside, who can tell?
Contrariwise, who needs be told 'The space
Which yields thee knowledge,—do its bounds embrace
Well-willing and wise-working, each at height?
Enough: beyond thee lies the infinite—
525 Back to thy circumscription!'

           "Back indeed!
Ending where I began—thus: retrocede,
Who will,—what comes first, take first, I advise!
Acquaint you with the body ere your eyes
Look upward: this Andromeda of mine—
530 Gaze on the beauty, Art hangs out for sign
There's finer entertainment underneath.
Learn how they ministrate to life and death—
Those incommensurably marvellous
Contrivances which furnish forth the house
535 Where soul has sway! Though Master keep aloof,
Signs of His presence multiply from roof
To basement of the building. Look around,

515| MS:evil, just alike §crossed out and replaced above by two words and comma§ the same,
1887:evil,—just   516| MS:Be §in margin§ Feigning §altered to§ feigning or be §inserted
above§   517| MS:Nowise my diffidence,—from   *1887*:Diffidence nowise if, from
518| MS:vantage not < > budge   *1887*:vantage, not < > budge.   519| MS:Nay, nor a
hair's breadth: all is wise   *1887*:All—for myself—seems ordered wise   520| MS:Inside
me,—what is outside   *1887*:Inside it,—what reigns outside   521| MS:told—"The
1887:told 'The   524| MS:Enough: thou hast conceived the   *1887*:Enough: beyond thee
lies the   525| MS:circumscription!" §¶§ Back indeed—   *1887*:circumscription' §¶§ < >
indeed!   *1889a*:circumscription.' §¶§ "Back   530| MS:Learn §crossed out and replaced
above by three words§ Gaze on the < > out the same §last two words crossed out§ for sign—
1887:sign   531| MS:Go inside and get knowledge. §last five words and period crossed out
and replaced above by four words§ There's finer entertainment underneath,—
1887:underneath.   532| MS:death   *1887*:death—   533| MS:Those unimaginably
marvellous   *1887*:Those incommensurably marvellous   535| MS:Wherein §altered to§
Where soul has fit §crossed out§ < > master   *1887*:sway! Though Master   536| MS:of his
1887:of His   537| MS:building: look around   *1887*:Building. Look around,

Learn thoroughly,—no fear that you confound
Master with messuage! He's away, no doubt,
540 But what if, all at once, you come upon
A startling proof—not that the Master gone
Was present lately—but that something—whence
Light comes—has pushed Him into residence?
Was such the symbol's meaning,—old, uncouth—
545 That circle of the serpent, tail in mouth?
Only by looking low, ere looking high,
Comes penetration of the mystery."

XI

Thanks! After sermonizing, psalmody!
Now praise with pencil, Painter! Fools attaint
550 Your fame, forsooth, because its power inclines
To livelier colours, more attractive lines
Than suit some orthodox sad sickly saint
—Grey male emaciation, haply streaked
Carmine by scourgings—or they want, far worse—
555 Some self-scathed woman, framed to bless not curse
Nature that loved the form whereon hate wreaked
The wrongs you see. No, rather paint some full
Benignancy, the first and foremost boon
Of youth, health, strength,—show beauty's May, ere June
560 Undo the bud's blush, leave a rose to cull

539| MS:messuage: he's <> doubt— *1887*:messuage! He's <> doubt, 541| MS:the
master *1887*:the Master 543| MS:The §crossed out§ light §altered to§ Light comes—
has §inserted above§ pushed him *1887*:pushed Him 544| MS:Ponder §crossed out and
replaced above by two words§ Was such <> meaning,—old §crossed out and replaced above by
so, and restored§ 545| MS:That circle of the §last three words inserted above§ serpent,
with the §last two words crossed out§ <> mouth,— §comma and dash altered to§ ?
546| MS:Begin §crossed out and replaced above by§ Only 547| MS:mystery—"
1887:mystery." 548| MS:And §crossed out and replaced above by word and exclamation
point§ Thanks! after §altered to§ After 549| MS:Praise with the pencil *1887*:Now praise
with pencil 552| MS:suit their orthodox *1887*:suit some orthodox 554| MS:by
drops §inserted above§ disciplinary,—worse— *1887*:by scourgings—or they want, far worse—
555| MS:woman—framed *1887*:woman, framed 557| MS:see: no <> paint the full
1887:see. No <> paint some full 559| MS:youth, and §crossed out§ health, and §crossed
out§ strength, and beauty's May ere *1887*:strength,—show beauty's May, ere

—No poppy, neither! yet less perfect-pure,
Divinely-precious with life's dew besprent.
Show saintliness that's simply innocent
Of guessing sinnership exists to cure
565　All in good time! In time let age advance
And teach that knowledge helps—not ignorance—
The healing of the nations. Let my spark
Quicken your tinder! Burn with—Joan of Arc!
Not at the end, nor midway when there grew
570　The brave delusions, when rare fancies flew
Before the eyes, and in the ears of her
Strange voices woke imperiously astir:
No,—paint the peasant girl all peasant-like,
Spirit and flesh—the hour about to strike
575　When this should be transfigured, that inflamed,
By heart's admonishing "Thy country shamed,
Thy king shut out of all his realm except
One sorry corner!" and to life forth leapt
The indubitable lightning "Can there be
580　Country and king's salvation—all through me?"
Memorize that burst's moment, Francis! Tush—
None of the nonsense-writing! Fitlier brush
Shall clear off fancy's film-work and let show
Not what the foolish feign but the wise know—
585　Ask Sainte-Beuve else!—or better, Quicherat,
The downright-digger into truth that's—Bah,

561|　MS:perfect-pure　*1887:*perfect-pure,　562|　MS:besprent,—　*1887:*besprent.
563|　MS:True saintliness　*1887:*Show saintliness　565|　MS:time—when needs must age
*1887:*time! In time let age　567|　MS:nations. Come—my　*1887:*nations. Let my
570|　MS:delusions, the rare　*1887:*delusions, when rare　571|　MS:eyes, while in
*1887:*eyes, and in　572|　MS:Great voices grew imperiously astir—　*1887:*Strange voices
woke imperiously astir:　573|　MS:No,—give the　*1887:*No,—paint the　575|　MS:this
shall be　*1887:*this should be　576|　MS:Yet neither yet so moved by country shamed
*1887:*By heart's admonishing "Thy county shamed,　577|　MS:And king　*1887:*Thy king
578|　MS:corner, that to life has leapt　*1887:*corner!" and to life forth leapt
579|　MS:lightning: "Shall there　*1887:*lightning "Can there　580|　MS:salvation—and
§crossed out and replaced above by§ all　582|　MS:nonsense writing　*1887:*nonsense-
writing　583|　MS:Clean away fancy's　*1887:*Shall clear off fancy's　585|　MS:Ask
Sainte Beuve else!—him deep in Quicherat　*1887:*Ask Sainte-Beuve else!—or better, Quicherat,
586|　MS:downright digger < > bah, §word altered to§ Bah,　*1887:*downright-digger

Bettered by fiction? Well, of fact thus much
Concerns you, that "of prudishness no touch
From first to last defaced the maid; anon,
590　Camp-use compelling"—what says D'Alençon
Her fast friend?—"though I saw while she undressed
How fair she was—especially her breast—
Never had I a wild thought!"—as indeed
I nowise doubt. Much less would she take heed—
595　When eve came, and the lake, the hills around
Were all one solitude and silence,—found
Barriered impenetrably safe about,—
Take heed of interloping eyes shut out,
But quietly permit the air imbibe
600　Her naked beauty till . . . but hear the scribe!
Now as she fain would bathe, one even-tide,
God's maid, this Joan, from the pool's edge she spied
The fair blue bird clowns call the Fisher-king:
And " 'Las," sighed she, "my Liege is such a thing
605　*As thou, lord but of one poor lonely place*
Out of his whole wide France: were mine the grace
To set my Dauphin free as thou, blue bird!"
Properly Martin-fisher—that's the word,
Not yours nor mine: folk said the rustic oath
610　In common use with her was—"By my troth"?
No,—"By my Martin"! Paint this! Only, turn
Her face away—that face about to burn

588| MS:that of　*1887:*that "of　　590| MS:compelling　*1887:*compelling"
591| MS:friend? "Though　*1887:*friend?—"though　　595| MS:At night-fall
when §last three words crossed out and replaced above by four words§ When eve came, and
the lake, and §crossed out and replaced above by§ the hills which bound §last two
words crossed out and replaced above by§ around　　596| MS:Walled in the §last three
words crossed out and replaced above by three words§ Were all one <> silence, walled her
round §last three words crossed out and replaced above by dash and word§ —found
597| MS:Barriered §in margin§ Impenetrably §altered to§ impenetrably　　600| MS:till . .
but　*1889a:*till . . . but　　601| MS:*even-tide　1887:even-tide,*　　604| MS:*And "'Las, sighed*
she, my　1887:And "'Las" sighed she, "my　　609| MS:mine: but since the　*1*
*887:*mine: folks said the　*1889a:*folk said　　610| MS:In common §inserted above§ <>
troth?"　*1889a:*troth"?　　611| MS:this! only　*1887:*this! Only

Into an angel's when the time is ripe!
That task's beyond you. Finished, Francis? Wipe
615   Pencil, scrape palette, and retire content!
"Omnia non omnibus"—no harm is meant!

613| MS:ripe: *1887*:ripe!   615| MS:content,   *1887*:content!   616| MS:*"Omnia* §in margin§ *Non*   *1887:"Omnia non*

WITH GERARD DE LAIRESSE

I

Ah, but—because you were struck blind, could bless
Your sense no longer with the actual view
Of man and woman, those fair forms you drew
In happier days so duteously and true,—
⁵ Must I account my Gerard de Lairesse
All sorrow-smitten? He was hindered too
—Was this no hardship?—from producing, plain
To us who still have eyes, the pageantry
Which passed and passed before his busy brain
¹⁰ And, captured on his canvas, showed our sky
Traversed by flying shapes, earth stocked with brood
Of monsters,—centaurs bestial, satyrs lewd,—
Not without much Olympian glory, shapes
Of god and goddess in their gay escapes
¹⁵ From the severe serene: or haply paced
The antique ways, god-counselled, nymph-embraced,
Some early human kingly personage.
Such wonders of the teeming poet's-age
Were still to be: nay, these indeed began—
²⁰ Are not the pictures extant?—till the ban
Of blindness struck both palette from his thumb
And pencil from his finger.

II

Blind—not dumb,
Else, Gerard, were my inmost bowels stirred
With pity beyond pity: no, the word
²⁵ Was left upon your unmolested lips:

WITH GERARD DE LAIRESSE   *Title*| MS:VI. §altered from illegible original numeral§
1889a:§numeral deleted§   ⁷| MS:producing plain,   *1887:*producing, plain
⁹| MS:Which ever passed   *1887:*Which passed and passed   ¹⁰| MS:showed the sky
*1887:*showed our sky   ¹⁸| MS:All wonders   *1887:*Such wonders
¹⁹| MS:These were to <> these to be began   *1887:*Were still to <> these indeed began—
²⁰| MS:Still are the <> exstant—till   *1887:*Are not the <> extant?—till
²¹| *1887:*palate   *1889a:*palette   ²⁵| MS:lips,   *1887:*lips:

Your mouth unsealed, despite of eyes' eclipse,
Talked all brain's yearning into birth. I lack
Somehow the heart to wish your practice back
Which boasted hand's achievement in a score
30 Of veritable pictures, less or more,
Still to be seen: myself have seen them,—moved
To pay due homage to the man I loved
Because of that prodigious book he wrote
On Artistry's Ideal, by taking note,
35 Making acquaintance with his artist-work.
So my youth's piety obtained success
Of all-too dubious sort: for, though it irk
To tell the issue, few or none would guess
From extant lines and colours, De Lairesse,
40 Your faculty, although each deftly-grouped
And aptly-ordered figure-piece was judged
Worthy a prince's purchase in its day.
Bearded experience bears not to be duped
Like boyish fancy: 'twas a boy that budged
45 No foot's breadth from your visioned steps away
The while that memorable "Walk" he trudged
In your companionship,—the Book must say
Where, when and whither,—"Walk," come what come may,
No measurer of steps on this our globe
50 Shall ever match for marvels. Faustus' robe,
And Fortunatus' cap were gifts of price:

---

^{26|} MS:And §crossed out and replaced above by§ Your   ^{28|} MS:the power to wish the
practice   *1887*:the heart to wish your practice   ^{29|} MS:boasted old §crossed out and
replaced above by§ hand's   ^{31|} MS:be judged §crossed out and replaced above by§ seen
<> have judged §crossed out and replaced above by§ seen   ^{34|} MS:§line added§
^{35|} MS:By fit §last two words crossed out and replaced by§ Making <> artist-work;
1887:artist-work.   ^{36|} MS:I and my §last three words crossed out and replaced above by
two words§ Whereby youth's   *1887*:So my youth's   ^{39|} MS:From extant §inserted
above§ <> colours, O my §last two words crossed out§   ^{40|} MS:Thy §crossed out and
replaced above by§ Your   ^{43|} MS:experience §followed by illegible word crossed out
and replaced above by§ bears   ^{44|} MS:boy who budged   *1887*:boy that budged
^{45|} MS:from thy §crossed out and replaced above by§ your   ^{47|} MS:In your §inserted
above§ company with thee §last two words crossed out and *company* altered above to§
companionship   ^{48|} MS:whither,—walk, come   *1887*:whither,—"Walk," come

But—oh, your piece of sober sound advice
That artists should descry abundant worth
In trivial commonplace, nor groan at dearth
55   If fortune bade the painter's craft be plied
In vulgar town and country! Why despond
Because hemmed round by Dutch canals? Beyond
The ugly actual, lo, on every side
Imagination's limitless domain
60   Displayed a wealth of wondrous sounds and sights
Ripe to be realized by poet's brain
Acting on painter's brush! "Ye doubt? Poor wights,
What if I set example, go before,
While you come after, and we both explore
65   Holland turned Dreamland, taking care to note
Objects whereto my pupils may devote
Attention with advantage?"

III

So commenced

That "Walk" amid true wonders—none to you,
But huge to us ignobly common-sensed,
70   Purblind, while plain could proper optics view
In that old sepulchre by lightning split,
Whereof the lid bore carven,—any dolt
Imagines why,—Jove's very thunderbolt:
You who could straight perceive, by glance at it,

---

⁵²| MS:oh, that §altered to§ thy §crossed out and replaced above by§ your < > of homely §crossed out and replaced above by§ sober   ⁵⁵| MS:If needs were that §last three words crossed out and replaced above by two words§ fortune bade   ⁵⁸| MS:actual §next word illegibly crossed out and replaced above by word and comma§ lo, on
⁶⁰| MS:Displays §altered to§ Displayed   ⁶²| MS:painter's hand §crossed out and replaced above by§ brush   ⁶³| MS:before *1887:*before,   ⁶⁸| MS:to thee §crossed out and replaced above by§ you— *1887:*you,   ⁶⁹| MS:huge §over illegible word§ < > common-sensed: *1887:*common-sensed,   ⁷⁰| MS:Purblind, alas §crossed out§ while thou couldst §altered to§ could plainly see §last four words crossed out and replaced above by seven words§ your §crossed out§ plain could your brave §last two words crossed out and replaced above by§ proper   ⁷³| MS:Could tell us why *1887:*Imagines why
⁷⁴| MS:For §crossed out and replaced above by§ You who could fast §crossed out and replaced above by§ straight perceive, at §crossed out and replaced above by§ by

75 This tomb must needs be Phaeton's! In a trice,
    Confirming that conjecture, close on hand,
    Behold, half out, half in the ploughed-up sand,
    A chariot-wheel explained its bolt-device:
    What other than the Chariot of the Sun
80 Ever let drop the like? Consult the tome—*
    I bid inglorious tarriers-at-home—
    For greater still surprise the while that "Walk"
    Went on and on, to end as it begun,
    Choke-full of chances, changes, every one
85 No whit less wondrous. What was there to baulk
    Us, who had eyes, from seeing? You with none
    Missed not a marvel: wherefore? Let us talk.

                         IV

    Say am I right? Your sealed sense moved your mind,
    Free from obstruction, to compassionate
90 Art's power left powerless, and supply the blind
    With fancies worth all facts denied by fate.
    Mind could invent things, add to—take away,
    At pleasure, leave out trifles mean and base
    Which vex the sight that cannot say them nay
95 But, where mind plays the master, have no place.
    And bent on banishing was mind, be sure,

* *The Art of Painting, &c.,* by Gerard de Lairesse. Translated by J. F. Fritsch. 1778.

75| MS:This tomb §inserted above§ must needs §inserted above§ be Phaeton's? In   *1887:*be
Phaeton's! In   78| MS:explained that bolt-device: *1887:*explained its bolt-device:
79| MS:the chariot §altered to§ Chariot of the sun §altered to§ Sun
80| MS:The Art of Painting &c by Gerard di Lairesse: Translated   *1887:The Art of Painting,
&c.,* by Gerard de Lairesse; translated   *1889a:*de Lairesse. Translated   81| MS:§line
added§ May all §last two words crossed out and replaced by two words§ I bid <> tarriers at
home—   *1887:*tarriers-at-home—   82| MS:surprises §altered to§ surprise as that §last
two words crossed out and replaced below by three words§ the while that
84| MS:Chokefull of chances and §crossed out§ changes, and §crossed out§   *1887:*chances,
changes   *1889a:*Choke-full   85| MS:wondrous—what   *1887:*wondrous. What
86| MS:seeing? Thou §crossed out and replaced above by§ You   88| MS:right? Thy
§crossed out and replaced above by§ Your <> moved the §crossed out and replaced above
by§ your   90| MS:A power   *1887:*Art's power   92| MS:add   *1889a:*and §emended
to§ add §see Editorial Notes§   93| MS:out all the mean   *1887:*out trifles mean

All except beauty from its mustered tribe
Of objects apparitional which lure
Painter to show and poet to describe—
100   That imagery of the antique song
Truer than truth's self. Fancy's rainbow-birth
Conceived mid clouds in Greece, could glance along
Your passage o'er Dutch veritable earth,
As with ourselves, who see, familiar throng
105   About our pacings men and women worth
Nowise a glance—so poets apprehend—
Since nought avails portraying them in verse:
While painters turn upon the heel, intend
To spare their work the critic's ready curse
110   Due to the daily and undignified.

V

I who myself contentedly abide
Awake, nor want the wings of dream,—who tramp
Earth's common surface, rough, smooth, dry or damp,
—I understand alternatives, no less
115   —Conceive your soul's leap, Gerard de Lairesse!
How were it could I mingle false with true,
Boast, with the sights I see, your vision too?
Advantage would it prove or detriment
If I saw double? Could I gaze intent
120   On Dryope plucking the blossoms red,
As you, whereat her lote-tree writhed and bled,
Yet lose no gain, no hard fast wide-awake
Having and holding nature for the sake

97| MS:All imagery   *1887:*All except beauty   100| MS:All imagery   *1887:*That imagery
101| MS:self, fancy's   *1887:*self. Fancy's   103| MS:Thy §crossed out and replaced above
by§ Your   104| MS:ourselves, the eyed, familiar   *1887:*ourselves, who see, familiar
106| MS:glance—our §crossed out and replaced above by§ so   107| MS:verse,   *1887:*verse:
115| MS:Conceive thy §crossed out and replaced above by§ your   *1887:*de Lairesse   *1889a:*—
Conceive <> de Lairesse!   117| MS:see, thy §crossed out and replaced above by§ your <>
too—   *1887:*too?   120| MS:On Dryope and watch her §last three words crossed out§ pluck
§altered to§ plucking the bough §crossed out and replaced above by two words§ blossoms red
*1887:*red,   121| MS:As you, §last two words and comma in margin§ whereat the lote-tree
<> bled, as thou— §last two words and dash crossed out§   *1887:*whereat her lote-tree

Of nature only—nymph and lote-tree thus
125   Gained by thy loss of fruit not fabulous,
Apple of English homesteads, where I see
Nor seek more than crisp buds a struggling bee
Uncrumples, caught by sweet he clambers through?
Truly, a moot point: make it plain to me,
130   Who, bee-like, sate sense with the simply true,
Nor seek to heighten that sufficiency
By help of feignings proper to the page—
Earth's surface-blank whereon the elder age
Put colour, poetizing—poured rich life
135   On what were else a dead ground—nothingness—
Until the solitary world grew rife
With Joves and Junos, nymphs and satyrs. Yes,
The reason was, fancy composed the strife
'Twixt sense and soul: for sense, my De Lairesse,
140   Cannot content itself with outward things,
Mere beauty: soul must needs know whence there springs—
How, when and why—what sense but loves, nor lists
To know at all.

VI

Not one of man's acquists

125| MS:by thy §crossed out and replaced above by *your*, then restored§ loss of §inserted
above§ red-cheeked not §last two words crossed out and replaced above by three words§ gold
§crossed out§ fruit not   *1887*:by the loss   *1889a*:by the §emended to§ thy §see Editorial
Notes§   127| MS:than its blossom which §last three words crossed out and replaced
above by two words§ crisp buds a struggling §inserted above§   128| MS:Crumples
§altered to§ Uncrumples, enclosed §crossed out and replaced above by§ caught <> through.
1887:through?   130| MS:sate my §crossed out§ sense with surface §crossed out and
replaced above by two words§ the simply truth §altered to§ true,   133| MS:The surface-
blank   *1887*:Earth's surface-blank   134| MS:poured that life   *1887*:poured rich life
136| MS:And so the   *1887*:Until the   137| MS:With god §crossed out and replaced
above by§ Joves and goddess §crossed out and replaced above by§ Junos <> and fauns—I
guess §last three words crossed out and replaced above by two words§ satyrs—yes
1887:satyrs. Yes,   138| MS:was, they so composed   *1887*:was, fancy composed
139| MS:twixt   *1887*:'Twixt   141| MS:beauty, but soul needs must know whence
springs—   *1887*:beauty: soul must needs know whence there springs—
142| MS:How, why, when, wherefore— §last three words and dash crossed out and replaced
above by three words and dash§ when and why—<> sense but §inserted above§

Ought he resignedly to lose, methinks:
145   So, point me out which was it of the links
Snapt first, from out the chain which used to bind
Our earth to heaven, and yet for you, since blind,
Subsisted still efficient and intact?
Oh, we can fancy too! but somehow fact
150   Has got to—say, not so much push aside
Fancy, as to declare its place supplied
By fact unseen but no less fact the same,
Which mind bids sense accept. Is mind to blame,
Or sense,—does that usurp, this abdicate?
155   First of all, as you "walked"—were it too late
For us to walk, if so we willed? Confess
We have the sober feet still, De Lairesse!
Why not the freakish brain too, that must needs
Supplement nature—not see flowers and weeds
160   Simply as such, but link with each and all
The ultimate perfection—what we call
Rightly enough the human shape divine?
The rose? No rose unless it disentwine
From Venus' wreath the while she bends to kiss
165   Her deathly love?

VII

Plain retrogression, this!

147| MS:and still §crossed out and replaced above by§ yet for thee §crossed out and replaced above by§ you   148| MS:still; efficient   *1887*:still efficient   149| MS:we could §crossed out and replaced above by§ can fancy still §crossed out and replaced above by§ too—but   *1887*:too! but   150| MS:Has §over illegible word§
151| MS:as to §inserted above§   155| MS:you walked—is §crossed out and replaced above by§ were   *1887*:you "walked"   156| MS:For me §crossed out and replaced above by§ us < > so I §crossed out and replaced above by§ we   157| MS:the sober §inserted above§ < > still, Gerard §crossed out§ de Lairesse!   *1887*:still, De   158| MS:brain as well §last two words crossed out and replaced above by§ too, that must §inserted above§
159-61| §added at bottom of page§   159| MS:Must glorify all §last three words crossed out and replaced above by§ Supplement nature—not see §last two words inserted above§
160| MS:Rather §crossed out§ simply §altered to§ Simply §next word illegibly crossed out§   162-80| MS:§added in right margin§   164| MS:bends above §crossed out and replaced above by two words§ to kiss   165| MS:Deathly Adonis? Rag-wort— §reading uncertain§   *1887*:Her deathly love? §¶§ Plain retrogression, this!

No, no: we poets go not back at all:
What you did we could do—from great to small
Sinking assuredly: if this world last
One moment longer when Man finds its Past
170   Exceed its Present—blame the Protoplast!
If we no longer see as you of old,
'Tis we see deeper. Progress for the bold!
You saw the body, 'tis the soul we see.
Try now! Bear witness while you walk with me,
175   I see as you: if we loose arms, stop pace,
'Tis that you stand still, I conclude the race
Without your company. Come, walk once more
The "Walk": if I to-day as you of yore
See just like you the blind—then sight shall cry
180   —The whole long day quite gone through—victory!

VIII

Thunders on thunders, doubling and redoubling
Doom o'er the mountain, while a sharp white fire
Now shone, now sheared its rusty herbage, troubling
Hardly the fir-boles, now discharged its ire
185   Full where some pine-tree's solitary spire
Crashed down, defiant to the last: till—lo,
The motive of the malice!—all a-glow,
Circled with flame there yawned a sudden rift
I' the rock-face, and I saw a form erect
190   Front and defy the outrage, while—as checked,
Chidden, beside him dauntless in the drift—

166| MS:§¶§ No *1887:*No   169| MS:when one finds *1887:*when Man finds
170| MS:§first three words illegibly crossed out and replaced above by three words§ Exceed its
Present   171| MS:old *1887:*old,   172| MS:Why, §word and comma crossed out
and replaced by§ 'Tis <> deeper: §next word illegibly crossed out§ the truth be bold—
*1887:*deeper. Progress for the bold!   173| MS:You §next word illegibly crossed out and
replaced above by§ saw the body, and §crossed out and replaced above by§ 'tis
174| MS:now! bear *1887:*now! Bear   175| MS:you: and when §crossed out and replaced
above by§ if we break, stop *1887:*you: if we loose arms, stop   176| MS:race, *1887:*race
178| MS:The walk, I'll see to day *1887:*The "Walk": if I to-day   179| MS:When you
declare you're blind—why then I'll cry *1887:*See just like you the blind—then sight shall cry
182| MS:while the sharp *1887:*while a sharp   186| MS:'till *1887:*till

Cowered a heaped creature, wing and wing outspread
In deprecation o'er the crouching head
Still hungry for the feast foregone awhile.

195 O thou, of scorn's unconquerable smile,
Was it when this—Jove's feathered fury—slipped
Gore-glutted from the heart's core whence he ripped—
This eagle-hound—neither reproach nor prayer—
Baffled, in one more fierce attempt to tear

200 Fate's secret from thy safeguard,—was it then
That all these thunders rent earth, ruined air
To reach thee, pay thy patronage of men?
He thundered,—to withdraw, as beast to lair,
Before the triumph on thy pallid brow.

205 Gather the night again about thee now,
Hate on, love ever! Morn is breaking there—
The granite ridge pricks through the mist, turns gold
As wrong turns right. O laughters manifold
Of ocean's ripple at dull earth's despair!

IX

210 But morning's laugh sets all the crags alight
Above the baffled tempest: tree and tree
Stir themselves from the stupor of the night
And every strangled branch resumes its right
To breathe, shakes loose dark's clinging dregs, waves free

215 In dripping glory. Prone the runnels plunge,
While earth, distent with moisture like a sponge,
Smokes up, and leaves each plant its gem to see,
Each grass-blade's glory-glitter. Had I known
The torrent now turned river?—masterful

220 Making its rush o'er tumbled ravage—stone
And stub which barred the froths and foams: no bull

---

¹⁹⁸| MS:prayer,— *1887*:prayer— ²⁰³| MS:withdraw in pale despair *1887*:withdraw, as beast to lair, ²⁰⁴| MS:brow: *1887*:brow. ²⁰⁶| MS:ever: morn *1887*:ever! Morn ²⁰⁷⁻⁹| MS:§added in right margin§ ²¹²| MS:Bestir them §last two words crossed out and replaced above by two words§ Stir themselves ²¹⁴| MS:dregs, make §crossed out and replaced above by§ waves ²¹⁶| MS:spunge, *1889a*:sponge, ²¹⁸| MS:grass-blade plain its glitter. Had *1887*:grass-blade's glory-glitter. Had ²²¹| MS:foams—no *1887*:foams: no

Ever broke bounds in formidable sport
More overwhelmingly, till lo, the spasm
Sets him to dare that last mad leap: report
225 Who may—his fortunes in the deathly chasm
That swallows him in silence! Rather turn
Whither, upon the upland, pedestalled
Into the broad day-splendour, whom discern
These eyes but thee, supreme one, rightly called
230 Moon-maid in heaven above and, here below,
Earth's huntress-queen? I note the garb succinct
Saving from smirch that purity of snow
From breast to knee—snow's self with just the tinct
Of the apple-blossom's heart-blush. Ah, the bow
235 Slack-strung her fingers grasp, where, ivory-linked
Horn curving blends with horn, a moonlike pair
Which mimic the brow's crescent sparkling so—
As if a star's live restless fragment winked
Proud yet repugnant, captive in such hair!
240 What hope along the hillside, what far bliss
Lets the crisp hair-plaits fall so low they kiss
Those lucid shoulders? Must a morn so blithe,
Needs have its sorrow when the twang and hiss
Tell that from out thy sheaf one shaft makes writhe
245 Its victim, thou unerring Artemis?
Why did the chamois stand so fair a mark
Arrested by the novel shape he dreamed
Was bred of liquid marble in the dark
Depths of the mountain's womb which ever teemed
250 With novel births of wonder? Not one spark
Of pity in that steel-grey glance which gleamed
At the poor hoof's protesting as it stamped

224| MS:leap—reports,— *1887*:leap: report   226| MS:silence! rather   *1887*:silence!
Rather   231| MS:huntress-queen: I   *1887*:huntress-queen? I   233| MS:breasts to
knees   *1887*:breast to knee   236| MS:moon-like   *1887*:moonlike   237| MS:mimic
where the crescent sparkles so—   *1887*:mimic the brow's crescent sparkling so—
238| MS:live restless §inserted above§   242| MS:shoulders—what, this §crossed
out and replaced above by§ a   *1887*:shoulders? Must a   243| MS:Must have   *1887*:Needs
have   244| MS:Tells §altered to§ Tell   248| MS:of marble, liquid in   *1887*:of liquid
marble in   249| *1887*:womb that ever   *1889a*:womb which ever

Idly the granite? Let me glide unseen
From thy proud presence: well mayst thou be queen
255 Of all those strange and sudden deaths which damped
So oft Love's torch and Hymen's taper lit
For happy marriage till the maidens paled
And perished on the temple-step, assailed
By—what except to envy must man's wit
260 Impute that sure implacable release
Of life from warmth and joy? But death means peace.

X

Noon is the conqueror,—not a spray, nor leaf,
Nor herb, nor blossom but has rendered up
Its morning dew: the valley seemed one cup
265 Of cloud-smoke, but the vapour's reign was brief,
Sun-smitten, see, it hangs—the filmy haze—
Grey-garmenting the herbless mountain-side,
To soothe the day's sharp glare: while far and wide
Above unclouded burns the sky, one blaze
270 With fierce immitigable blue, no bird
Ventures to spot by passage. E'en of peaks
Which still presume there, plain each pale point speaks
In wan transparency of waste incurred
By over-daring: far from me be such!
275 Deep in the hollow, rather, where combine
Tree, shrub and briar to roof with shade and cool
The remnant of some lily-strangled pool,
Edged round with mossy fringing soft and fine.
Smooth lie the bottom slabs, and overhead
280 Watch elder, bramble, rose, and service-tree

254| MS:may'st *1889a:*mayst 259| MS:what but §crossed out and replaced above by two words§ except to envy can our human §last three words crossed out and replaced above by two words§ must man's 260| MS:Impute to §crossed out§ that sure §inserted above§ 265| MS:cloud-smoke but *1887:*cloud-smoke, but 271| MS:passage: e'en the peaks *1887:*passage. E'en of peaks 272| MS:there: plain *1887:*there, plain 276| MS:to keep §crossed out and replaced above by§ roof 278| MS:with mosses shaggy §crossed out and replaced above by§ fringy soft and fine; *1887:*with mossy fringing soft and fine. 280| MS:elder, bramble, §word and comma inserted above§ dogrose §altered to§ rose, and §inserted above§

And one beneficent rich barberry
Jewelled all over with fruit-pendents red.
What have I seen! O Satyr, well I know
How sad thy case, and what a world of woe
²⁸⁵ Was hid by the brown visage furry-framed
Only for mirth: who otherwise could think—
Marking thy mouth gape still on laughter's brink,
Thine eyes a-swim with merriment unnamed
But haply guessed at by their furtive wink?
²⁹⁰ And all the while a heart was panting sick
Behind that shaggy bulwark of thy breast—
Passion it was that made those breath-bursts thick
I took for mirth subsiding into rest.
So, it was Lyda—she of all the train
²⁹⁵ Of forest-thridding nymphs,—'twas only she
Turned from thy rustic homage in disdain,
Saw but that poor uncouth outside of thee,
And, from her circling sisters, mocked a pain
Echo had pitied—whom Pan loved in vain—
³⁰⁰ For she was wishful to partake thy glee,
Mimic thy mirth—who loved her not again,
Savage for Lyda's sake. She couches there—
Thy cruel beauty, slumberously laid
Supine on heaped-up beast-skins, unaware
³⁰⁵ Thy steps have traced her to the briery glade,
Thy greedy hands disclose the cradling lair,
Thy hot eyes reach and revel on the maid!

XI

Now, what should this be for? The sun's decline
Seems as he lingered lest he lose some act

---

²⁸¹| MS:one beneficent §inserted above§   ²⁸⁴| MS:case and   *1887*:case, and
²⁸⁶| MS:Only §in margin§ For §altered to§ for mirth: alone §crossed out§ <> think
1887:think—   ²⁸⁷| MS:brink *1887*:brink,   ²⁸⁹| MS:But no less §last two words
crossed out and replaced above by§ haply <> wink— *1887*:wink?   ²⁹²| MS:it proves, that
1887:it was that   ²⁹⁴| MS:So it *1887*:So, it   ³⁰⁰| MS:glee *1887*:glee,
³⁰²| MS:couches *1887*:crouches *1889a*:crouches §emended to§ couches §see Editorial
Notes§   ³⁰⁷| MS:§bottom of page cut off after l. 307 and lines apparently deleted§

³¹⁰ Dread and decisive, some prodigious fact
Like thunder from the safe sky's sapphirine
About to alter earth's conditions, packed
With fate for nature's self that waits, aware
What mischief unsuspected in the air
³¹⁵ Menaces momently a cataract.
Therefore it is that yonder space extends
Untrenched upon by any vagrant tree,
Shrub, weed well nigh; they keep their bounds, leave free
The platform for what actors? Foes or friends,
³²⁰ Here come they trooping silent: heaven suspends
Purpose the while they range themselves. I see!
Bent on a battle, two vast powers agree
This present and no after-contest ends
One or the other's grasp at rule in reach
³²⁵ Over the race of man—host fronting host,
As statue statue fronts—wrath-molten each,
Solidified by hate,—earth halved almost,
To close once more in chaos. Yet two shapes
Show prominent, each from the universe
³³⁰ Of minions round about him, that disperse
Like cloud-obstruction when a bolt escapes.
Who flames first? Macedonian is it thou?
Ay, and who fronts thee, King Darius, drapes
His form with purple, fillet-folds his brow.

XII

³³⁵ What, then the long day dies at last? Abrupt
The sun that seemed, in stooping, sure to melt
Our mountain ridge, is mastered: black the belt

---

^{313|} MS:waits aware *1887:*waits, aware   ^{314|} MS:Mischief all unsuspected   *1887:*What
mischief unsuspected   ^{320|} MS:silent, heaven   *1887:*silent: heaven
^{321|} MS:while: they <> themselves: I see—   *1887:*while they <> themselves. I see!
^{324|} MS:Each §crossed out and replaced above by§ One   ^{326|} MS:Still as two statues
might—wrath-molten   *1887:*As statue statue fronts—wrath-molten   ^{327|} MS:hate,—the
world huge §last three words crossed out and replaced above by§ earth   ^{329|} MS:each
mid §crossed out and replaced above by§ from   ^{331|} MS:escapes: *1887:*escapes.
^{335|} MS:last? The sun §last two words crossed out and replaced above by§ Abrupt
^{337|} MS:mountain-ridge is   *1887:*mountain-ridge, is   *1889a:*mountain ridge

107

Of westward crags, his gold could not corrupt,
Barriers again the valley, lets the flow
340 Of lavish glory waste itself away
—Whither? For new climes, fresh eyes breaks the day!
Night was not to be baffled. If the glow
Were all that's gone from us! Did clouds, afloat
So filmily but now, discard no rose,
345 Sombre throughout the fleeciness that grows
A sullen uniformity. I note
Rather displeasure,—in the overspread
Change from the swim of gold to one pale lead
Oppressive to malevolence,—than late
350 Those amorous yearnings when the aggregate
Of cloudlets pressed that each and all might sate
Its passion and partake in relics red
Of day's bequeathment: now, a frown instead
Estranges, and affrights who needs must fare
355 On and on till his journey ends: but where?
Caucasus? Lost now in the night. Away
And far enough lies that Arcadia.
The human heroes tread the world's dark way
No longer. Yet I dimly see almost—
360 Yes, for my last adventure! 'Tis a ghost.
So drops away the beauty! There he stands
Voiceless, scarce strives with deprecating hands.

XIII

Enough! Stop further fooling, De Lairesse!
My fault, not yours! Some fitter way express
365 Heart's satisfaction that the Past indeed
Is past, gives way before Life's best and last,
The all-including Future! What were life

338| MS:crags his < > corrupt   *1887*:crags, his < > corrupt,   341| MS:day—   *1887*:day!
343| MS:us! But §crossed out and replaced above by§ Did   354| MS:Frightens §crossed
out and replaced above by word and comma§ Estranges, and   356| MS:Olympus
§crossed out and replaced above by§ Caucasus   359| MS:longer: yet   *1887*:longer. Yet
362| MS:hand . . .   *1887*:hands.   *1889a*:hands §emended to§ hands. §see Editorial Notes§

Did soul stand still therein, forego her strife
Through the ambiguous Present to the goal
370 Of some all-reconciling Future? Soul,
Nothing has been which shall not bettered be
Hereafter,—leave the root, by law's decree
Whence springs the ultimate and perfect tree!
Busy thee with unearthing root? Nay, climb—
375 Quit trunk, branch, leaf and flower—reach, rest sublime
Where fruitage ripens in the blaze of day!
O'erlook, despise, forget, throw flower away,
Intent on progress? No whit more than stop
Ascent therewith to dally, screen the top
380 Sufficiency of yield by interposed
Twistwork bold foot gets free from. Wherefore glozed
The poets—"Dream afresh old godlike shapes,
Recapture ancient fable that escapes,
Push back reality, repeople earth
385 With vanished falseness, recognize no worth
In fact new-born unless 'tis rendered back
Pallid by fancy, as the western rack
Of fading cloud bequeaths the lake some gleam
Of its gone glory!"

XIV

Let things be—not seem,
390 I counsel rather,—do, and nowise dream!
Earth's young significance is all to learn:
The dead Greek lore lies buried in the urn

368| MS:forego his §crossed out and replaced above by§ her   372| MS:leave §over
illegible erasure§   375| MS:Leave §crossed out and replaced above by§ Quit < > branch,
rest not till thou reach §last five words crossed out and replaced above by five words§ leaf and
flower—reach, rest   377| MS:flowers §altered to§ flower away *1887*:away,
379| MS:Ascent therewith §inserted above§ to dally, with them §last two words crossed out§
381| MS:Twistwork bold §inserted above§ foot §next word illegibly crossed out§
382| MS:The simple §crossed out and replaced above by§ poets—"Dream again §altered to§
afresh of §crossed out and replaced above by§ old   386| MS:fact around §crossed out and
replaced above by§ newborn unless it render back *1887*:unless 'tis rendered back
387| MS:Pallidly fancy *1887*:Pallid by fancy   389| MS:Of the §crossed out and replaced
above by§ its   391| MS:Earth's new §crossed out and replaced above by§ young < >
learn— *1887*:learn: 392| MS:The old §crossed out and replaced above by§ dead

Where who seeks fire finds ashes. Ghost, forsooth!
What was the best Greece babbled of as truth?
395   "A shade, a wretched nothing,—sad, thin, drear,
Cold, dark, it holds on to the lost loves here,
If hand have haply sprinkled o'er the dead
Three charitable dust-heaps, made mouth red
One moment by the sip of sacrifice:
400   Just so much comfort thaws the stubborn ice
Slow-thickening upward till it choke at length
The last faint flutter craving—not for strength,
Not beauty, not the riches and the rule
O'er men that made life life indeed." Sad school
405   Was Hades! Gladly,—might the dead but slink
To life back,—to the dregs once more would drink
Each interloper, drain the humblest cup
Fate mixes for humanity.

XV

Cheer up,—
Be death with me, as with Achilles erst,

394| MS:of in youth §last two words crossed out and replaced above by two words§ as truth?
395| MS:nothing,—sad, §word and comma inserted above§ thin, cold §crossed out§ drear
*1887:*drear,   396| MS:Cold §over *And*§ dark < > here   *1887:*Cold, dark < > here,
397| MS:By help of §last three words crossed out and replaced above by§ If hand that §crossed
out and replaced above by two words§ have haply   398| MS:Its §crossed out and replaced
above by§ Three < > dust; §semi-colon crossed out and word altered to§ dust-heaps: were pale
lips §last three words crossed out and replaced above by two words§ mouth made §transposed
to§ made mouth   *1887:*dust-heaps, made   399| MS:sacrifice   *1887:*sacrifice:
400| MS:How near would §last three words crossed out and replaced above by three words§ And
so much   *1887:*Just so   401| MS:That §crossed out and replaced above by§ Slow thickens
§altered to§ thickening < > choak   *1887:*Slow-thickening < > choke   402| MS:The still-
aspirant §crossed out and replaced above by two words§ last faint flutter craving—§word and
dash inserted above§   404| MS:indeed: sad   *1887:*indeed." Sad §for comment on
placement of these quotation marks see Editorial Notes§   405| MS:Is §crossed out and
replaced above by§ Their Hades!—taught there, might < > but §crossed out§ slink   *1887:*Was
Hades! Gladly,— might < > but slink   406| MS:back, gladly to the dregs would
*1887:*back,—to the dregs once more would   407| MS:The §crossed out and replaced above
by§ Each interloper of the humblest   *1887:*interloper, drain the humblest
408| MS:humanity."   *1887:*humanity.   409| MS:Why, §word and comma
crossed out and replaced above by§ Be Death §next word illegibly crossed out§ with us now
§last two words crossed out and replaced above by§ me, as with pagans §crossed out and
replaced above by§ Achilles   *1887:*death   410| MS:Of man's   *1887:*Of Man's

410 Of Man's calamities the last and worst:
　　Take it so! By proved potency that still
　　Makes perfect, be assured, come what come will,
　　What once lives never dies—what here attains
　　To a beginning, has no end, still gains
415 And never loses aught: when, where, and how—
　　Lies in Law's lap. What's death then? Even now
　　With so much knowledge is it hard to bear
　　Brief interposing ignorance? Is care
　　For a creation found at fault just there—
420 There where the heart breaks bond and outruns time,
　　To reach, not follow what shall be?

XVI

Here's rhyme
Such as one makes now,—say, when Spring repeats
That miracle the Greek Bard sadly greets:
"Spring for the tree and herb—no Spring for us!"
425 Let Spring come: why, a man salutes her thus:

Dance, yellows and whites and reds,—
Lead your gay orgy, leaves, stalks, heads
Astir with the wind in the tulip-beds!
There's sunshine; scarcely a wind at all
430 Disturbs starved grass and daisies small
On a certain mound by a churchyard wall.

Daisies and grass be my heart's bedfellows
On the mound wind spares and sunshine mellows:
Dance you, reds and whites and yellows!

418|　MS:The interposing ignorance? Thou Care　*1887*:Brief interposing ignorance? Is care
419|　MS:For thy creation　*1887*:For a creation　　421|　MS:To face not　*1887*:To reach not
1889a:reach, not　　　422|　MS:as a man §last two words crossed out and replaced above by§
one < > now,—say, §dash, word and comma inserted above§

WITH CHARLES AVISON

I

How strange!—but, first of all, the little fact
Which led my fancy forth. This bitter morn
Showed me no object in the stretch forlorn
Of garden-ground beneath my window, backed
5   By yon worn wall wherefrom the creeper, tacked
To clothe its brickwork, hangs now, rent and racked
By five months' cruel winter,—showed no torn
And tattered ravage worse for eyes to see
Than just one ugly space of clearance, left
10   Bare even of the bones which used to be
Warm wrappage, safe embracement: this one cleft—
—O what a life and beauty filled it up
Startlingly, when methought the rude clay cup
Ran over with poured bright wine! 'Twas a bird
15   Breast-deep there, tugging at his prize, deterred
No whit by the fast-falling snow-flake: gain
Such prize my blackcap must by might and main—
The cloth-shred, still a-flutter from its nail
That fixed a spray once. Now, what told the tale
20   To thee,—no townsman but born orchard-thief,—
That here—surpassing moss-tuft, beard from sheaf
Of sun-scorched barley, horsehairs long and stout,
All proper country-pillage—here, no doubt,
Was just the scrap to steal should line thy nest
25   Superbly? Off he flew, his bill possessed
The booty sure to set his wife's each wing
Greenly a-quiver. How they climb and cling,
Hang parrot-wise to bough, these blackcaps! Strange
Seemed to a city-dweller that the finch

WITH CHARLES AVISON   *Title*| MS:VII.   *1889a:*§numeral deleted§
7| MS:no sign §crossed out and replaced above by§ torn   11| MS:cleft   *1887:*cleft—
13| MS:Suddenly §crossed out and replaced above by§ Startlingly when   *1887:*Startlingly,
when   17| MS:blackcap would—by   *1887:*blackcap must by
22| MS:O' the sun-spoilt §altered to§ sun-scorched   *1887:*Of sun-scorched

30   Should stray so far to forage: at a pinch,
     Was not the fine wool's self within his range
     —Filchings on every fence? But no: the need
     Was of this rag of manufacture, spoiled
     By art, and yet by nature near unsoiled,
35   New-suited to what scheming finch would breed
     In comfort, this uncomfortable March.

                              II

     Yet—by the first pink blossom on the larch!—
     This was scarce stranger than that memory,—
     In want of what should cheer the stay-at-home,
40   My soul,—must straight clap pinion, well nigh roam
     A century back, nor once close plume, descry
     The appropriate rag to plunder, till she pounced—
     Pray, on what relic of a brain long still?
     What old-world work proved forage for the bill
45   Of memory the far-flyer? "March" announced,
     I verily believe, the dead and gone
     Name of a music-maker: one of such
     In England as did little or did much,
     But, doing, had their day once. Avison!
50   Singly and solely for an air of thine,
     Bold-stepping "March," foot stept to ere my hand
     Could stretch an octave, I o'erlooked the band
     Of majesties familiar, to decline
     On thee—not too conspicuous on the list
55   Of worthies who by help of pipe or wire
     Expressed in sound rough rage or soft desire—
     Thou, whilom of Newcastle organist!

38| MS:was no §crossed out and replaced above by§ scarce <> memory,   *1887*:memory,—
39| cheer this §crossed out and replaced above by§ the   40| MS:soul, must
1887:soul,—must   41| MS:plume,—descry   *1887*:plume, descry
43| MS:still—   *1887*:still?   46| MS:beleive   *1887*:believe
51| MS:Strong-stepping "march §altered to§ "March," I stept   *1887*:Bold-stepping "March,"
foot stept   57| MS:Thou—whileom   *1887*:Thou, whilom   *1889a*:whilom

III

So much could one—well, thinnish air effect!
Am I ungrateful? for, your March, styled "Grand,"
60 Did veritably seem to grow, expand,
And greaten up to title as, unchecked,
Dream-marchers marched, kept marching, slow and sure,
In time, to tune, unchangeably the same,
From nowhere into nowhere,—out they came,
65 Onward they passed, and in they went. No lure
Of novel modulation pricked the flat
Forthright persisting melody,—no hint
That discord, sound asleep beneath the flint,
—Struck—might spring spark-like, claim due tit-for-tat,
70 Quenched in a concord. No! Yet, such the might
Of quietude's immutability,
That somehow coldness gathered warmth, well nigh
Quickened—which could not be!—grew burning-bright
With fife-shriek, cymbal-clash and trumpet-blare,
75 To drum-accentuation: pacing turned
Striding, and striding grew gigantic, spurned
At last the narrow space 'twixt earth and air,
So shook me back into my sober self.

IV

And where woke I? The March had set me down
80 There whence I plucked the measure, as his brown
Frayed flannel-bit my blackcap. Great John Relfe,
Master of mine, learned, redoubtable,
It little needed thy consummate skill
To fitly figure such a bass! The key

58| MS:effect! *1889a:*effect §emended to§ effect! §see Editorial Notes§
59| MS:ungrateful?—for *1887:*ungrateful? for   69| MS:—Struck
§dash in margin§ <> spark-like, need due *1887:*spark-like, claim due
72| MS:That coldness somehow *1887:*That somehow coldness
78-79| MS:self—/And <> march *1887:*self. / §¶§ And <> March   81| MS:flannel-bit
the blackcap *1887:*flannel-bit my blackcap   82| MS:Master of §inserted above§ mine,
learned, and §crossed out§   84| MS:bass: the *1887:*bass! The

85 Was—should not memory play me false—well, C.
Ay, with the Greater Third, in Triple Time,
Three crotchets to a bar: no change, I grant,
Except from Tonic down to Dominant.
And yet—and yet—if I could put in rhyme
90 The manner of that marching!—which had stopped
—l wonder, where?—but that my weak self dropped
From out the ranks, to rub eyes disentranced
And feel that, after all the way advanced,
Back must I foot it, I and my compeers,
95 Only to reach, across a hundred years,
The bandsman Avison whose little book
And large tune thus had led me the long way
(As late a rag my blackcap) from to-day
And to-day's music-manufacture,—Brahms,
100 Wagner, Dvorak, Liszt,—to where—trumpets, shawms,
Show yourselves joyful!—Handel reigns—supreme?
By no means! Buononcini's work is theme
For fit laudation of the impartial few:
(We stand in England, mind you!) Fashion too
105 Favours Geminiani—of those choice
Concertos: nor there wants a certain voice
Raised in thy favour likewise, famed Pepusch
Dear to our great-grandfathers! In a bush
Of Doctor's wig, they prized thee timing beats
110 While Greenway trilled "Alexis." Such were feats
Of music in thy day—dispute who list—

85| MS:Was—but §crossed out§ should not §inserted above§ <> false!—well, G §crossed out
and replaced above by§ C. *1887*:false—well   88| MS:to Dominant,— *1887*:to
Dominant.   93| MS:And feel §inserted above§   96| MS:band's man *1889a*:bandsman
98| MS:late his §crossed out and replaced above by§ a   100| MS:Wagner, and §crossed out
and replaced above by word and comma§ Dvorak, Liszt,—to where— §followed by illegible
erasure§   103| MS:For the §crossed out and replaced above by§ fit   104| MS:in
England only.) Judgment too *1887*:in England, mind you!) Fashion too
107| MS:likewise,—famed Pepush *1887*:likewise, famed Pepusch   108| MS:great-
grandfathers: in that §crossed out and replaced above by§ a *1887*:great-grandfathers! In
109| MS:wig, who §crossed out and replaced above by§ they saw thee time the beats, *1887*:they
prized thee timing beats   110| MS:trilled "Alexis"—such *1887*:trilled "Alexis." Such

Avison, of Newcastle organist!

V

And here's your music all alive once more—
As once it was alive, at least: just so
115   The figured worthies of a waxwork-show
Attest—such people, years and years ago,
Looked thus when outside death had life below,
—Could say "We are now," not "We were of yore,"
—"Feel how our pulses leap!" and not "Explore—
120   Explain why quietude has settled o'er
Surface once all-awork!" Ay, such a "Suite"
Roused heart to rapture, such a "Fugue" would catch
Soul heavenwards up, when time was: why attach
Blame to exhausted faultlessness, no match
125   For fresh achievement? Feat once—ever feat!
How can completion grow still more complete?
Hear Avison! He tenders evidence
That music in his day as much absorbed
Heart and soul then as Wagner's music now.
130   Perfect from centre to circumference—
Orbed to the full can be but fully orbed:
And yet—and yet—whence comes it that "O Thou"—
Sighed by the soul at eve to Hesperus—
Will not again take wing and fly away
135   (Since fatal Wagner fixed it fast for us)
In some unmodulated minor? Nay,
Even by Handel's help!

VI

I state it thus:

---

¹¹²⁻¹³| MS:§B numbered this paragraph as 4, and paragraph 6 (l. 137) as 5, then stopped numbering paragraphs§   ¹¹⁸| MS:—Could §dash in margin§ <> now" not   *1889a*:now," not   ¹²⁹| MS:now: *1887*:now.   ¹³⁴| MS:Will never §crossed out and replaced above by two words§ not again more take   *1887*:again take   ¹³⁵| MS:§line added§ fatal Wagner came and set it us)   *1887*:fatal Wagner fixed it fast for us)   ¹³⁶| MS:minor—? Nay §last two words altered to§ minor—Nay,   *1887*:minor? Nay,   ¹³⁷| MS:help?   *1887*:help!

There is no truer truth obtainable
By Man than comes of music. "Soul"—(accept
140   A word which vaguely names what no adept
In word-use fits and fixes so that still
Thing shall not slip word's fetter and remain
Innominate as first, yet, free again,
Is no less recognized the absolute
145   Fact underlying that same other fact
Concerning which no cavil can dispute
Our nomenclature when we call it "Mind"—
Something not Matter)—"Soul," who seeks shall find
Distinct beneath that something. You exact
150   An illustrative image? This may suit.

VII

We see a work: the worker works behind,
Invisible himself. Suppose his act
Be to o'erarch a gulf: he digs, transports,
Shapes and, through enginery—all sizes, sorts,
155   Lays stone by stone until a floor compact
Proves our bridged causeway. So works Mind—by stress
Of faculty, with loose facts, more or less,
Builds up our solid knowledge: all the same,
Underneath rolls what Mind may hide not tame,
160   An element which works beyond our guess,
Soul, the unsounded sea—whose lift of surge,

144| MS:Shall §in margin§ still be felt fact—substantial §last two words crossed out and replaced above by two words§ the very absolute   *1887*:Is no less recognised the absolute   *1889a*:recognized   148| MS:not Matter, §altered to§)— §inserted above§ "Soul," then, is to §last three words crossed out and replaced above by three words§ who seeks shall   149| MS:Distinct §in margin§ Somehow §inserted above and crossed out§ Beneath §altered to§ beneath that something: how? §word and question mark crossed out§   *1887*:something. You   150-51| MS:suit./We   *1887*:suit./ §¶§ We   152| MS:himself. Suppose our act   *1887*:himself. Suppose his act   153| MS:gulf: we dig, transport,   *1887*:gulf: he digs, transports,   154| MS:Shape < > enginery of every sort,   *1887*:Shapes < > enginery—all sizes, sorts,   155| MS:Lay < > floor's compact: *1887*:Lays < > floor compact   156| MS:There's our < > causeway: so §last two words altered to§ causeway. So < > Mind, by   *1887*:Proves our < > Mind—by   157| MS:faculty sufficient, more or less   *1887*:faculty, with loose facts, more or less,   158| MS:up the solid structure §crossed out and replaced above by§ knowledge   *1887*:up our solid

Spite of all superstructure, lets emerge,
In flower and foam, Feeling from out the deeps
Mind arrogates no mastery upon—
165   Distinct indisputably. Has there gone
To dig up, drag forth, render smooth from rough
Mind's flooring,—operosity enough?
Still the successive labour of each inch,
Who lists may learn: from the last turn of winch
170   That let the polished slab-stone find its place,
To the first prod of pick-axe at the base
Of the unquarried mountain,—what was all
Mind's varied process except natural,
Nay, easy, even, to descry, describe,
175   After our fashion? "So worked Mind: its tribe
Of senses ministrant above, below,
Far, near, or now or haply long ago
Brought to pass knowledge." But Soul's sea,—drawn whence,
Fed how, forced whither,—by what evidence
180   Of ebb and flow, that's felt beneath the tread,
Soul has its course 'neath Mind's work overhead,—
Who tells of, tracks to source the founts of Soul?
Yet wherefore heaving sway and restless roll
This side and that, except to emulate
185   Stability above? To match and mate
Feeling with knowledge,—make as manifest
Soul's work as Mind's work, turbulence as rest,
Hates, loves, joys, woes, hopes, fears, that rise and sink
Ceaselessly, passion's transient flit and wink,
190   A ripple's tinting or a spume-sheet's spread

162| MS:of the superstructure   *1887*:of all superstructure   163| MS:from out §inserted above§   167| MS:Mind's making,—operosity   *1887*:Mind's flooring, —operosity
168| MS:inch   *1887*:inch,   170| MS:lets   *1887*:let   175| MS:After poor human §last two words crossed out and replaced above by§ our < > Mind—its   *1887*:worked Mind: its
176| MS:Below   *1887*:below,   177| MS:ago,   *1887*:ago   180| MS:flow that's felt beneath §inserted above§ the tread,—   *1887*:flow, that's < > tread,   181| MS:course with Mind's   *1887*:course 'neath Mind's   182| MS:Who shall describe the §crossed out and replaced above by§ such processes of   *1887*:Who tells of, tracks to source the founts of
183| MS:Yet why the §last two words crossed out and replaced above by§ wherefore
185| MS:above: to §last two words altered to§ above? To   187| MS:as mind's   *1887*:as Mind's

Whitening the wave,—to strike all this life dead,
Run mercury into a mould like lead,
And henceforth have the plain result to show—
How we Feel, hard and fast as what we Know—
195   This were the prize and is the puzzle!—which
Music essays to solve: and here's the hitch
That baulks her of full triumph else to boast.

VIII

All Arts endeavour this, and she the most
Attains thereto, yet fails of touching: why?
200   Does Mind get Knowledge from Art's ministry?
What's known once is known ever: Arts arrange,
Dissociate, re-distribute, interchange
Part with part, lengthen,broaden, high or deep
Construct their bravest,—still such pains produce
205   Change, not creation: simply what lay loose
At first lies firmly after, what design
Was faintly traced in hesitating line
Once on a time, grows firmly resolute
Henceforth and evermore. Now, could we shoot
210   Liquidity into a mould,—some way
Arrest Soul's evanescent moods, and keep
Unalterably still the forms that leap
To life for once by help of Art!—which yearns
To save its capture: Poetry discerns,
215   Painting is 'ware of passion's rise and fall,

191| MS:the waters,—strike   *1887*:the wave,—to strike   193| MS:show   *1887*:show—
195| MS:That §crossed out and replaced above by§ This   197-98| MS:Which §crossed out and replaced above by§ That <> boast./All Arts endeavour, she of all the   *1887*:boast./ §¶§ All Arts endeavour this, and she the   199| MS:fails to touch: for why?   *1887*:fails of touching: why?   200| MS:Has Mind got Knowledge from their ministry?   *1887*:Does Mind get knowledge from Art's ministry?   201| MS:arrange   *1887*:arrange, 203| MS:lengthen, highten §crossed out and replaced above by§ broaden <> deep, *1887*:deep   204| MS:still Art's pains   *1887*:still such pains 206| MS:after—what   *1887*:after, what   210| MS:mould,—this way   *1887*:mould,—some way   211| MS:moods,—so keep   *1887*:moods, and keep   212| MS:Always unchanged, §last two words and comma crossed out and replaced above by two words§ Unalterably still the §crossed out and restored§   215| MS:ware   *1887*:'ware

Bursting, subsidence, intermixture—all
A-seethe within the gulf. Each Art a-strain
Would stay the apparition,—nor in vain:
The Poet's word-mesh, Painters sure and swift
220   Colour-and-line-throw—proud the prize they lift!
Thus felt Man and thus looked Man,—passions caught
I' the midway swim of sea,—not much, if aught,
Of nether-brooding loves, hates, hopes and fears,
Enwombed past Art's disclosure. Fleet the years,
225   And still the Poet's page holds Helena
At gaze from topmost Troy—"But where are they,
My brothers in the armament I name
Hero by hero? Can it be that shame
For their lost sister holds them from the war?"
230   —Knowing not they already slept afar
Each of them in his own dear native land.
Still on the Painter's fresco, from the hand
Of God takes Eve the life-spark whereunto
She trembles up from nothingness. Outdo
235   Both of them, Music! Dredging deeper yet,
Drag into day,—by sound, thy master-net,—
The abysmal bottom-growth, ambiguous thing
Unbroken of a branch, palpitating
With limbs' play and life's semblance! There it lies,
240   Marvel and mystery, of mysteries
And marvels, most to love and laud thee for!
Save it from chance and change we most abhor!
Give momentary feeling permanence,

217| MS:gulf,—each   *1887*:gulf. Each   218| MS:To §crossed out and replaced above by§
Would   219| MS:word-mesh—painter's §next word illegibly crossed out§ throw §crossed
out and replaced above by two words§ sure and   *1887*:word-mesh, Painter's
220| MS:Colour-and-line—behold §last word and dash crossed out and replaced above by two
words and hyphen§ -throw—proud   221| MS:So felt men and so looked men,—passions
1887:Thus felt Man and thus looked Man,—passions   226| MS:topmost tower §crossed
out and replaced above by§ Troy   230| MS:afar,   *1887*:afar   232| MS:fresco—from
1887:fresco, from   235| MS:yet   *1887*:yet,   236| MS:sound,—thy   *1887*:sound, thy
237| MS:abymal   *1887*:abysmal   239| MS:semblance—there §last two words altered to§
semblance! There   240| MS:mystery of   *1887*:mystery, of   241| MS:marvels most
<> for—   *1887*:marvels, most <> for!   242| MS:Only, from <> abhor,   *1887*:Save it
from <> abhor!   243| MS:feeling safety, §last word and comma crossed out§

So that thy capture hold, a century hence,
245   Truth's very heart of truth as, safe to-day,
The Painter's Eve, the Poet's Helena,
Still rapturously bend, afar still throw
The wistful gaze! Thanks, Homer, Angelo!
Could Music rescue thus from Soul's profound,
250   Give feeling immortality by sound,
Then were she queenliest of Arts! Alas—
As well expect the rainbow not to pass!
"Praise 'Radaminta'—love attains therein
To perfect utterance! Pity—what shall win
255   Thy secret like 'Rinaldo'?"—so men said:
Once all was perfume—now, the flower is dead—
They spied tints, sparks have left the spar! Love, hate,
Joy, fear, survive,—alike importunate
As ever to go walk the world again,
260   Nor ghost-like pant for outlet all in vain
Till Music loose them, fit each filmily
With form enough to know and name it by
For any recognizer sure of ken

244| MS:hold a <> hence   *1887:*hold, a <> hence,   245| MS:truth plain §crossed out and replaced above by§ safe as to-day.   *1887:*truth as, safe to-day,   246| MS:The §crossed out and replaced by§ When §over illegible erasure§ Painter's Eve, the §last word and comma crossed out and replaced above by§ and <> Helena, §crossed out§   *1887:*The Painter's Eve the Poet's Helena   *1889a:*The Painter's Eve, the Poet's Helena,   247| MS:Still kneel §crossed out and replaced above by two words and comma§ rapturously bend, afar §inserted above§   248| MS:gaze! Thanks, Homer—Angelo!   *1887:*gaze! Thanks, Homer, Angelo!   249| MS:Ah, §word and comma crossed out§ couldst §altered to§ Could then §crossed out§ Music §inserted above§   250| MS:Thus make an immortality by sound   *1887:*Give feeling immortality by sound,   251| MS:Then, Music §crossed out§ wert §altered to§ were thou §crossed out and replaced above by§ she   *1889a:*Then were   252| MS:rainbow will §crossed out§ not to §inserted above§   256| MS:Once they found perfume, but §crossed out and replaced above by word and comma§ now, the   *1887:*Once all was perfume—now, the   257| MS:Spied §in margin§ Tints, but the §crossed out§ spark §altered to§ sparks has §altered to§ have <> spar. Love   *1887:*They spied tints, sparks <> spar! Love   258| MS:fear, remain §crossed out and replaced above by word, comma and dash§ survive,—no less importunate   *1887:*survive,—alike importunate   259| MS:again   *1887:*again,   260| MS:for liberty §crossed out and replaced above by two words§ outlet all   261| MS:Till Music re-embody §crossed out and replaced above by four words§ loose them, fit each   262| MS:Yet §crossed out and replaced above by§ With <> by.   *1887:*by   263| MS:Be but the §last three words crossed out and replaced above by two words§ To any <> ken,   *1887:*For any <> ken

And sharp of ear, no grosser denizen
265   Of earth than needs be. Nor to such appeal
Is Music long obdurate: off they steal—
How gently, dawn-doomed phantoms! back come they
Full-blooded with new crimson of broad day—
Passion made palpable once more. Ye look
270   Your last on Handel? Gaze your first on Gluck!
Why wistful search, O waning ones, the chart
Of stars for you while Haydn, while Mozart
Occupies heaven? These also, fanned to fire,
Flamboyant wholly,—so perfections tire,—
275   Whiten to wanness, till . . . let others note
The ever-new invasion!

IX

I devote

Rather my modicum of parts to use
What power may yet avail to re-infuse
(In fancy, please you!) sleep that looks like death
280   With momentary liveliness, lend breath
To make the torpor half inhale. O Relfe,
An all-unworthy pupil, from the shelf
Of thy laboratory, dares unstop
Bottle, ope box, extract thence pinch and drop
285   Of dusts and dews a many thou didst shrine
Each in its right receptacle, assign
To each its proper office, letter large
Label and label, then with solemn charge,
Reviewing learnedly the list complete
290   Of chemical reactives, from thy feet

267| MS:phantoms—back   *1887:*phantoms! back   268| MS:with the §crossed out and replaced above by§ new   269| MS:more: ye §altered to§ Ye   *1887:*more. Ye
271| MS:search, you §crossed out and replaced above by§ O   272| MS:while Haydn, nay, §last word crossed out and replaced above by§ while, Mozart   *1887:*while Mozart
273| MS:heaven? Who §crossed out and replaced above by§ These <> fire   *1887:*fire,
275| MS:till . . let   *1887:*till . . . let   278| MS:What means may   *1887:*What power may
281| MS:That makes the   *1887:*To make the   282| MS:Thy all-unworthy pupil from   *1887:*An all-unworthy pupil, from   283| MS:laboratory dares   *1887:*laboratory, dares
284| MS:extract the §altered to§ thence pinch or drop   *1887:*pinch and drop

Push down the same to me, attent below,
Power in abundance: armed wherewith I go
To play the enlivener. Bring good antique stuff!
Was it alight once? Still lives spark enough
295   For breath to quicken, run the smouldering ash
Red right-through. What, "stone-dead" were fools so rash
As style my Avison, because he lacked
Modern appliance, spread out phrase unracked
By modulations fit to make each hair
300   Stiffen upon his wig? See there—and there!
I sprinkle my reactives, pitch broadcast
Discords and resolutions, turn aghast
Melody's easy-going, jostle law
With licence, modulate (no Bach in awe),
305   Change enharmonically (Hudl to thank),
And lo, upstart the flamelets,—what was blank
Turns scarlet, purple, crimson! Straightway scanned
By eyes that like new lustre—Love once more
Yearns through the Largo, Hatred as before
310   Rages in the Rubato: e'en thy March
My Avison, which, sooth to say—(ne'er arch
Eyebrows in anger!)—timed, in Georgian years
The step precise of British Grenadiers
To such a nicety,—if score I crowd,
315   If rhythm I break, if beats I vary,—tap
At bar's off-starting turns true thunder-clap,
Ever the pace augmented till—what's here?
Titanic striding toward Olympus!

293| MS:enlivener. Bring but §inserted above§ antique   *1887*:enlivener. Bring good antique
294| MS:once? Still there's §crossed out and replaced above by§ lives
295| MS:Dormant to   *1887*:For breath to   296| MS:right-through. So, §last word and
comma crossed out and replaced above by word and comma§ What, "stone-dead
299| MS:modulations that had made each   *1887*:modulations fit to make each
301| MS:broad-cast   *1887*:broadcast   304| MS:awe)   *1889a*:awe),
305| MS:enharmonically (Hudl in hand §last two words crossed out and replaced above by two
words§ to thank)   *1889a*:thank),   308| MS:that like §crossed out and replaced above by§
need new lustre—love §altered to§ Love   *1887*:that like new   316| MS:turns a thunder-
clap,   *1887*:turns true thunder-clap,   318| MS:toward Olympus?   *1887*:toward Olympus!

X

Fear

No such irreverent innovation! Still
³²⁰ Glide on, go rolling, water-like, at will—
Nay, were thy melody in monotone,
The due three-parts dispensed with!

XI

This alone
Comes of my tiresome talking: Music's throne
Seats somebody whom somebody unseats,
³²⁵ And whom in turn—by who knows what new feats
Of strength,—shall somebody as sure push down,
Consign him dispossessed of sceptre, crown,
And orb imperial—whereto?—Never dream
That what once lived shall ever die! They seem
³³⁰ Dead—do they? lapsed things lost in limbo? Bring
Our life to kindle theirs, and straight each king
Starts, you shall see, stands up, from head to foot
No inch that is not Purcell! Wherefore? (Suit
Measure to subject, first—no marching on
³³⁵ Yet in thy bold C major, Avison,
As suited step a minute since: no: wait—
Into the minor key first modulate—
Gently with A, now—in the Lesser Third!)

XII

Of all the lamentable debts incurred

---

³²²| MS:with! This *1887*:with! §¶§ This ³²³| MS:of the §crossed out and replaced
above by§ my ³²⁵| MS:turn shall §crossed out§ <> what new §inserted above§
³²⁶| MS:strength, shall *1887*:strength,—shall ³²⁷| MS:Consign all disposed
1887:Consign him dispossessed ³²⁸| MS:whereto? Never *1889a*:whereto?—Never
³³⁰| MS:they? §next word illegibly crossed out and replaced above by§ lapsed ³³¹| MS:Your
§crossed out and replaced above by§ Our <> theirs and *1887*:theirs, and ³³⁵| MS:bold
§capital letter illegibly crossed out and replaced above by letter and period§ C. major
1887:C major ³³⁷| MS:key we §crossed out and replaced above by§ first
³³⁸| MS:with §followed by capital letter illegibly crossed out§ then §crossed out; letter and word
replaced above by capital letter and word§ A, now <> lesser third!) *1887*:<> Lesser Third!)

340 By Man through buying knowledge, this were worst:
That he should find his last gain prove his first
Was futile—merely nescience absolute,
Not knowledge in the bud which holds a fruit
Haply undreamed of in the soul's Spring-tide,
345 Pursed in the petals Summer opens wide,
And Autumn, withering, rounds to perfect ripe,—
Not this,—but ignorance, a blur to wipe
From human records, late it graced so much.
"Truth—this attainment? Ah, but such and such
350 Beliefs of yore seemed inexpugnable
When we attained them! E'en as they, so will
This their successor have the due morn, noon,
Evening and night—just as an old-world tune
Wears out and drops away, until who hears
355 Smilingly questions—'This it was brought tears
Once to all eyes,—this roused heart's rapture once?'
So will it be with truth that, for the nonce,
Styles itself truth perennial: 'ware its wile!
Knowledge turns nescience,—foremost on the file,
360 Simply proves first of our delusions."

XIII

Now—
Blare it forth, bold C Major! Lift thy brow,
Man, the immortal, that wast never fooled
With gifts no gifts at all, nor ridiculed—
Man knowing—he who nothing knew! As Hope,

341| MS:find the §crossed out and replaced above by§ his < > prove the §crossed out and
replaced above by§ his   342| MS:Was ever futile—nescience absolute: *1887*:Was
futile—merely nescience absolute,   347| MS:ignorance—a   *1887*:ignorance, a
348| MS:From Man's §crossed out and replaced above by§ human   351| MS:As I §crossed
out and replaced above by§ we < > them: e'en   *1887*:When we < > them! E'en
352| MS:have it due   *1887*:have the due   353| MS:And §in margin§ Evening §altered
to§ Eve and   *1887*:Evening and   360| MS:of thy §crossed out and replaced above by§
our delusions.'   *1887*:delusions."   361| MS:forth, §followed by illegible cross-out§ flat
§crossed out; crossed out words replaced above by letter and word§ C. Major   *1887*:bold C
Major   364| MS:The §crossed out and replaced above by§ As knowing one §crossed out
and replaced above by word and dash§ —he < > hope,   *1887*:Man knowing < > Hope,

365 Fear, Joy, and Grief,—though ampler stretch and scope
They seek and find in novel rhythm, fresh phrase,—
Were equally existent in far days
Of Music's dim beginning—even so,
Truth was at full within thee long ago,
370 Alive as now it takes what latest shape
May startle thee by strangeness. Truths escape
Time's insufficient garniture: they fade,
They fall—those sheathings now grown sere, whose aid
Was infinite to truth they wrapped, saved fine
375 And free through March frost: May dews crystalline
Nourish truth merely,—does June boast the fruit
As—not new vesture merely but, to boot,
Novel creation? Soon shall fade and fall
Myth after myth—the husk-like lies I call
380 New truth's corolla-safeguard: Autumn comes,
So much the better!

XIV

Therefore—bang the drums,
Blow the trumpets, Avison! March-motive? that's
Truth which endures resetting. Sharps and flats,
Lavish at need, shall dance athwart thy score
385 When ophicleide and bombardon's uproar

365| MS:Fear, §word and comma in margin§ Joy, and Grief, though   *1887:*and Grief,—
though   366| MS:phrase,   *1887:*phrase,—   367| MS:in those days   *1887:*in far
days   369| MS:Was truth at   *1887:*Truth was at   370| MS:Even as alive it
*1887:*Alive as now it   371| MS:strangeness: truths §colon and word altered to§
strangeness! Truths   *1887:*strangeness. Truths   372| MS:The insufficient garniture,—
they   *1887:*Time's insufficient garniture: they   374| MS:wrapped so fine
*1887:*wrapped,saved fine   375| MS:And safe through   *1887:*And free through
376| MS:Nourish it merely   *1887:*Nourish truth merely   377| MS:As it were—not new-
vestured but   *1887:*As— not new vesture merely but   378| MS:Summer's creation
*1887:*Novel creation   379| MS:husklike   *1887:*husk-like
380| MS:truth's unworn corolla—autumn §altered to§ Autumn   *1887:*truth's corolla-
safeguard: Autumn   381| MS:better! §¶§ Therefore—beat §crossed out and replaced
above by§ bang   382| MS:Bray the march §crossed out and replaced above by§ trumps,
Avison! its §altered to§ Its subject? that   *1887:*Blow the trumps, Avison! March-motive? that's
*1889a:*Blows §emended to§ Blow the trumpets, Avison §see Editorial Notes§
383| MS:resetting: sharps   *1887:*resetting. Sharps

Mate the approaching trample, even now
Big in the distance—or my ears deceive—
Of federated England, fitly weave
March-music for the Future!

XV

Or suppose

390 Back, and not forward, transformation goes?
Once more some sable-stoled procession—say,
From Little-ease to Tyburn—wends its way,
Out of the dungeon to the gallows-tree
Where heading, hacking, hanging is to be
395 Of half-a-dozen recusants—this day
Three hundred years ago! How duly drones
Elizabethan plain-song—dim antique
Grown clarion-clear the while I humbly wreak
A classic vengeance on thy March! It moans—
400 Larges and Longs and Breves displacing quite
Crotchet-and-quaver pertness—brushing bars
Aside and fillling vacant sky with stars
Hidden till now that day returns to night.

XVI

Nor night nor day: one purpose move us both,
405 Be thy mood mine! As thou wast minded, Man's
The cause our music champions: I were loth
To think we cheered our troop to Preston Pans
Ignobly: back to times of England's best!
Parliament stands for privilege—life and limb

388| MS:federated England—fitly *1887*:federated England, fitly 389| MS:the Future?
§¶§ Or *1887*:the Future! §¶§ Or 390| MS:goes— *1887*:goes? 392| MS:to
Tyburn wends *1889a*:to Tyburn—wends 398| MS:while I humbly §inserted above§
399| MS:thy March: it *1887*:thy March! It 402| MS:and bringing out a host of stars
1887:and filling vacant sky with stars 404| MS:We'll neither: one intent shall move
1887:Nor night nor day: one purpose move 405| MS:mine! as <> minded, Charles
§crossed out§ *1887*:mine! As <> minded, Man's 406| MS:Champion we some great
cause! for I *1887*:The cause our music champions: I 409| MS:privelege *1887*:privilege

410   Guards Hollis, Haselrig, Strode, Hampden, Pym,
       The famous Five. There's rumour of arrest.
       Bring up the Train Bands, Southwark! They protest:
       Shall we not all join chorus? Hark the hymn,
       —Rough, rude, robustious—homely heart a-throb,
415   Harsh voice a-hallo, as beseems the mob!
       How good is noise! what's silence but despair
       Of making sound match gladness never there?
       Give me some great glad "subject," glorious Bach,
       Where cannon-roar not organ-peal we lack!
420   Join in, give voice robustious rude and rough,—
       Avison helps—so heart lend noise enough!

       Fife, trump, drum, sound! and singers then,
       Marching, say "Pym, the man of men!"
       Up, heads, your proudest—out, throats, your loudest—
425   "Somerset's Pym!"

       Strafford from the block, Eliot from the den,
       Foes, friends, shout "Pym, our citizen!"
       Wail, the foes he quelled,—hail, the friends he held,
       "Tavistock's Pym!"

430   Hearts prompt heads, hands that ply the pen
       Teach babes unborn the where and when
       —Tyrants, he braved them,—patriots, he saved them—
       "Westminster's Pym!"

411| MS:arrest: *1887:*arrest.   414| *1887:*a throb,   *1889a:*a-throb,   417| MS:Of finding match for gladness   *1887:*Of making sound match gladness   421| MS:so you lend   *1887:*so heart lend   422| MS:then   *1889a:*then,   423| MS:Marching shout §crossed out and replaced above by§ say   *1889a:*Marching, say   425| *1887:*'Somerset's *1889a:*"Somerset's   427| MS:friends, sing §crossed out and replaced above by§ shout < > citizen!   *1887:*citizen!"   433| MS:"England's own §last two words crossed out and replaced above by§ "Westminster's

Music MS:§followed by B's note to printers§ Print the above in small type (as in "Dramatic Idyls." Vol. II./page 111.

FUST AND HIS FRIENDS

AN EPILOGUE

Inside the House of Fust, Mayence, 1457

FIRST FRIEND

Up, up, up—next step of the staircase
Lands us, lo, at the chamber of dread!

SECOND FRIEND

Locked and barred?

THIRD FRIEND

Door open—the rare case!

FOURTH FRIEND

Ay, there he leans—lost wretch!

FIFTH FRIEND

                 His head
5   Sunk on his desk 'twixt his arms outspread!

SIXTH FRIEND

Hallo,—wake, man, ere God thunderstrike Mayence
   —Mulct for thy sake who art Satan's, John Fust!
Satan installed here, God's rule in abeyance,
   Mayence some morning may crumble to dust.
10 Answer our questions thou shalt and thou must!

SEVENTH FRIEND

Softly and fairly! Wherefore a-gloom?
   Greet us, thy gossipry, cousin and sib!
Raise the forlorn brow, Fust! Make room—

FUST AND HIS FRIENDS   5| MS:outspread   *1887:*outspread!
12| MS:us thy   *1887:*us, thy

Let daylight through arms which, enfolding thee, crib
15 From those clenched lids the comfort of sunshine!

FIRST FRIEND

So glib

Thy tongue slides to "comfort" already? Not mine!
　Behoves us deal roundly: the wretch is distraught
—Too well I guess wherefore! Behoves a Divine
　—Such as I, by grace, boast me—to threaten one caught
20 In the enemy's toils,—setting "comfort" at nought.

SECOND FRIEND

Nay, Brother, so hasty? I heard—nor long since—
　Of a certain Black Artsman who,—helplessly bound
By rash pact with Satan,—through paying—why mince
　The matter?—fit price to the Church,—safe and sound
25 Full a year after death in his grave-clothes was found.

Whereas 'tis notorious the Fiend claims his due
　During lifetime,—comes clawing, with talons a-flame,
The soul from the flesh-rags left smoking and blue:
　So it happed with John Faust; lest John Fust fare the same,—
30 Look up, I adjure thee by God's holy name!

For neighbours and friends—no foul hell-brood flock we!
　Saith Solomon "Words of the wise are as goads:"
Ours prick but to startle from torpor, set free
　Soul and sense from death's drowse.

FIRST FRIEND

And soul, wakened, unloads
35 Much sin by confession: no mere palinodes!

22| MS:certain Black Art's man   *1889a*:certain Black Artsman   27| MS:life-time < >
clawing with < > a-flame   *1887*:clawing, with < > a-flame,   *1889a*:lifetime
34| MS:drowse!   *1889a*:drowse.   35| MS:palinodes   *1887*:palinodes!

—"I was youthful and wanton, am old yet no sage:
    When angry I cursed, struck and slew: did I want?
Right and left did I rob: though no war I dared wage
    With the Church (God forbid!)—harm her least ministrant—
40   Still I outraged all else. Now that strength is grown scant,

I am probity's self "—no such bleatings as these!
    But avowal of guilt so enormous, it baulks
Tongue's telling. Yet penitence prompt may appease
    God's wrath at thy bond with the Devil who stalks
45   —Strides hither to strangle thee!

FUST

Childhood so talks.

Not rare wit nor ripe age—ye boast them, my neighbours!—
    Should lay such a charge on your townsman, this Fust
Who, known for a life spent in pleasures and labours
    If freakish yet venial, could scarce be induced
50   To traffic with fiends.

FIRST FRIEND

So, my words have unloosed

A plie from those pale lips corrugate but now?

FUST

Lost count me, yet not as ye lean to surmise.

FIRST FRIEND

To surmise? to establish! Unbury that brow!
    Look up, that thy judge may read clear in thine eyes!

36| MS:sage,—   *1887*:sage: 45| MS:talks—   *1887*:talks.   46| MS:wit and ripe <>
boast of, my neibours!—   *1887*:wit nor ripe <> boast them, my neighbours!—

SECOND FRIEND

55 By your leave, Brother Barnabite! Mine to advise!

—Who arraign thee, John Fust! What was bruited erewhile
    Now bellows through Mayence. All cry —thou hast trucked
Salvation away for lust's solace! Thy smile
    Takes its hue from hell's smoulder!

FUST

Too certain! I sucked
60 —Got drunk at the nipple of sense.

SECOND FRIEND

Thou hast ducked—

Art drowned there, say rather! Faugh—fleshly disport!
    How else but by help of Sir Belial didst win
That Venus-like lady, no drudge of thy sort
    Could lure to become his accomplice in sin?
65 Folk nicknamed her Helen of Troy!

FIRST FRIEND

Best begin

At the very beginning. Thy father,—all knew,
    A mere goldsmith . . .

FUST

Who knew him, perchance may know this—
He dying left much gold and jewels no few:
    Whom these help to court with but seldom shall miss

---

⁶⁰| MS:ducked   *1887*:ducked—   ⁶¹| MS:—Nay, drowned   *1887*:Art drowned
⁶³| MS:lady no   *1887*:lady, no   ⁶⁵| MS:Folks   *1889a*:Folk   ⁶⁵⁻⁶⁶| MS:§stanza ends
at bottom of page§   *1887*:§no line space between stanzas§   *1889a*:§no line space between
stanzas;line space restored; see Editorial Notes§   ⁶⁷| MS:goldsmith . . Who
1889a:goldsmith . . . Who   ⁶⁹| MS:with, but   *1889a*:with but

70   The love of a leman: true witchcraft, I wis!

FIRST FRIEND

Dost flout me? 'Tis said, in debauchery's guild
    Admitted prime guttler and guzzler—O swine!—
To honour thy headship, those tosspots so swilled
    That out of their table there sprouted a vine
75 Whence each claimed a cluster, awaiting thy sign

To out knife, off mouthful: when—who could suppose
    Such malice in magic?—each sot woke and found
Cold steel but an inch from the neighbour's red nose
    He took for a grape-bunch!

FUST

                                    Does that so astound
80 Sagacity such as ye boast,—who surround

Your mate with eyes staring, hairs standing erect
    At his magical feats? Are good burghers unversed
In the humours of toping? Full oft, I suspect,
    Ye, counting your fingers, call thumbkin their first,
85 And reckon a groat every guilder disbursed.

What marvel if wags, while the skinker fast brimmed
    Their glass with rare tipple's enticement, should gloat
—Befooled and beflustered—through optics drink-dimmed—
    On this draught and that, till each found in his throat
90 Our Rhenish smack rightly as Raphal? For, note—

They fancied—their fuddling deceived them so grossly—
    That liquor sprang out of the table itself
Through gimlet-holes drilled there,—nor noticed how closely
    The skinker kept plying my guests, from the shelf

---

⁷³| MS:honor *1887*:honour   ⁷⁹⁻⁸⁰| MS:§line space between last two lines of stanza§
1889a:§no line space between last two lines of stanza§   ⁷⁶| MS:knife and off
1887:knife, off   ⁸⁵| MS:gilder *1887*:guilder

⁹⁵   O'er their heads, with the potable madness. No elf

Had need to persuade them a vine rose umbrageous,
    Fruit-bearing, thirst-quenching! Enough! I confess
To many such fool-pranks, but none so outrageous
    That Satan was called in to help me: excess
¹⁰⁰ I own to, I grieve at—no more and no less.

SECOND FRIEND

Strange honours were heaped on thee—medal for breast,
    Chain for neck, sword for thigh: not a lord of the land
But acknowledged thee peer! What ambition possessed
    A goldsmith by trade, with craft's grime on his hand,
¹⁰⁵ To seek such associates?

FUST

Spare taunts! Understand—

I submit me! Of vanities under the sun,
    Pride seized me at last as concupiscence first,
Crapulosity ever: true Fiends, every one,
    Haled this way and that my poor soul: thus amerced—
¹¹⁰ Forgive and forget me!

FIRST FRIEND

Had flesh sinned the worst,

Yet help were in counsel: the Church could absolve:
    But say not men truly thou barredst escape
By signing and sealing . . .

---

⁹⁵| MS:madness: no   *1887*:madness. No   ¹⁰⁰| *1887*:less   *1889a*:less.
¹⁰¹| MS:honors   *1889a*:honours   ¹⁰⁸| MS:ever: such fiends, every one,
1887:ever: true Fiends, everyone,   *1889a*:everyone, §emended to§ every one, §see Editorial
Notes§   ¹¹⁰| MS:sinned its worst,   *1887*:sinned the worst,
¹¹³| MS:sealing . . On   *1889a*:sealing . . . On

SECOND FRIEND

On me must devolve
The task of extracting . . .

FIRST FRIEND

Shall Barnabites ape
115   Us Dominican experts?

SEVENTH FRIEND

Nay, Masters,—agape

When Hell yawns for a soul, 'tis myself claim the task
Of extracting, by just one plain question, God's truth!
Where's Peter Genesheim thy partner? I ask
Why, cloistered up still in thy room, the pale youth
120   Slaves tongue-tied—thy trade brooks no tattling forsooth!

No less he, thy *famulus,* suffers entrapping,
Succumbs to good fellowship: barrel a-broach
Runs freely nor needs any subsequent tapping:
Quoth Peter "That room, none but I dare approach,
125   Holds secrets will help me to ride in my coach."

He prattles, we profit: in brief, he assures
Thou hast taught him to speak so that all men may hear
—Each alike, wide world over, Jews, Pagans, Turks, Moors,
The same as we Christians—speech heard far and near
130   At one and the same magic moment!

FUST

That's clear!

Said he—how?

---

¹¹⁴| MS:extracting . . Shall   *1889a:*extracting . . . Shall   ¹²⁴| MS:but I may approach,
*1887:*but I dare approach,   ¹²⁶| MS:profit—in   *1887:*profit: in   ¹³⁰⁻³¹| MS:§line
space between stanzas§   *1887:*§no line space between stanzas§   *1889a:*§No line space
between stanzas; emended to restore line space; see Editorial Notes§   ¹³¹| MS:how?

SEVENTH FRIEND

Is it like he was licensed to learn?
Who doubts but thou dost this by aid of the Fiend?
Is it so? So it is, for thou smilest! Go, burn
    To ashes, since such proves thy portion, unscreened
135 By bell, book and candle! Yet lately I weened

Balm yet was in Gilead,—some healing in store
    For the friend of my bosom. Men said thou wast sunk
In a sudden despondency: not, as before,
    Fust gallant and gay with his pottle and punk,
140 But sober, sad, sick as one yesterday drunk!

FUST

Spare Fust, then, thus contrite!—who, youthful and healthy,
    Equipped for life's struggle with culture of mind,
Sound flesh and sane soul in coherence, born wealthy,
    Nay, wise—how he wasted endowment designed
145 For the glory of God and the good of mankind!

That much were misused such occasions of grace
    Ye well may upbraid him, who bows to the rod.
But this should bid anger to pity give place—
    He has turned from the wrong, in the right path to plod,
150 Makes amends to mankind and craves pardon of God.

Yea, friends, even now from my lips the "*Heureka*—
    Soul saved!" was nigh bursting—unduly elate!
Have I brought Man advantage, or hatched—so to speak—a
    Strange serpent, no cygnet? 'Tis this I debate
155 Within me. Forbear, and leave Fust to his fate!

Very like <> licenced to learn!   *1887*:how? Is it like <> learn?   *1889a*:licensed
¹³²| MS:the fiend   *1887*:the Fiend   ¹³⁹| MS:punk   *1887*:punk,   ¹⁴⁰| MS:drunk. .
1887:drunk!   ¹⁴³| MS:wealthy   *1887*:wealthy,   ¹⁴⁷| MS:rod: *1887*:rod.
¹⁴⁹| MS:wrong in   *1887*:wrong, in   ¹⁵³| MS:*Have*   *1889a*:Have

FIRST FRIEND

So abject, late lofty? Methinks I spy respite.
    Make clean breast, discover what mysteries hide
In thy room there!

SECOND FRIEND

                    Ay, out with them! Do Satan despite!
    Remember what caused his undoing was pride!

FIRST FRIEND

160   Dumb devil! Remains one resource to be tried!

SECOND FRIEND

Exorcize!

SEVENTH FRIEND

                    Nay, first—is there any remembers
    In substance that potent "*Ne pulvis*"—a psalm
Whereof some live spark haply lurks mid the embers
    Which choke in my brain. Talk of "Gilead and balm"?
165   I mind me, sung half through, this gave such a qualm

To Asmodeus inside of a Hussite, that, queasy,
    He broke forth in brimstone with curses. I'm strong
In—at least the commencement: the rest should go easy,
    Friends helping. "*Ne pulvis et ignis*" . . .

SIXTH FRIEND

                                        All wrong!

FIFTH FRIEND

158| MS:despite! *1889a*:despite §emended to§ despite! §see Editorial Notes§
160| MS:tried— *1887*:tried!   164| MS:Brain chokes with. Talk not of your "Gilead and
balm"— *1887*:Which choke in my brain. Talk of "Gilead and balm"?   166| MS:a
Hussite that *1887*:a Hussite, that   169| MS:*ignis* . . All *1889a*:*ignis*" . . . All

¹⁷⁰ I've conned till I captured the whole.

SEVENTH FRIEND

Get along!

"*Ne pulvis et cinis superbe te geras,*
   Nam fulmina" . . .

SIXTH FRIEND

Fiddlestick! Peace, dolts and dorrs!
Thus runs it "*Ne Numinis fulmina feras*"—
Then "*Hominis perfidi justa sunt sors*
¹⁷⁵ *Fulmen et grando et horrida mors.*"

SEVENTH FRIEND

You blunder. "*Irati ne*" . . .

SIXTH FRIEND

Mind your own business!

FIFTH FRIEND

I do not so badly, who gained the monk's leave
To study an hour his choice parchment. A dizziness
   May well have surprised me. No Christian dares thieve,
¹⁸⁰ Or I scarce had returned him his treasure. These cleave:

"*Nos pulvis et cinis, trementes, gementes,*
   Venimus"—some such word—"*ad te, Domine.*
Da lumen, juvamen, ut sancta sequentes
   Cor . . . *corda* . . ." Plague take it!

---

^{172|} MS:*fulmina*" . . Fiddlestick   *1889a:fulmina*" . . . Fiddlestick   ^{176|} MS:*ne* . . Mind
1887:ne." . . . Mind   *1889a:*ne" . . . Mind   ^{182|} MS:*te, Domine!*   *1889a:te, Domine.*
^{184|} MS:*Cor* . . *corda* . ." Plague   *1889a:Cor* . . . *corda* . . ." Plague

SEVENTH FRIEND

—*"erecta sint spe:"*

¹⁸⁵ Right text, ringing rhyme, and ripe Latin for me!

SIXTH FRIEND

A Canon's self wrote it me fair: I was tempted
To part with the sheepskin.

SEVENTH FRIEND

Didst grasp and let go
Such a godsend, thou Judas? My purse had been emptied
Ere part with the prize!

FUST

Do I dream? Say ye so?
¹⁹⁰ Clouds break, then! Move, world! I have gained my *"Pou sto"*!

I am saved: Archimedes, salute me!

OMNES

Assistance!
Help, Angels! He summons . . . Aroint thee!—by name,
His familiar!

FUST

Approach!

OMNES

Devil, keep thy due distance!

FUST

Be tranquillized, townsmen! The knowledge ye claim

---

¹⁹⁰| MS:then: move §colon and word altered to§ then! Move
¹⁹²| MS:summons . . Aroint   *1889a*:summons . . . Aroint

195   Behold, I prepare to impart. Praise or blame,—

Your blessing or banning, whatever betide me,
   At last I accept. The slow travail of years,
The long-teeming brain's birth—applaud me, deride me,—
   At last claims revealment. Wait!

SEVENTH FRIEND

Wait till appears
200   Uncaged Archimedes cooped-up there?

SECOND FRIEND

Who fears?

Here's have at thee!

SEVENTH FRIEND

Correctly now! *"Pulvis et cinis"* . . .

FUST

The verse ye so value, it happens I hold
In my memory safe from *initium* to *finis*.
   Word for word, I produce you the whole, plain enrolled,
205   Black letters, white paper—no scribe's red and gold!

OMNES

Aroint thee!

195| MS:blame,   *1887*:blame,—   196| MS:banning, whatever   *1889a*:banning whatever §emended to§ banning, whatever §see Editorial Notes§   197| MS:accept. The *1889a*:accept The §emended to§ accept. The §see Editorial Notes§   199-200| MS:revealment. Wait!/Uncaged   *1887*:revealment. Wait! Wait till appears/Uncaged 200-201| MS:§no line space between stanzas§   *1889a*:§no line space between stanzas; emended to add line space; see Editorial Notes§   201| MS:*cinis*" . .   *1889a:cinis*" . . . 203| MS:fi*nis*   *1887*:fi*nis*.   204| MS:whole plain   *1887*:whole, plain

FUST

I go and return.   [*He enters the inner rooms.*

FIRST FRIEND

Ay, 'tis "*ibis*"
No doubt: but as boldly "*redibis*"—who'll say?
I rather conjecture "*in Orco peribis!*"

SEVENTH FRIEND

Come, neighbours!

SIXTH FRIEND

I'm with you! Show courage and stay
²¹⁰ Hell's outbreak? Sirs, cowardice here wins the day!

FIFTH FRIEND

What luck had that student of Bamberg who ventured
    To peep in the cell where a wizard of note
Was busy in getting some black deed debentured
    By Satan? In dog's guise there sprang at his throat
²¹⁵ A flame-breathing fury. Fust favours, I note,

An ugly huge lurcher!

SEVENTH FRIEND

If I placed reliance
As thou, on the beads thou art telling so fast,
I'd risk just a peep through the keyhole.

SIXTH FRIEND

Appliance
Of ear might be safer. Five minutes are past.

---

²⁰⁸| MS:"in   *1887:*"in   ²¹⁴| MS:by Satan: in   *1887:*By Satan? In

OMNES

²²⁰ Saints, save us! The door is thrown open at last!

FUST   (*re-enters, the door closing behind him*).

As I promised, behold I perform! Apprehend you
    The object I offer is poison or pest?
Receive without harm from the hand I extend you
    A gift that shall set every scruple at rest!
²²⁵ Shrink back from mere paper-strips? Try them and test!

Still hesitate? Myk, was it thou who lamentedst
    Thy five wits clean failed thee to render aright
A poem read once and no more?—who repentedst
    Vile pelf had induced thee to banish from sight
²³⁰ The characters none but our clerics indite?

Take and keep!

FIRST FRIEND

Blessed Mary and all Saints about her!

SECOND FRIEND

What imps deal so deftly,—five minutes suffice
To play thus the penman?

THIRD FRIEND

By Thomas the Doubter,
    Five minutes, no more!

FOURTH FRIEND.

Out on arts that entice
²³⁵ Such scribes to do homage!

---

^{232|} MS:deftly, five   *1887*:deftly,—five

FIFTH FRIEND

Stay! Once—and now twice—

Yea, a third time, my sharp eye completes the inspection
Of line after line, the whole series, and finds
Each letter join each—not a fault for detection!
Such upstrokes, such downstrokes, such strokes of all kinds
240 In the criss-cross, all perfect!

SIXTH FRIEND

There's nobody minds

His quill-craft with more of a conscience, o'erscratches
A sheepskin more nimbly and surely with ink,
Than Paul the Sub-Prior: here's paper that matches
His parchment with letter on letter, no link
245 Overleapt—underlost!

SEVENTH FRIEND

No erasure, I think—

No blot, I am certain!

FUST

Accept the new treasure!

SIXTH FRIEND

I remembered full half!

SEVENTH FRIEND

But who other than I
(Bear witness, bystanders!) when he broke the measure
Repaired fault with "*fulmen*"?

---

[236] MS:eyes §altered to§ eye complete *1887*:completes   [237] MS:line—the
1887:line, the   [241] MS:conscience—o'erscratches *1887*:conscience, o'erscratches

FUST

Put bickerings by!
₂₅₀ Here's for thee—thee—and thee, too: at need a supply
[*distributing Proofs.*

For Mayence, though seventy times seven should muster!
How now? All so feeble of faith that no face
Which fronts me but whitens—or yellows, were juster?
Speak out lest I summon my Spirits!

OMNES

Grace—grace!
₂₅₅ Call none of thy—helpmates! We'll answer apace!

My paper—and mine—and mine also—they vary
In nowise—agree in each tittle and jot!
Fust, how—why was this?

FUST

Shall such *"Cur"* miss a *"quare"*?
Within, there! Throw doors wide! Behold who complot
₂₆₀ To abolish the scribe's work—blur, blunder and blot!
[*The doors open, and the Press is discovered in operation.*

Brave full-bodied birth of this brain that conceived thee
In splendour and music,—sustained the slow drag
Of the days stretched to years dim with doubt,—yet believed thee,
Had faith in thy first leap of life! Pulse might flag—
₂₆₅ —Mine fluttered how faintly!—Arch-moment might lag

Its longest—I bided, made light of endurance,
Held hard by the hope of an advent which—dreamed,
Is done now: night yields to the dawn's reassurance:

_{254|} MS:my spirits *1887*:my Spirits   _{258|} MS:Fust, why—why *1887*:Fust, how—why
_{265|} MS:faintly—The arch-moment lag *1887*:Faintly!—Arch-moment might lag
_{268|} MS:reassurance, *1887*:reassurance:

I have thee—I hold thee—my fancy that seemed,
270   My fact that proves palpable! Ay, Sirs, I schemed

Completion that's fact: see this Engine—be witness
    Yourselves of its working! Nay, handle my Types!
    Each block bears a Letter: in order and fitness
    I range them. Turn, Peter, the winch! See, it gripes
275   What's under! Let loose—draw! In regular stripes

Lies plain, at one pressure, your poem—touched, tinted,
    Turned out to perfection! The sheet, late a blank,
    Filled—ready for reading,—not written but PRINTED!
    Omniscient omnipotent God, Thee I thank,
280   Thee ever, Thee only!—Thy creature that shrank

From no task Thou, Creator, imposedst! Ceation
    Revealed me no object, from insect to Man,
    But bore Thy hand's impress: earth glowed with salvation:
    "Hast sinned? Be thou saved, Fust! Continue my plan,
285   Who spake and earth was: with my word things began.

"As sound so went forth, to the sight be extended
    Word's mission henceforward! The task I assign,
    Embrace—thy allegiance to evil is ended!
    Have cheer, soul impregnate with purpose! Combine
290   Soul and body, give birth to my concept—called thine!

"Far and wide, North and South, East and West, have dominion
    O'er thought, winged wonder, O Word! Traverse world
In sun-flash and sphere-song! Each beat of thy pinion
    Bursts night, beckons day: once Truth's banner unfurled,
295   Where's Falsehood? Sun-smitten, to nothingness hurled!"

More humbly—so, friends, did my fault find redemption.
    I sinned, soul-entoiled by the tether of sense:

279| MS:Omniscient §over illegible erasure§ < > thank   *1887*:thank,
280| MS:only!—thy   *1887*:only!—Thy

My captor reigned master: I plead no exemption
    From Satan's award to his servant: defence
300 From the fiery and final assault would be—whence?

By making—as man might—to truth restitution!
    Truth is God: trample lies and lies' father, God's foe!
Fix fact fast: truths change by an hour's revolution:
    What deed's very doer, unaided, can show
305 How 'twas done a year—month—week—day—minute ago?

At best, he relates it—another reports it—
    A third—nay, a thousandth records it: and still
Narration, tradition, no step but distorts it,
    As down from truth's height it goes sliding until
310 At the low level lie-mark it stops—whence no skill

Of the scribe, intervening too tardily, rescues
    —Once fallen—lost fact from lie's fate there. What scribe
—Eyes horny with poring, hands crippled with desk-use,
    Brains fretted by fancies—the volatile tribe
315 That tease weary watchers—can boast that no bribe

Shuts eye and frees hand and remits brain from toiling?
    Truth gained—can we stay, at whatever the stage,
Truth a-slide,—save her snow from its ultimate soiling
    In mire,—by some process, stamp promptly on page
320 Fact spoiled by pen's plodding, make truth heritage

Not merely of clerics, but poured out, full measure,
    On clowns—every mortal endowed with a mind?
Read, gentle and simple! Let labour win leisure
    At last to bid truth do all duty assigned,
325 Not pause at the noble but pass to the hind!

How bring to effect such swift sure simultaneous
    Unlimited multiplication? How spread

315| MS:teaze   *1889a*:tease   317| MS:We gain—can   *1887:*Truth gained—can
321| MS:clerics but   *1889a:*clerics, but

By an arm-sweep a hand-throw—no helping extraneous—
 Truth broadcast o'er Europe? "The goldsmith," I said,
330 "Graves limning on gold: why not letters on lead?"

So, Tuscan artificer, grudge not thy pardon
 To me who played false, made a furtive descent,
Found the sly secret workshop,—thy genius kept guard on
 Too slackly for once,—and surprised thee low-bent
335 O'er thy labour—some chalice thy tool would indent

With a certain free scroll-work framed round by a border
 Of foliage and fruitage: no scratching so fine,
No shading so shy but, in ordered disorder,
 Each flourish came clear,—unbewildered by shine,
340 On the gold, irretrievably right, lay each line.

How judge if thy hand worked thy will? By reviewing,
 Revising again and again, piece by piece,
Tool's performance,—this way, as I watched. 'Twas through glueing
 A paper-like film-stuff—thin, smooth, void of crease,
345 On each cut of the graver: press hard! at release,

No mark on the plate, but the paper showed double:
 His work might proceed: as he judged—space or speck
Up he filled, forth he flung—was relieved thus from trouble
 Lest wrong—once—were right never more: what could check
350 Advancement, completion? Thus lay at my beck—

At my call—triumph likewise! "For," cried I, "what hinders
 That graving turns Printing? Stamp one word—not one
But fifty such, phœnix-like, spring from death's cinders,—
 Since death is word's doom, clerics hide from the sun
355 As some churl closets up this rare chalice." Go, run

329| MS:goldsmith" I said *1889a*:goldsmith," I said,   330| MS:gold—why *1887*:gold:
why   333| MS:work-shop *1889a*:workshop   337| MS:fruitage—no *1887*:fruitage:
no   338| MS:shy, §comma crossed out§   340| MS:gold—irretrievably right—lay
1887:gold, irretrievably right, lay   346| MS:plate but *1889a*:plate, but
351| MS:likewise! "For" cried I "what *1889a*:likewise! "For," cried I, "what

148

Thy race now, Fust's child! High, O Printing, and holy
    Thy mission! These types, see, I chop and I change
Till the words, every letter, a pageful, not slowly
    Yet surely lies fixed: last of all, I arrange
360 A paper beneath, stamp it, loosen it!

FIRST FRIEND

Strange!

SECOND FRIEND

How simple exceedingly!

FUST

Bustle, my Schœffer!
Set type,—quick, Genesheim! Turn screw now!

THIRD FRIEND

Just that!

FOURTH FRIEND

And no such vast miracle!

FUST

"Plough with my heifer,
    Ye find out my riddle," quoth Samson, and pat
365 He speaks to the purpose. Grapes squeezed in the vat

Yield to sight and to taste what is simple—a liquid
    Mere urchins may sip: but give time, let ferment—
You've wine, manhood's master! Well, "*rectius si quid*
    Novistis im-per-ti-te!" Wait the event,

361| MS:my Schoefer! *1889a:*my Schoeffer!   364| MS:quoth Sampson *1887:*quoth
Samson   368| MS:master! Well, "*rectius si quid* §last four words over illegible erasure§
369| MS:*Novistis impertite!*" §next two words and punctuation added above after *or* in margin§
Novisti—imperti?— Wait §altered to§ Await *1887:impertite!*" Wait *1889a:*im-per-ti-te

370   Then weigh the result! But whate'er Thy intent,

O Thou, the one force in the whole variation
    Of visible nature,—at work—do I doubt?—
From Thy first to our last, in perpetual creation—
    A film hides us from Thee—'twixt inside and out,
375   A film, on this earth where Thou bringest about

New marvels, new forms of the glorious, the gracious,
    We bow to, we bless: for no star bursts heaven's dome
But Thy finger impels it, no weed peeps audacious
    Earth's clay-floor from out, but Thy finger makes room
380   For one world's-want the more in Thy Cosmos: presume

Shall Man, Microcosmos, to claim the conception
    Of grandeur, of beauty, in thought, word or deed?
I toiled, but Thy light on my dubiousest step shone:
    If I reach the glad goal, is it I who succeed
385   Who stumbled at starting tripped up by a reed,

Or Thou? Knowledge only and absolute, glory
    As utter be Thine who concedest a spark
Of Thy spheric perfection to earth's transitory
    Existences! Nothing that lives, but Thy mark
390   Gives law to—life's light: what is doomed to the dark?

Where's ignorance? Answer, creation! What height,
    What depth has escaped Thy commandment—to Know?
What birth in the ore-bed but answers aright
    Thy sting at its heart which impels—bids "E'en so,
395   Not otherwise move or be motionless,—grow,

"Decline, disappear!" Is the plant in default
    How to bud, when to branch forth? The bird and the beast

370| MS:result! But, whate'er   *1889a:*result! But whate'er   377| *1889a:*bless for: no
§emended to§ bless: for no §see Editorial Notes§   380| MS:in Thy cosmos §altered to§
Cosmos   384-86| MS:succeed/Or   *1887:*succeed/Who stumbled at
starting tripped up by a reed,/Or   387| MS:concededst   *1887:*concedest
394| MS:impels it? "E'en   *1887:*impels—bids "E'en

—Do they doubt if their safety be found in assault
    Or escape? Worm or fly, of what atoms the least
400 But follows light's guidance,—will famish, not feast?

In such various degree, fly and worm, ore and plant,
    All know, none is witless: around each, a wall
Encloses the portion, or ample or scant,
    Of Knowledge: beyond which one hair's breadth, for all
405 Lies blank—not so much as a blackness—a pall

Some sense unimagined must penetrate: plain
    Is only old licence to stand, walk or sit,
Move so far and so wide in the narrow domain
    Allotted each nature for life's use: past it
410 How immensity spreads does he guess? Not a whit.

Does he care? Just as little. Without? No, within
    Concerns him: he Knows. Man Ignores—thanks to Thee
Who madest him know, but—in knowing—begin
    To know still new vastness of knowledge must be
415 Outside him—to enter, to traverse, in fee

Have and hold! "Oh, Man's ignorance!" hear the fool whine!
    How were it, for better or worse, didst thou grunt
Contented with sapience—the lot of the swine
    Who knows he was born for just truffles to hunt?—
420 Monks' Paradise—"*Semper sint res uti sunt!*"

No, Man's the prerogative—knowledge once gained—
    To ignore,—find new knowledge to press for, to swerve
In pursuit of, no, not for a moment: attained—
    Why, onward through ignorance! Dare and deserve!
425 As still to its asymptote speedeth the curve,

402| MS:is ignorant: round each   *1889a*:is witless: around each   405| MS:One blank
1887:Lies blank   408| MS:far, so   *1887*:far and so   409| MS:use—past   *1887*:use:
past   412| MS:him: he knows. Man ignores   *1887*:him: he Knows. Man Ignores
1889a:him? he §emended to§ him: he §see Editorial Notes§

So approximates Man—Thee, who, reachable not,
   Hast formed him to yearningly follow Thy whole
Sole and single omniscience!
                      Such, friends, is my lot:
   I am back with the world: one more step to the goal
430 Thanks for reaching I render—Fust's help to Man's soul!

Mere mechanical help? So the hand gives a toss
   To the falcon,—aloft once, spread pinions and fly,
Beat air far and wide, up and down and across!
   My Press strains a-tremble: whose masterful eye
435 Will be first, in new regions, new truth to descry?

Give chase, soul! Be sure each new capture consigned
   To my Types will go forth to the world, like God's bread
—Miraculous food not for body but mind,
   Truth's manna! How say you? Put case that, instead
440 Of old leasing and lies, we superiorly fed

These Heretics, Hussites . . .

FIRST FRIEND

                      First answer my query!
If saved, art thou happy?

FUST

I was and I am.

FIRST FRIEND

Thy visage confirms it: how comes, then, that—weary
   And woe-begone late—was it show, was it sham?—
445 We found thee sunk thiswise?

432| MS:alift *1887*:aloft   441| MS:These Heretics, Hussites . . First
*1889a:*These Heretics, Hussites . . . First

SECOND FRIEND

—In need of the dram

From the flask which a provident neighbour might carry!

FUST

Ah, friends, the fresh triumph soon flickers, fast fades!
I hailed Word's dispersion: could heartleaps but tarry!
　　Through me does Print furnish Truth wings? The same aids
450　Cause Falsehood to range just as widely. What raids

On a region undreamed of does Printing enable
　　Truth's foe to effect! Printed leasing and lies
May speed to the world's farthest corner—gross fable
　　No less than pure fact—to impede, neutralize,
455　Abolish God's gift and Man's gain!

FIRST FRIEND

Dost surmise

What struck me at first blush? Our Beghards, Waldenses,
　　Jeronimites, Hussites—does one show his head,
Spout heresy now? Not a priest in his senses
　　Deigns answer mere speech, but piles faggots instead,
460　Refines as by fire, and, him silenced, all's said.

Whereas if in future I pen an opuscule
　　Defying retort, as of old when rash tongues
Were easy to tame,—straight some knave of the Huss-School
　　Prints answer forsooth! Stop invisible lungs?
465　The barrel of blasphemy broached once, who bungs?

SECOND FRIEND

Does my sermon, next Easter, meet fitting acceptance?

455-56|　MS:gain!/What　*1887*:gain! Dost surmise/What　　464|　MS:Prints an answer
1887:Prints answer　　466|　MS:acceptance　*1887*:acceptance?

Each captious disputative boy has his quirk
"An cuique credendum sit?" Well the Church kept *"ans"*
In order till Fust set his engine at work!
470 What trash will come flying from Jew, Moor and Turk

When, goosequill, thy reign o'er the world is abolished!
Goose—ominous name! With a goose woe began:
Quoth Huss—which means "goose" in his idiom unpolished—
"Ye burn now a Goose: there succeeds me a Swan
475 Ye shall find quench your fire!"

FUST

I foresee such a man.

468| MS:*sit.*" well <> "ans"   *1887:sit?*" Well <> "*ans*"   469| MS:until Fust set engine
*1887:*till Fust set his engine   474| MS:a Goose—there   *1887:*a Goose: there

§This and the following pages reproduce the "Prefatory Note" that B inserted in Smith, Elder & Co.'s 1887 collection, *Poems by Elizabeth Barrett Browning*.§

In a recent "Memoir of Elizabeth Barrett Browning," by John H. Ingram, it is observed that "such essays on her personal history as have appeared, either in England or elsewhere, are replete with mistakes or misstatements." For these he proposes to substitute "a correct if short memoir:" but, kindly and appreciative as may be Mr. Ingram's performance, there occur not a few passages in it equally "mistaken and misstated."

1. "Elizabeth, the eldest daughter of Edward Moulton Barrett, was born in London on the 4th of March, 1809." Elizabeth was born, March 6, 1806, at Coxhoe Hall, county of Durham, the residence of her father.[1] "Before she was eleven she composed an epic on "Marathon.'" She was then fourteen.

2. "It is said that Mr. Barrett was a man of intellect and culture, and therefore able to direct his daughter's education; but be that so or not, he obtained for her the tutorial assistance of the well-known Greek scholar Hugh Stuart Boyd ... who was also a writer of fluent verse: and his influence and instruction doubtless confirmed Miss Barrett in her poetical aspirations." Mr. Boyd, early deprived of sight from over-study, resided at Malvern, and cared for little else than Greek literature, especially that of the "Fathers." He was about or over fifty, stooped a good deal, and was nearly bald. His daily habit was to sit for hours before a table, treating it as a piano with his fingers, and reciting Greek—his memory for which was such that, on a folio column of his favourite St. Gregory being read to him, he would repeat it without missing a syllable. Elizabeth, then residing in Herefordshire, visited him frequently, partly from her own love of Greek, and partly from a desire for the congenial society of one to whom her attendance might be helpful. There was nothing in the least "tutorial" in this relation— merely the natural feeling of a girl for a blind and disabled scholar in

[1]The entry in the Parish Register of Kelloe Church is as follows:—
Elizabeth Barrett Moulton Barrett, daughter and first child of Edward Barrett Moulton Barrett, of Coxhoe Hall, native of St. James's, Jamaica, by Mary, late Clarke, native of Newcastle-upon-Tyne, was born, March 6th, 1806, and baptized 10th of February, 1808.

whose pursuits she took interest. Her knowledge of Greek was origi-
nally due to a preference for sharing with her brother Edward in the
instruction of his Scottish tutor Mr. M'Swiney rather than in that of
her own governess Mrs. Orme: and at such lessons she constantly as-
sisted until her brother's departure for the Charter House—where he
had Thackeray for a schoolfellow. In point of fact, she was self-taught
in almost every respect. Mr. Boyd was no writer of "fluent verse,"
though he published an unimportant volume, and the literary sympa-
thies of the friends were exclusively bestowed on Greek.

3. "Edward, the eldest of the family," was Elizabeth's younger by
nearly two years. He and his companions perished, not "just off Teign-
mouth," but in Babbicombe Bay. The bodies drifted up channel, and
were recovered three days after.

4. "Her father's fortune was considerably augmented by his acces-
sion to the property of his only brother Richard, for many years
Speaker of the House of Assembly at Jamaica." Mr. Edward Moulton,
by the will of his grandfather, was directed to affix the name of Barrett
to that of Moulton, upon succeeding to the estates in Jamaica. Richard
was his cousin, and by his death Mr. Barrett did not acquire a shilling.
His only brother was Samuel, sometime M.P. for Richmond. He had
also a sister who died young, the full-length portrait of whom by Sir
Thomas Lawrence (the first exhibited by that painter) is in the posses-
sion of Octavius Moulton-Barrett at Westover, near Calbourne, in the
Isle of Wight. With respect to the "semi-tropical taste" of Mr. Barrett,
so characterised in the "Memoir," it may be mentioned that, on the
early death of his father, he was brought from Jamaica to England
when a very young child, as a ward of the late Chief Baron Lord
Abinger, then Mr. Scarlett, whom he frequently accompanied in his
post-chaise when on Circuit. He was sent to Harrow, but received there
so savage a punishment for a supposed offence ("burning the toast")
by the youth whose "fag" he had become, that he was withdrawn from
the school by his mother, and the delinquent was expelled. At the age
of sixteen he was sent by Mr. Scarlett to Cambridge, and thence, for an
early marriage, went to Northumberland. After purchasing the estate
in Herefordshire, he gave himself up assiduously to the usual duties
and occupations of a country gentleman,—farmed largely, was an ac-
tive magistrate, became for a year High Sheriff, and in all county con-
tests busied himself as a Liberal. He had fine taste for landscape-gar-
dening, planted considerably, loved trees—almost as much as his

friend, the early correspondent of his daughter, Sir Uvedale Price— and for their sake discontinued keeping deer in the park.

Many other particulars concerning other people, in other "Biographical Memoirs which have appeared in England or elsewhere" for some years past, are similarly "mistaken and misstated:" but they seem better left without notice by anybody.

R. B.

29 DE VERE GARDENS, W.
December 10, 1887

§This and the following pages reproduce the title pages, B's dedication
and notes, and the tables of contents of his *Poetical Works* of 1888-89.§

ROBERT BROWNING'S

POETICAL WORKS

VOL. I

THE POETICAL WORKS

OF

ROBERT BROWNING

VOL. I

PAULINE—SORDELLO

LONDON

SMITH, ELDER, & CO., 15 WATERLOO PLACE

1888

¹⁻⁵| *1889*:§Series binding only; replaced for separately-titled binding by four lines§
PAULINE / SORDELLO / BY / ROBERT BROWNING   ⁸| *1888-89a*:§Vols.
1-8; replaced for vols. 9-16 by§ 1889   *1889*:§all vols.§ 1889

§Dedication as 1863; prefatory note as 1868; see Vol. 6.160, 367. The following note is appended in 1888.§

    I preserve, in order to supplement it, the foregoing preface. I had thought, when compelled to include in my collected works the poem to which it refers, that the honest course would be to reprint, and leave mere literary errors unaltered. Twenty years' endurance of an eyesore seems more than sufficient: my faults remain duly recorded against me, and I claim permission to somewhat diminish these, so far as style is concerned, in the present and final edition where "Pauline" must needs, first of my performances, confront the reader. I have simply removed solecisms, mended the metre a little, and endeavoured to strengthen the phraseology—experience helping, in some degree, the helplessness of juvenile haste and heat in their untried adventure long ago.

    The poems that follow are again, as before, printed in chronological order; but only so far as proves compatible with the prescribed size of each volume, which necessitates an occasional change in distribution of its contents. Every date is subjoined as before.

R. B.

LONDON: *February* 27, 1888.

CONTENTS

VOLUME I

PAULINE
SORDELLO

VOLUME II

PARACELSUS
STRAFFORD

VOLUME III

§Frontispiece: engraving of Beard's 1835 sketch of B; see Editorial Notes§
PIPPA PASSES
KING VICTOR AND KING CHARLES
THE RETURN OF THE DRUSES
A SOUL'S TRAGEDY

VOLUME IV

A BLOT IN THE 'SCUTCHEON
COLOMBE'S BIRTHDAY
MEN AND WOMEN
    §Contents as 1868; see Vol. 6.371§

VOLUME V

DRAMATIC ROMANCES
    §Contents as 1868; see Vol. 6:370-71§
CHRISTMAS-EVE AND EASTER-DAY

VOLUME VI

DRAMATIC LYRICS
§Contents as 1868; note as 1863; see Vol. 6.165, 369-70§
LURIA

VOLUME VII

§Frontispiece: engraving of Talfourd's 1859 portrait of B; see Editorial Notes§
IN A BALCONY
DRAMATIS PERSONAE
§Contents as 1868; see Vol. 6:371-72§

VOLUME VIII

§Frontispiece: engraving of coin bearing image of Pope Innocent XII; see Editorial Notes§
THE RING AND THE BOOK
    I. THE RING AND THE BOOK
    II. HALF-ROME
    III. THE OTHER HALF-ROME
    IV. TERTIUM QUID

VOLUME IX

THE RING AND THE BOOK
    V. COUNT GUIDO FRANCESCHINI
    VI. GIUSEPPI CAPONSACCHI
    VII. POMPILIA
    VIII. DOMINUS HYACINTHUS DE ARCHANGELIS

VOLUME X

§Frontispiece: engraving of drawing of Guido Franceschini; see Editorial Notes§
THE RING AND THE BOOK
    IX. JURIS DOCTOR JOHANNES-BAPTISTA BOTTINIUS
     X. THE POPE
    XI. GUIDO
    XII. THE BOOK AND THE RING

VOLUME XI

BALAUSTION'S ADVENTURE
PRINCE HOHENSTIEL-SCHWANGAU
FIFINE AT THE FAIR

VOLUME XII

RED COTTON NIGHT-CAP COUNTRY
THE INN ALBUM

VOLUME XIII

ARISTOPHANES' APOLOGY
THE AGAMEMNON OF AESCHYLUS

VOLUME XIV

PACCHIAROTTO
LA SAISIAZ
THE TWO POETS OF CROISIC

Poetical Works

VOLUME XV

DRAMATIC IDYLLS: FIRST SERIES
DRAMATIC IDYLLS: SECOND SERIES
JOCOSERIA

VOLUME XVI

§Frontispiece: engraving of R. W. B. Browning's 1882 portrait of B;
see Editorial Notes§
FERISHTAH'S FANCIES
PARLEYINGS WITH CERTAIN PEOPLE OF IMPORTANCE IN
    THEIR DAY

Photograph of Robert Browning and Joseph Milsand looking at a painting by
Robert Wiedemann Barrett (Pen) Browning. Ca. 1884.

Perseus and Andromeda. Engraving by Giovanni Volpato, 1772, of a sixteenth-century fresco by Polidoro da Caravaggio.

Preliminary sketch by Max Beerbohm for his cartoon titled "Mr. Browning taking tea with the Browning Society." Ca. 1904. [Armstrong Browning Library]

Joan of Arc and the Kingfisher. Painting by Robert Wiedemann Barrett (Pen) Browning, 1886.

PARLEYINGS WITH CERTAIN PEOPLE OF IMPORTANCE IN THEIR DAY

Emendations to the Text

The following emendations have been made to the 1889a copy-text:

Apollo and the Fates, Title page: MS-1887 placed a comma after each of the first six poems. The comma after *Dodington* became a period in 1889a. The comma is restored.

Apollo and the Fates, l. 98: MS-1887 *of* became *off* in 1889a; *of* is required by syntax and sense and is restored.

Apollo and the Fates, l. 141: The comma in MS-1887 after the exclamation *What* was lost in 1889a, though the space for it remains. The comma is restored.

Bernard de Mandeville, l. 25: MS *when* became *if* in 1887. The original *when* clause was parallel with the *when* clause l. 22, and both clauses balance and explain the main clause and *soul and body* (l. 22). B's revision of *when* to *if* in 1887 obscured a parallelism between ll. 22 and 25, a parallelism that his simultaneous revisions to punctuation seem intended to emphasize. For the sake of syntactic clarity, the MS reading *when* is restored.

Bernard de Mandeville, l. 140: The MS-1887 question mark at the end of the line was lost in 1889a; the question mark is restored.

Bernard de Mandeville, l. 150: MS closes the quotation with a single quotation mark after *worked?* The quotation mark was not printed in 1887 or 1889a. P-C close the quote after *minute?* l. 149; other modern editions close the quote at the end of l. 150 or at the end of the section at l. 170. But the sentence *Man's fancy makes the fault!* l. 150 is clearly a bridge to the counter-argument of ll. 151-55 and a response to the preceding quoted argument, not a part of the quote. The friend characterizes the argument by Design as flawed human projection. The MS quotation mark after *worked?* is restored in this edition.

Bernard de Mandeville, l. 160: MS *discretely* became *discreetly* in 1887 and

1889a. The phrase *discretely side by side* and the passage emphasize the presumed separation-in-parallelism of human and divine orders, not the judgment or restraint of either. MS *discretely* is restored.

Bernard de Mandeville, l. 229: MS *who scowls, all he can*, was revised in MS to *who, all scowling*, by crossing out *scowls* and *he* and replacing *can* above by *scowling*. The revision was apparently never completed, and the reading in 1887-1889a is ungrammatical and nonsensical in context. The original MS reading *Who scowls, all he can*, is restored.

With Daniel Bartoli, footnote l. 6: The MS-1887 apostrophe in *l'animo*, lost in 1889a, is restored.

With Daniel Bartoli, l. 47: The MS-1887 quotation marks after *vain* are missing in 1889a and are restored.

With Daniel Bartoli, l. 213: The MS-1887 comma after *again*, which indicates the appositive nature of the following phrase, is missing in 1889; the comma is restored.

With Christopher Smart, l. 265: The quotation marks required at the end of the line, which concludes the speech beginning l. 254, are not present in MS, 1887 or 1889a. The text has been emended to add them.

With George Bubb Dodington, l. 39: The punctuation at the end of the line was lost in 1889a. The 1887 colon is restored.

With George Bubb Dodington, l. 52: MS *shiny* was misread by printers as *slimy* and the word remained uncorrected in 1887 and 1889a. The reference in l. 50 to Darwin's bower-birds and the *sparkling* decoration of their *platform-stage* makes clear that their *rubbish* is *shiny*, not *slimy*; *shiny* is restored.

With George Bubb Dodington, ll. 63, 65: The closing quotation marks for Dodington's speech beginning l. 58 are missing in MS and 1887. Quotation marks were inserted in 1889a at the end of l. 63, but this was an apparent error. It is clear that the next two lines also belong to the speech. Moreover, the MS-1887 exclamation point at the end of l. 65 was lost in 1889a. What may have happened was that the picker working on the stereo plate took out the exclamation point as the first step in correcting the punctuation, intending to add the quotation marks (!"), and then lost his place, inserting the quotation marks at l. 63. The 1889a text is emended to restore the MS-1887 exclamation point at the end of l. 65, and to move the 1888-89 closing quotation marks at the end of l. 63 to the end of line 65.

With George Bubb Dodington, l. 89: The MS closing parenthesis after *populace* appears at the end of the line in 1887 and 1889a. *People or populace* refers to *rabble-rout* l. 87 above, while *for praise or blame* modifies *labour* l. 88 and should be outside the parentheses. The 1889a text is emended to complete the parenthesis after *populace*, following MS.

With George Bubb Dodington, l. 160: The MS-1887 exclamation point at the end of the line was lost in 1889a and is restored.

With George Bubb Dodington, l. 280: The MS colon after *conception* is missing in 1887 and 1889a, though a space for it remains in 1887. The colon is restored.

With George Bubb Dodington, l. 290: The 1887 comma at the end of the line is required by syntax but is missing in 1889a. It is restored.

With Francis Furini, l. 129: The MS-1887 comma after *Creator*, required by syntax, was lost in 1889a. The comma is restored.

With Francis Furini, l. 201: MS *souls'* was printed *soul's* in 1887 and 1889a. The plural sense of *souls* in the passage requires the plural possessive. MS *souls'* is restored.

With Francis Furini, l. 467: The paragraph break in the middle of l. 467 is indicated in the margin in MS. Quotation marks at the beginning of the paragraph signaling a continuing speech are present (though faint) in MS but are missing in 1887 and 1889a. The MS quotation marks are restored.

With Gerard de Lairesse, l. 92: MS-1887 *add* became *and* in 1889a. Sense and syntax require the verb; *add* is restored in this edition.

With Gerard de Lairesse, l. 125: In a sequence of revisions to this line B replaced *thy* with *your* and then restored the cancelled reading by a marginal note. MS *thy* became *the* in 1887 and 1888-89. The emphasis of this passage on seeing double, through de Lairesse's blind eyes and the speaker's own, is obscured by *the* and clarified by *thy*; MS *thy* is restored in this edition.

With Gerard de Lairesse, l. 302: MS-1887 *couches* became *crouches* in 1889a. The "supine" and "slumberously laid" Lyda is clearly not crouching; *couches* is restored.

With Gerard de Lairesse, l. 362: The MS-1887 period at the end of the line was lost in 1889a and is restored.

With Charles Avison, l. 58: The MS-1887 exclamation point at the end of the line was lost in 1889a and is restored.

With Charles Avison, l. 382: MS-1887 *Blow* became *Blows* in 1889a. *Blow* is required by syntax and is restored.

Fust and His Friends, ll. 65-66: In the MS, the stanza ends at the bottom of a page; the line space between stanzas was lost in 1887 and 1889a. The line space is restored.

Fust and His Friends, l. 108: MS spacing between the words *every* and *one* is ambiguous, and in 1887 and 1889a the two words were printed as *everyone*. Sense and syntax require that the appositive *every one* refer to each and all of *Pride, concupiscence*, and *Crapulosity* in ll. 107-8. Since the pronoun *everyone* is inappropriate, the MS reading is restored.

Fust and His Friends, ll. 130-31: The MS line space between stanzas was lost in 1887 and 1889a. The line space is restored.

Fust and His Friends, l. 158: The MS-1887 exclamation point at the end of the line was lost in 1889a and is restored.

Fust and His Friends, l. 196: The MS-1887 comma after *banning* was lost in 1889a, although the space remains. The comma is restored.

Fust and His Friends, l. 197: The MS-1887 period after *accept* was lost in 1889a, although the space remains. The period is restored.

Fust and His Friends, ll. 200-201: The line space between stanzas is not present MS-1889a. The 1889a text is emended to add the line space.

Fust and His Friends, l. 377: In the MS B placed a colon after *for*, though in the name of sense and idiom it clearly should have followed *bless*. Though other errors in this passage were corrected in 1887 and 1889a, this one was not; the text is emended to read *bless: for*.

Fust and His Friends, l. 412: The MS-1887 colon after *him* became a question-mark in 1889a. The sentence is not a question; the colon is restored.

In MS and 1887, each parleying had a separate half-title page; in 1889a, these titles were placed at the head of the first page of text. The variant listings for the titles record only verbal variants and manuscript alterations.

Composition and Publication]

Published in two editions in B's lifetime, the first in 1887 and the second in the collected edition of 1889-89, *Parleyings With Certain People of Importance in Their Day* was written over about fourteen months, from September 1885 to December of 1886. Scattered external and internal indications suggest a fairly clear sequence of composition. The first available reference to composition is in a letter to F.J. Furnivall from a remote village of Val d'Aosta in the Italian Alps where B and his sister had returned for a five- or six-week stay in mid-August 1885. The letter has vivid and enthusiastic descriptions of the village environs and of the poet's and Sarianna's marathon walks, with an abrupt interjection that is characteristically reticent about the work in progress. In reply to an earlier inquiry from Furnivall B remarks, "Yes,—I am writing another poem" (7 September 1885, *B's Trumpeter*, 116).

"With Charles Avison," which appears from internal evidence (see *Composition* note to that poem) to have been written early, in Warwick Crescent in March of 1886, was eventually placed last in the series. "With Francis Furini" is centrally concerned with circumstances surrounding a May 1886 exhibit in London of Pen Browning's "Joan of

Arc and the Kingfisher." "Furini" is dated 30 September (1886) in MS and was probably the last poem of the sequence to be finished, but it was eventually placed fifth in the series. Joseph Milsand, to whom *Parleyings* is dedicated, died on 4 September 1886. De Vane speculates plausibly that the framing dialogues were written last, the initial one, "Apollo and the Fates," in response to Milsand's death. B wrote to Furnivall 9 December 1886, "My poem [*Parleyings*] is gone to press a week ago." Furnivall's presentation copy was inscribed with the date of publication, 28 January 1887 (*Reconstruction*, C448).

More revealing than surviving documentation about the actual writing of *Parleyings* are the fuller context and background of its composition. Both the prominence of the Browning Society, founded in 1881, and Mrs. Orr's *A Handbook to the Works of Robert Browning*, prepared with B's collaboration and published in 1885, shed light on the writing of *Parleyings*. Frederick Furnivall, founder and leader of the Browning Society, persistently urged B to provide for his readers and for posterity a portrait of himself and his age, emphasizing that the indirect approach of the dramatic monologue and its use of irony in point of view left readers like himself dissatisfied with B's propensity— in Furnivall's phrase—"to whitewash a blackguard" (*B's Trumpeter*, xxxiii). To counterbalance the remoteness of the subject matter of *The Ring and the Book*, Furnivall recommended treating blackguards closer to home, suggesting, for example, such a one as Disraeli. B took up Furnivall's challenge in both general spirit and particular case, offering in *Parleyings* a poem in his own voice about positive and negative events and figures in his life and including in his rogues' gallery an unnamed but recognizable Disraeli—though not, it appears, recognizable to Furnivall (see *Composition* note to "With George Bubb Dodington"). In the same letter in which he announced *Parleyings*, B gave permission to Furnivall to "biographize" about him (7 September 1885; *B's Trumpeter*, 115). But if he implicitly accepted the challenge to offer a form of autobiography in his next work, it was not to be without irony and indirection. Indeed, the poem serves less as consent and more as corrective to the demand for biographical disclosure personified by Mrs. Orr and by Furnivall and his Browning Society.

In the deeper background behind *Parleyings* are other biographical milestones. In the years prior to the writing of the poem, and increasingly within B's circle, the intellectual giants of the age were dying, and their reputations sometimes dying with them. Examples of betrayal by biography, as it seemed to many at the time, were J. A. Froude's *Reminiscences of Carlyle* (1881) and his *Letters and Memorials of Jane Carlyle* (1883), both published after Carlyle's death in 1881.

Froude's exposure of the deep unhappiness expressed by Jane Carlyle in her diaries and letters was a lesson evidently instructive and irritating to the conscience of many a male writer at the time.

But the main current of B's life in the mid-80's was prosperous and positive: his career was still ripening toward further poetic harvest and critical esteem ahead, and the fruition of hopes for Pen Browning appeared imminent. B continued to write and publish steadily, and the two collections of poems that appeared just prior to *Parleyings*, *Jocoseria* (1883) and *Ferishtah's Fancies* (1885), quickly sold out three editions in their first year of publication. By November of 1887, ten months after *Parleyings* was published, B was correcting poems for the collected edition of 1888-1889. Social life and family affairs were active and secure as well. Pen Browning was gaining recognition as a painter. The November 1885 purchase of the Palazzo Rezzonico in Venice as Pen's residence was followed in 1887 by his marriage to Fannie Coddington. Travelling, writing, and being lionized effusively at home and abroad, B in these years inspired a shrewd member of his circle, Henry James, then forty-nine, to speculate in "The Private Life" that this English poet had a ghostly second self who produced his work quite independently of the social lion, raconteur, and ladies' man.

James's fantasy of a dual-voiced B is a useful model for the speaker of *Parleyings*. The narrative voice in individual poems in the series is typically dual, embedding a voice which is unnamed but in contrast to the title subject of the poem, a counter-voice which is mediated, parodied, and ventriloquized by the narrator. Without identification of these counter-voices, the reader may be left in Furnivall's or Christopher Smart's case, holding a key to B's intellectual biography in his hand but powerless to use it (see *Composition* notes to "With Christopher Smart" and "With George Bubb Dodington").

Sources and Backgrounds]

The fullest exploration of the sources of *Parleyings* is William Clyde DeVane's *Browning's Parleyings: The Autobiography of a Mind* (1964). As DeVane establishes, the sources of *Parleyings* are, with one exception ("With Francis Furini"), books that B knew as a boy, books associated with shaping influences in his thought, with music, and with painting. Most of these books were in B's father's library (see *Reconstruction*, Section A), where B could and did return to them repeatedly.

Curiously, in later life the strong early impressions that B formed in his reading became an almost principled defense against rereading. An early letter of 11 March 1845 to EBB about Aeschylus' *Prometheus* asserts categorically, "(I never look at books I loved once—it was your mention of the translation that brought out the old fast fading outlines of the Poem in my brain.)" (Kintner, 38). And indeed a number of the sources for *Parleyings* do not appear to have been consulted in the writing of the poems, and do appear to have been imperfectly remembered. In "With Bernard de Mandeville," for example, B imposes his own faith in the benign tension between error and effort in the moral development of humankind, upon Mandeville's more cynical eighteenth-century satirist's view of human nature, apparently failing to recollect either the moral or the pervasive irony of the original *Fable*. In the same parleying, the devil's advocate figure countering Mandeville's presumed optimism is a recognizable but distorted Thomas Carlyle, the great Victorian moral activist and friend of B's, who is given the moral skepticism that more properly belongs to Mandeville himself.

Indeed one of the most striking features of these autobiographical poems is their free license with facts, chronology, and interpretation. The dramatic monologue in B's hands, of course, combines historical authenticity, daring originality, and poetic license, but the poems in *Parleyings* are not dramatic monologues. The license toward sources in *Parleyings* is distinct in the B canon, in view of B's declared purpose to offer a truthful autobiographical account of his earliest, formative, and lasting intellectual influences. B's lifelong interest in painting, music, religion, politics, were awakened and shaped by Bernard de Mandeville, Christopher Smart, Gerard de Lairesse, Charles Avison, among others, and he seems to have wished to express his debts with candor and clarity. Nonetheless, the persons addressed in these poems are consistently and radically recast by the very homage or damage with which they are linked in the poems. To discern and trace the factual divergences between the originals of these poems and B's versions of them, and to identify the tonal complexities and defining importance of the narrative voice, are significant challenges to reader and editor.

Title]

The title phrase is B's own translation of a sardonic understatement by Dante. In *The Vita Nuova*, Dante describes how his thoughts were interrupted by "certain people of importance"—namely, the targets of the *Inferno*, in B's reading. See B's use of the phrase in "One Word More," l. 56 (in Vol. 6 of this edition, 143 and 419n.). B's addition "in their day" to Dante's phrase adds emphasis to Dante's irony—in another

179

time these figures may no longer have importance at all—while also suggesting that B's own interest is in their very unimportance, their difficulty or obscurity for a later age. Writing in his late maturity, B's projection of figures such as Mandeville, Smart, Lairesse and Avison, derives as much from the difference B found in them from Victorian art and thought as from the powerful attraction he once felt toward them. In varying ways, all the title figures in *Parleyings* share this dual quality of importance faded and unimportance celebrated.

Dedication]

Absens . . . videtque "The absent one hears and sees him who is absent" (Virgil, *Aeneid*, 4.1.83).

APOLLO AND THE FATES; A PROLOGUE

Sources and Backgrounds] The debate between Apollo and the Fates concerns their opposing positive and negative views of human destiny. The argument sets a tone and a theme for the series of poems in *Parleyings*, and recalls the variations on the struggle between good and evil, truth and lie, illumination and mystery, real and ideal, that persist in B's work throughout his career. The treatment of mythological and classical sources in the Prologue involves, as does the use of sources in *Parleyings* generally, a balance and assimilation among source, adaptation, and purpose.

B's headnote cites passages from a *Hymn to Mercury* attributed to Homer, Aeschylus' *Eumenides*, and Euripides' *Alcestis*. All of the passages refer to the function of the Fates in determining human birth, destiny, and death, and to the story of Apollo's successful ruse to deceive the Fates into sparing the life of his friend Admetus, whose wife Alcestis died in his stead and was later returned to life from the underworld by Hercules. (B translated most of Euripides' *Alcestis*, which tells of her rescue, in *Balaustion's Adventure*, 1871.) The brief passages cited from the *Hymn* and from *Eumenides* are translated as follows:

> From their home they fly now here, now there, feeding on honeycomb and bringing all things to pass. And when they are inspired through yellow honey, they are willing to speak truth.
> (*Hymn to Mercury*, ll. 558-60; Loeb Classical Library)

> Such was thy style of action also in the house of Pheres, when thou didst move the Fates to make mortals free from death . . . .

Thou it was in truth who didst beguile with wine those ancient
goddesses and thus abolish the dispensations of eld.
(addressed by the Furies to Apollo in Aeschylus,
Eumenides, ll. 723-24, 737-38; Loeb Classical Library)

We give the passages from *Alcestis* both in the Loeb Classical Library
translation and in B's adaptation in *Balaustion's Adventure*.

The son of Pheres; him I snatched from death,
Cozening the Fates: the Sisters promised me—
"Admetus shall escape the imminent death
If he for ransom gives another life."
(Apollo in *Alcestis*, ll. 11-14)

Whence I deceived the Moirai, drew from death
My master, this same son of Pheres,—ay,
The Goddesses conceded him escape
From Hades, when the fated day should fall,
Could he exchange lives, find some friendly one
Ready, for his sake, to content the grave.
(*Balaustion's Adventure*, ll. 383-88)

Did this not suffice thee, to thwart that doom
Of Admetus when, all by thy cunning beguiled
Were the Fates?
(Addressed to Apollo in *Alcestis*, ll. 32-34)

Was't not enough for thee to have delayed
Death from Admetos,—with thy crafty art
Cheating the very Fates,—
(*Balaustion's Adventure* ll. 434-36)

B's adaptations of his sources are as significant as his borrowings.
In the *Prologue*, the tipsy sisters' instantaneous conversion to optimism
under the influence of wine is at once delirious and spurious. Their
readiness to draw a moral opposite to Apollo's, after they sober up and
witness the birth of "knowledge," entails for B a vivid recasting of both
character and myth (see ll. 221 and following). The occasional
conflation of the judicious Furies and the cruel Fates in the descriptive
passages and in the role of the Chorus is also characteristic of B's free
use of sources. Finally, the ironic end of the play and the laughter of
the Fates at the apparent collapse of Apollo's hopeful construction of

a world made new by love, is a typical "parleying" or negotiating with sources.

1] *Flame . . . Apollo* The scene appears to be sunrise on Parnassus, a mountain in Greece sacred to the gods. Apollo, god of light and music, drove the chariot of the sun. But the reference to Apollo's *foot-fall* suggests that the god brings only his own essential effulgence into the dark underworld.

3-4] *depths . . . Ones* The Fates resided in the underworld.

5] *Admetus . . . seek* King of Thessaly, Admetus was condemned to die by Artemis (or Diana, as she was known in Roman myth) in punishment for failing to sacrifice to her on Admetus's wedding day. See also ll. 28-29nn. below.

6-7] *Dragonwise . . . Night* The Fates were the daughters of one of the Titans, Themis, who belonged to a pre-Olympian era of Greek religion which was strongly matriarchal. Themis was a goddess of justice. The Fates are also known as the daughters of night, after Hesiod. They are traditionally depicted as having human shape.

13] *bronze lip* The figure may derive from the indifference and lack of feeling of the "cruel" Fate's pronouncements; to be made of bronze is to be impervious to sympathy.

15] *Woe-purfled, weal-prankt* Chequered (see l. 27) by misfortune and fortune. The participles denote ornamentation and embroidery of woven fabric.

18] *thumb and finger* The thread is formed by being turned from the spindle between thumb and finger of the spinner.

23] *Moirai* Greek word for Fates.

28-30] *slaved . . . Dead?"* Admetus' "chequered" or mixed fate entailed on the one hand a god's help to secure Admetus' marriage to Alcestis, and on the other premature death. The god Apollo was sentenced by Zeus to serve as Admetus' slave for a year as a consequence of a quarrel over Apollo's son Asclepius, a physician and mortal whom Zeus ordered to be killed by a thunderbolt for his usurpation of god-like power over life and death. Apollo retaliated by killing the forger of the thunderbolt. As his punishment, Apollo was made to serve Admetus, and assisted Admetus in winning Alcestis as his bride. When Admetus failed to sacrifice properly to Artemis on his wedding day, the goddess sent snakes to the wedding chamber. Apollo (brother to Artemis) restored peace between the king and the goddess. But Admetus was cut off in his prime by the Fates' sentence of death.

43] *encumber* Limit. The word has a legal sense of undeserved or imposed debt; see *annulled* l. 47 for a continuation of the figure.

47, 66, 81]   *Boy / boy-thing*   Apollo is traditionally represented as youthful, associated with beauty and dawn light. Here the Fates associate his youth with inexperience and naivete.

55]   *threescore and ten*   Apollo cites the Biblical lifespan as another kind of law, counter to the Fates' powers. "The days of our years are threescore years and ten" (Ps. 90:10).

56-59]   *Disaster . . . we*   See. ll. 28-29n.

82]   *owns*   Admits.

116-17]   *honeycombs . . . amiss*   B contrasts the Fates' pessimism and their food, honey (see *Sources* above), with Apollo's optimism and the effects of wine. Apollo invokes a rosy version of the proverbial "in vino veritas" to challenge the Fates.

120]   *allow*   Concede.

121]   *Unhook . . . brows*   See *Sources* above. In myth and poetry the three Fates are often conflated with the Furies, whose function is more punitive and less abstract than that of the Fates. The Furies are winged, and the Fates are often represented as hooded figures.

122]   *fond*   Deluded, doting on illusion rather than on truth.

123]   *leaps*   Invites or excites, as in "makes the pulse leap"; Atropos responds to Lachesis' recognition of the sensuous appeal of wine, in contrast to the truth-revealing property of honey.

126]   *Trine*   Trinity.

127]   *Bacchus-prompted*   God of wine, Bacchus-Dionysus was the son of Zeus and Semele, a mortal woman. Apollo argues that wine is divinely inspired. See below ll. 147-60 for elaboration of the symbolic role of wine in the mixed and ambiguous experience of humankind.

136-40]   *pied . . . white*   Now that she has drunk wine she can make the patterns of dark and light less mixed and unpredictable, with white as the dominant color.

137]   *hair's breadth*   A pun on the weaver's thread and the proverbial expression connoting narrow escape from danger; under the influence of wine Lachesis becomes whimsical.

147-60]   *youngest . . . change*   See l. 127n. The individual powers, attributes, and gifts of the gods taken together presumably compose and account for the full range of creation and history. Bacchus, coming last in the genealogy of the gods, made a contribution to civilization, progress, and harmony between past and present that was appropriate to his late arrival. Apollo assigns a civilizing and reconciling symbolism to wine without denying man's *mixed woe and weal* and his capacity for illusion and error. The mixture of divine and human are reflected in Bacchus' origins. Bacchus' mortal mother *Semele*, unable to bear the sight of Zeus' glory when she insisted that he reveal it to her, was consumed by fire, and the infant Bacchus was rescued from her body by Zeus.

173] *cluster* I.e., of wine grapes.

187] *Not . . . incept* "Are" is understood, parallel with l. 186. The terms refer back to ll. 156-57.

  incept Inception, beginning (a B coinage).

192] *cummers* Wise women, witches (ironic). The word means co-mothers, godmothers.

198] *collyrium* From the Greek, eye-wash or salve. As father of Ascle-pius (ll. 28-29 n.), Apollo is also father of medicine—though the diag-nosis and prescription here are ironic.

200] *CHORUS* See *Sources* for the combined and differentiated voices of the Furies and the Fates in this poem. The Chorus in Greek tragedy interposes comment upon the action of the play. Here, as in Aeschylus' *Eumenides*, the Chorus confirms insights and motives (Apollo's).

221] *Stage direction* Earth's volcanic response to the millenial com-promise heralded by the Chorus is ambiguous, at once destructive and transforming. Cf. the ambiguous power of the printing press in the Epilogue, "Fust and His Friends."

227-29] *portent . . . uncouth* A *bantling* is a child, with the connota-tion of bastard. The unenlightened Fates see a different meaning in the *portent* of the explosion and its image of humanity as without cer-tainty of origins or of hope, capable of knowing only its own unknow-ing, *uncouth* state.

236] *nor . . . nor* Neither . . . nor.

247] *doom* The word is close to the meaning of "fate" or "destiny," but signifies that which is beyond even the Fates themselves. .

254] *infinite* Not finite; unrealized, indeterminate (*OED*).

256] *griesly* Grisly.

261] *Pherae* Capital city of Thessaly, where Admetus ruled and where Apollo served him.

258-65] *subjects . . . ha* No one but Admetus' wife Alcestis volun-teers to sacrifice life for him, and he does not *spurn the exchange*. The Fates have the last laugh for the present. B implies, as he did earlier in *Balaustion's Adventure* (1871), that Admetus shows human fallibility and weakness in accepting Alcestis' sacrifice.

WITH BERNARD DE MANDEVILLE

Sources and Backgrounds] A native of Dort or Dordrecht in Holland, Bernard de Mandeville (c. 1670-1733) attended the Erasmus School in

Rotterdam and took the degree of doctor of medicine at Leyden before settling in England. In 1705, he published a satirical work of 433 lines of doggerel verse, *The Grumbling Hive, or Knaves turned Honest.* In 1714 this was republished as an expanded volume under the title *The Fable of the Bees, or Private Vices, Publick Benefits.* Prose essays of commentary, including a "Vindication," were added by the author, all suggesting controversy the book had aroused. A 1795 edition of *The Fable* was given to B by his father in 1833, presumably for the poet's twenty-first birthday and in recognition of the hundredth anniversary of Mandeville's death (*Reconstruction*, A1534). B was sufficiently struck by the book's argument and ingenious use of paradox to imitate it in some early contributions to an amateur magazine called *The Trifler*, edited by some friends. Cast as a fable about bees, Mandeville's book argues that human nature is naturally self-serving and depraved, but that human vices generate both a thriving marketplace and a society concerned to protect its economy by adequate laws and customs. Without thievery, prostitution, gin, and other depravities, a well-governed society would have no meaning, according to *The Fable*. Legislators and criminals serve similar ends:

> As sharpers, parasites, pimps, players,
> Pickpockets, coiners, quacks, soothsayers . . .
> These were called knaves, but bar the name,
> The grave industrious were the same.
>
> (ll. 49-50, 55-56)

In *The Fable of the Bees*, the stable balance between widespread knavery and a well-ordered state is upset by the enforcement of sweeping reform among the bees and followed by the swift decline of both prosperity and morality. Mandeville extends his satire to Christian faith, arguing that to pretend that human nature can be other than self-serving is to encourage hypocrisy, a worse danger than admission of vice. "The imaginary notions that men may be virtuous without self-denial, are a vast inlet to hypocrisy; which being once made habitual, we must not only deceive others, but likewise become altogether unknown to ourselves." ("Search Into the Nature of Society," 1795 edition of *Fable*, 210)

In his 1724 "Vindication" Mandeville claimed that his intention was satirical, and that he meant his fable to be read as corrective exaggeration. But some fifty years after his first reading of Mandeville in 1833, B's selective memory provided quite another meaning for the *Fable*, and a purposeful connection between Mandeville and B's own view of the function of temptation, error and sin in individual moral development.

B takes more conscious liberties with the point of view he appoints as a contrast to Mandeville's. Though unnamed in the parleying, the voice raised in skeptical counterpoint to B's and Mandeville's affirmative world view is clearly intended to be Thomas Carlyle's, directly evoking as it does Carlyle's principles, views, writings, style, even personal mannerisms. Carlyle's powerful moral outlook, his assertion of the prevalence of human weakness in the world, his combative, direct way of delivering his views whether in public debate or *ad hominem,* and his distrust of poetry (early in his career B had been charged by Carlyle to give up poetry for prose), were all well known. In Carlyle's last years these qualities were linked with a confirmed melancholy; W. Allingham, a close friend of Carlyle's, gives first-hand witness of these years in *A Diary* (London, 1907). In this parleying, Carlyle's dogmatic moral polemic is represented as squeamish and escapist beside Mandeville's robust affirmation. The Carlyle-voice is likewise measured and found wanting beside a master of imaginative achievement in B's personal canon, Euripides, whose mythic intuition of divinity dwarfs the Carlylean distrust of imaginative extensions of reality. Such invidious contrasts for the Victorian prophet of meliorism, work, and Natural Supernaturalism seem unjust. Yet B not only revises but revives Carlyle's cultural presence, especially his devil's advocacy, the vigor of Carlylean debate, and the indelible Carlylese of the voice in that debate (see ll. 235-300 and n.). The interplay of memory and revision, the dynamics of evolving and eroding views of truth, define this parleying and those to follow.

5] *loaded line* A cord weighted with lead to take depth soundings; also a pun on the probing lines of this poem; see next n.
18-34] *doubtful . . . magnificence* In its incremental thought, fragmented syntax and opposed concepts, the passage offers a calculated model of both "turbidity" (l. 5) and triumphant truth, as expressed by the "sage dead," Mandeville (l. 10). The oppositions in this passage, between revealed truth (*full disclosure*) and the *doubtful doctrine* and earthly law of *probative* moral *growth* by hard spiritual exercise amid human error(*foiled darings, fine faults, brave sins*) strain against sense and rhetorical balance until the redemptive closure of the final line. This first parleying thus expresses in its own beginning a theme about beginnings that will remain a pattern and a purpose for other parleyings.
36] *stung* A pun. In B's selective memory of Mandeville's fable the

theme of temptation as a spur or sting toward moral growth was dominant. See *Sources* above. This indirect reference to bees may be the closest allusion B makes in this parleying to Mandeville's actual fable; it is a reminder of how far B is willing to depart from his announced sources in *Parleyings*.

37]   *race-ground* Field of trial.

40-41]   *Objected . . . antithesis* Here an unnamed opponent of Mandeville's supposed faith in the triumph of good over evil is introduced. B invokes the spirit of his old friend Thomas Carlyle, who had died in 1881 (*yesterday*), as the voice of skepticism, pessimism, and agnosticism countering Mandeville's purposeful optimism and religious faith.

43-61]   *No . . . release* The speech invokes Carlyle's fear that if *justice bears no sword, if justice swerves from dealing doom*, if democracy is not limited by strong leadership and moral behavior is not enforced by disciplinary action, civilization will collapse.

    groaned he Carlyle's utterances typically retained the declamatory stamp of his early training for ministry and of the rhetorical traditions of dissenting Scottish protestantism.

44]   *God's finger* The finger of God is a repeated figure in the OT for God's wrath or will. At Exod. 8:19, a plague of lice in Egypt is called the "finger of God"; see also Exod. 31:18 and Deut. 9:10.

64-68]   *Thunderbolts . . . shoe* One reference here is to Jove's thunderbolt dispatched when the god was angered. The *parlous friend*, however, is Jove-like only in his bluster, and cowers from a *puny straw*. Carlyle's autocratic personal style in both writing and speaking were well known. Less well known, until Jane Carlyle's diaries were used in J.A. Froude's scandal-raising biography of her husband (1881), were Carlyle's domestic tyranny and petty despotism over household details; an allusion to that domestic situation is implicit here. Carlyle's melancholy contrition when he learned after Jane's death of her unhappiness in their marriage was a sad refrain in his conversation with his friends; Allingham's *Diary* is a clear record of this aspect of Carlyle's late years (see *Sources* above). B, however, never an admirer of Jane's nor she of him, may have been entirely unsympathetic with Jane and with his friend's sore conscience. As Betty Miller writes, B "regarded Thomas, and not Jane, as the true martyr of the marriage" (*Robert Browning, A Portrait* [New York, 1953], 55). B's impatience with Carlyle's inability to kick a domestic straw out of the way may well be the subtext here.

69-70]   *pooh-pooh . . . preachment* A reference to an anecdote in Samuel Johnson's *Life of Addison*, in which Mandeville comments dismissively about Joseph Addison, well known for his essays in *The Specta-tor.* Mandeville describes Addison as "a parson in a tye-wig." A *tye-wig* was an elaborate formal wig gathered and tied with ribbon at the back. *Parson* is used in a generalized and deprecating sense here to contrast with *tye-wig* and to indicate that to Mandeville's eye for falsity and pre-tense, Addison was mutton dressed as veal, a preacher-moralist with pretensions to elegance. The analogy is between Addison's and Car-lyle's self-important "magisterial" (l. 41) voices for their generations.

71] *groan . . . guffaw* Typical verbal mannerisms of Carlyle's; see ll. 43-61n. In a letter to J. Nettleship dated Aug. 31, 1889, B speaks of his use of Carlyle's *guffaw* as an unmistakably identifying feature. "I thought I had distinguished him sufficiently by the mention of his 'guffaw'" (*Meeting the Brownings,* ed. Michael Meredith [Waco, Texas: Armstrong Browning Library, 1986], 118).

73] *bilious mood* Another reference to Carlyle, who not only suf-fered from a troublesome digestive system, but used gastric distress as a metaphor in *Sartor Resartus.*

75] *preference* Precedence, superiority. In this speech Carlyle gives the argument for rule by authority and dogma, against trust in individ-ual judgment and experience.

94] *friend . . . fables* Carlyle's anecdotal style is famously illus-trated in both his long and his shorter works, but with particular vivid-ness in *Sartor Resartus.*

102] *spud* A cutting tool.

123-26] *burgeon . . . mandrake-monster* The poisonous mandrake has a thick, forked root. It has uses in witchcraft and is often used figu-ratively in literature. Here, B has Mandeville argue that to prune the buds and shoots (*burgeon*) of evil is necessary in order to protect life's good, but to take out the roots would be "folly" (l. 120).

127-29] *It . . . vain* The subjunctives are elided in these lines, whose sense is, "if you purged the field of the roots of evil, the sower would behold his law repealed, and his ordinance would prove vain."

132-38] *Still . . . tares* The friend (Carlyle) points out that the Biblical parable of the wheat and the tares has a quite different moral from that of Mandeville's agricultural fable. Matt. 13:24-30 says that the tares (weeds) sowed by the devil will be burned on the day of judg-ment. Since the intermixed *crop and weeds . . . once planted* cannot be separated, surely, argues Carlyle, it would be better to avoid the begin-nings of evil than to indulge the fancy (*vain pretence*) that it is all part of the divine plan. Carlyle, again, questions optimism about humanity's capacity for free moral choice. In the letter to J. Nettleship cited above l. 71n. B specifies, "My 'pessemistic' friend was Carlyle—whose words

on the subject of his dispondency [sic] at no direct and apparent in-
terference with, or punishment of, evil are recorded by Froude."

136, 141, 150-55]   *Vain pretence . . . Man's play . . . Man's fancy . .
. understanding*   The repeated questions and varied refrains in answer
reinforce the speaker's skepticism about humanity's capacity to grasp
providential design. The statement *Man's fancy makes the fault* (the
error, the faulty interpretation) introduces the summary and charac-
teristically ironic Carlylean statement about man's urge to overreach
his limitations. Carlyle's position is sharply opposed to B's embrace of
imperfection as the opportunity for moral and imaginative develop-
ment.

154-55]   *Since . . . understanding*   St. Paul's promise of "the peace
of God, which passeth understanding" (Phil. 4:7) was an assurance of
transcendence of earthly troubles through prayer, not a warning
against understanding. As with the parable of the wheat and the tares
ll. 132-38, the speaker—like the devil—can quote scripture to his pur-
pose.

155-66]   *So . . . space*   The lines are a loose, ironic paraphrase of
the creation of man and the fall as told in Genesis. Some relevant pas-
sages are Gen. 1:6-25; 3:5, 8, 19: the creation of man in God's image;
the order of creation; the temptation, fall, and punishment.

176]   *Goethe's . . . Weimar*   Carlyle was a student of German roman-
tic literature and thought, and was strongly influenced by Johann Wolf-
gang von Goethe (1749-1832), whom he translated and helped to in-
troduce to Victorian readers and writers. B chooses the example of
Goethe's great house in Weimar, the city where Goethe lived during
his long renown, to point out to his friend the difference between sym-
bol and reality, just as Carlyle had used Goethe in *On Heroes, Hero-Wor-
ship, and the Heroic in History* (1841) as the type of the Man of Letters.

180-97]   *Do . . . ken*   The example of the *ground-plan* (l. 174) of the
estate and of the *constellation* Orion are instructively chosen to suggest
that earthly and heavenly orders may indeed be parallel. But the most
typical application of the kind of analysis under discussion here is not
directly mentioned. The German school of thought known as the
Higher Criticism, which questioned the literal truth of the Bible and
its miracles while affirming its mythical truth and which B explored in
Christmas-Eve and Easter-Day (1850), lies behind the argument of this
passage. See the notes to that poem in this edition, Vol. 5, 340-49.

inane   The void of empty space (*OED*).

198-201]   *Fitlier . . . Will*   I. e., "It would be better, more fitting,
that man accept by report on good authority [*on tongue*] the attributes
of God." See above 136, 141, 150-55 and n.

204-6]   *A myth* . . . *Aeschylus*   B translated both Greek tragic
dramatists and considered Euripides the greater teacher, although the
critical estimate of his generation ranked Euripides below Sophocles
and Aeschylus. In *The Ring and the Book*, the Pope conjures the spirit of
Euripides for counsel in his vigil as he considers how to judge the mur-
derer Guido. Advising him, Euripides says of his plays, "They might
please, they may displease, they shall teach, / For truth's sake."
(10.1710-11). B dedicated his *Agamemnon of Aeschylus* (1877) to Carlyle,
who had said to him after the publication of *Aristophanes' Apology*
(1875), "Ye won't mind me, though it's the last advice I may give ye;
but ye ought to translate the whole of the Greek tragedians—that's
your vocation" (Maisie Ward, *Robert Browning and His World*, [New
York, 1969], 2. 91]. As this parleying reveals, however, the tensions be-
tween Carlyle and B that developed in the late years of their lives,
while not destroying the friendship, colored all of their exchanges.
Carlyle was openly critical of the *Agamemnon of Aeschylus*, and B clearly
found Carlyle incapable of appreciating either Euripides or Mande-
ville.

207-27]   *Boundingly* . . . *praise*   The lines offer a heightened style
and language that in its pictorial values, attention to setting, and
mythic style seem to emulate Euripides.

221-22]   *ore* . . . *crystal*   The passage offers a poetic description of
specific geological materials and properties. Certain minerals such as
feldspar or *spar* have a low melting point (*ran liquid*) and form large
branching crystals. B shared the Victorian interest in geology and the
geological evidence for evolution, and here the geological references
reinforce the primitivism of the setting and theme.

235-300]   *Man* . . . *Man*   In these lines Carlyle's voice is recast as
prototypical man's, and elements of his style, language, and thought
are ingeniously synthesized and incorporated into the argument of the
poem. The passage, a riposte to the mythic Euripidean celebration of
sun and landscape of ll. 207-227, invokes the themes of transcenden-
talism and natural supernaturalism (especially ll. 268-75) and vitalism
(especially ll. 268-81). "Carlylese," the author's eccentric, alliterative
language studded with animal and naturalist imagery, is especially evi-
dent in ll. 254-62. See n. following and *Sartor Resartus*, Book II, chapter
9, "The Everlasting Yea," and Book III, chapter 8, "Natural Supernatu-
ralism," for the sorts of Carlylean arguments expressed in Carlylese
that B is imitating here.

254-64]   *Let* . . . *All-incomplete*   This poetic evocation of the orders
and ranks of insentient nature is a splendid evocation of natural su-
pernaturalism and its search for the way that human consciousness

and imagination crown the created world and reach beyond to a higher consciousness. In his quest for enlightenment and certainty B's Carlylean speaker interestingly invokes B's own esthetic and moral doctrine of the *incomplete,* but without B's positive associations with the concept.

301-9] *Prometheus . . . sight* Prometheus' theft of fire from the gods to aid mankind's progress is a favorite myth among poets and prose writers, especially in the Romantic period, when the Promethean rebel had special historical and imaginative resonance. B's incorporation of a magnifying glass both to focus the sun's rays and to focus and enlarge the message of his myth is an anachronism but one typical of nineteenth-century adaptations of the Prometheus myth; see, for example, Shelley's *Prometheus Unbound* (1820) and EBB's translation of Aeschylus's *Prometheus Bound,* published in *Prometheus Bound and Other Poems* (1833).

318] *Little* An intended echo of "little" in l. 304 above, but without the macrocosmic sense of that line; here the stubbornly worldly "less is more" moral of "Andrea de Sarto" is invoked.

WITH DANIEL BARTOLI

Sources and Backgrounds] Daniel Bartoli's *De' Simboli Transportati al Morale,* originally published in the seventeenth century, was edited and reissued by B's Italian tutor Angelo Cerutti in 1830 and studied by B as a model for Italian prose. Cerutti's lively teaching style and his influence on the young B are detailed by Maynard (*B's Youth,* 304-7); teacher and pupil were apparently very compatible in their temperaments and their enthusiasm for literature. B must have known Cerutti's edition of Bartoli well; it was with him on his first and second trips to Italy in 1838 and 1844 and it was in the inner cover of *De' Simboli* that he wrote "How They Brought the Good News from Ghent to Aix" and "Home-Thoughts, from the Sea" in 1844. B owned two copies of *De' Simboli*; see *Reconstruction,* A167, 168.

Daniel Bartoli (1609-85) was a Jesuit scholar whose writings, together with those of other Jesuits during the counter-Reformation of the later sixteenth and early seventeenth century, were a major instrument in the revitalization and reform of the Roman Catholic Church. Bartoli's three-volume treatise offers many learned examples of the wonders of history and creation. Some of the curiosities in Bartoli's examples from classical and natural history must have held interest for B, but apparently he did not revisit his source for the brief anecdote that he represents as Bartoli's, Saint Scholastica taming the lion (ll. 245-50). Indeed the saint's name (surely a *nom de plume* for the pedantic Bartoli himself), and the generic miracle suggesting yet another Christian martyrdom played out, seem intended to be taken as parodic.

While Cerutti and his pupil apparently respected Bartoli's style, neither apparently held Bartoli's content in the same esteem. B included an editorial note by Cerutti in his parleying which acknowledged the "intolerable nuisance" of Bartoli's long-windedness, his superstition, and his relentless moralizing. Bartoli's *De' Simboli* is thus merely the occasion for this parleying, and the poem does not require a close acquaintance with the source.

"With Daniel Bartoli" is almost pure narrative, its dialogue dramatic, not discursive. The parleying falls into a three-part structure, each section typologically distinct, each employing a different style of expression. The three effects and their relative weight are introduced in the first stanza: poetry, history, and legend. The poet invokes "historians' skill" in behalf of his art, and proceeds to demonstrate history's superiority to legend by telling the story of Marianne Pajot, a beautiful woman of lowly birth who refused a duke's proposal of marriage because there were dishonorable conditions attached. This tale is then contrasted to a brief conventional saint's tale, which is in turn followed by a vituperative episode dealing with the duke's romantic history after Marianne's rejection. The tone of the latter passage is strikingly harsh, and it is likely that B's anxieties over a proposal of marriage to Louisa Lady Ashburton in 1869 joined forces with his story at this point.

The main narrative of the parleying derives from sources favored by B. Led by a condensed account of the story of Marianne Pajot in the life of Charles, Duke of Lorraine, in the *Biographie Universelle*, to the fuller version in the *Memoires* of the Marquis de Lassay (1756), and to the *Causerie* on de Lassay in Sainte-Beuve's *Causeries* (1851-70), B worked again some of the same materials he had used in "Colombe's Birthday" (1844), "The Glove" (1845), and "The Flight of the Duchess" (1845). But while the conflict between love and honor are similar in all the adaptations of the source, in the parleying the manipulative role and speechifying of the evil minister dominate, emphasizing still more than formerly the intuitive courage and insight of the innocent, defenseless Marianne and her ability to cut through hypocrisy and guile and to act unhesitatingly.

Marianne's sacrifice of wealth and her refusal to sacrifice honor, her marriage to a suitor who loves her for that honor, and the duke's failure to honor her memory, form a chain of events in the story linked to B's life as well as to his work. Unlike the fickle, forsworn duke, B narrowly escaped a "bold she-shape" (l. 287) in the person of Louisa Lady Ashburton. Many of the details of this experience remain speculative for biographers and editors of the letters, but the available evidence and its implications are recounted in Hood, Appendix, 325-38, and in Irvine and Honan, Chapter 24, "Some Faint Show of Bigamy," 443-70.

Whatever autobiographical references and parallels there may be in this parleying among the chronicle, the legend, and the personal history of the poet, within the collection it is one of the freest in its uses of its title source. Revisions to the MS suggest attempts to foreground Bartoli more decisively. An original title is illegibly erased, and further revisions within the poem were made either to justify a revised title, or to remind the reader of Bartoli's importance to the poem. See textual variants ll. 1, 239.

B's Footnote]   *'Fu Gesuita . . . avanti'* The quotation is taken directly from Cerutti's editorial preface to the *Simboli*; see *Sources* above. "He was a Jesuit and a historian of the Society; so that he wrote voluminous histories, that would be read if they were not filled to overflowing with all kinds of superstitions . . . He has stuffed them so full of unbelievable miracles, that it becomes an unbearably boring experience to anyone who would want to read those histories: and even I do not have enough desire or energy to continue farther."

1]   *Don* Bartoli. From being a signifier of rank in Spanish usage, the term Don became a generalized title of courtesy and respect in Italy, particularly applied to priests and teachers. B would have called Cerutti "Don." MS replaces "Sir" with *Don*, perhaps, as DeVane argues, when B changed the addressee of the poem from another figure to Bartoli (De Vane, *Hbk.*, 501). The revision seems less a change of address, however, than an added emphasis on the instructive role of the teacher-subject, in preparation for the role reversal to be assumed by the pupil-speaker.

2]   *saints . . . talked* B's talks were with his tutor Cerutti, not Bartoli. This conflation of identities and temporalities is typical of the treatment of "certain people of importance in their day" in *Parleyings*.

3]   *My saint* Marianne Pajot, the heroine of the story to follow.

4-5]   *pity . . . chronicle* The contrast between historical truth (*chronicle*) and undocumented legend introduces the tale to follow, drawn largely from the *Memoires* of the Marquis de Lassay (1756) and from the *Biographie Universelle*, both distinguished *chronicles* (see *B's Parleyings*, 63). The unrevised reading of l. 4 was "'Tis pity poets lack historians' skill," a reading which makes more immediate sense than B's revision *lack* to *need*.

6-13]   *lord . . . kingship*   Like a number of other powerful nobles of
the period, the Duke of Lorraine, a former ally of Spain and enemy of
Louis XIV, forfeited large territories to the French king in the Treaty
of the Pyrenees (1659), after which Louis established his reputation as
absolute monarch (*craver of Kingship*) in the most powerful country in
Europe. Louis XIV's long and prosperous reign (1643-1713) was in
large part due to the ambition and skill of two illustrious clerics, Car-
dinal Richelieu and Cardinal Mazarin, and it was a representative of
Cardinal Mazarin, Michel le Tellier, who acted as *the king's minister* in
the story of Marianne and the Duke.

13-15]   *"Let . . . devil*   "Unto every one that hath shall be given,
and he shall have abundance: but from him that hath not shall be
taken away even that which he hath" (Matt. 25:29). But B reminds us in
an oblique allusion to Shakespeare's *The Merchant of Venice* that "The
devil can cite Scripture for his purpose," as Antonio says of Shylock
(1.3.99), and as the demonic minister does here.

17]   *Duchess herself*   The Duchess of Orleans, an ally of the king
rather than of her brother.

24-34]   *a girl . . . you*   Marianne Pujot was a commoner and the
daughter of an apothecary, a detail found only in the *Biographie Uni-
verselle* account. Druggists often served as doctors before the advance
of medical science in the seventeenth century, and Marianne's father
was apothecary to the Duchess's husband, hence Marianne's presence
at court. *Manna and senna* are medicinal herbs; *manna* was used as a
laxative, *senna* as an emetic.

27-30]   *pearl . . . costly*   Possible references to both Matt. 13:46 and
7:6. Marianne is a pearl of great price, but a pearl cast before swine,
who can only regard her as fake.

40-41]   *state . . . license*   One of several references in the poem to
the concept of *droit du seigneur,* the feudal allowance for sexual ad-
vances conceded to nobility; see ll. 67-75 and 133 and n. *State* here
means "rank." Presumably the duke's sister, who has made a political
marriage, knows whereof she speaks.

42]   *rate*   Scold.

48-50]   *contract . . . rite*   This contract appears to be the proposal
and its acceptance. There was also a marriage contract stating the
terms of the treaty between the duke and the king and barring the suc-
cession of children to the duke's property. The banns published be-
fore an intended marriage were announcements for the purpose of
bringing forward any evidence which might forbid the marriage. They
were published three times, usually on successive Sundays, before the
ceremony.

58-77]   *He smiled . . . smiled he*   B frames the duke's speech contrasting written and unwritten law with God's law and the lovers' *vow* by a signal (*he smiled*) that his categories are facile and self-serving. He is more naive than his bride. The duke was much older than Marianne and had heard this advice more than once (*Long ago / 'Twas rounded in my ears*) in connection with two former marriages to women of nobility, one of whom was still living (see the passage quoted from de Lassay in *B's Parleyings*, 76, n.59). While these facts remain only a subtext in the poem, B does appear to suggest them.

78]   *minister*   Le Tellier; see ll. 6-13n.

85]   *upstart . . . sun-absorbed*   The imagery contrasts the folk image "ignis fatuus" or will o' the wisp, an atmospheric phenomenon manifested as a moving phosphorescent light seen after dark on marshy ground and superstitiously supposed to be a temptation to destruction, with the divine light of the Sun-King, the "solar monarch" (l. 91).

91]   *solar monarch's* Louis XIV was called the Sun-King, a designation reflecting his claim to divine right and the splendor of his long reign (1643-1715). Louis shed his light on the arts, of which he was a great patron, and basked in turn in their reflected light: during his reign Versailles was built; the French Academy established French as the language of culture and diplomacy in Europe; and science and literature flourished.

96-98]   *contract . . . contract*   "Pari passu" means "with equal step." The Latin expression signifies divergent schemes moving at the same pace. The minister suggests that rather than forbidding the marriage, the king can make the two contracts compatible.

105]   *mulct . . . amercing*   Tit for tat. If the king forbids the marriage, the duke will not forfeit the dukedoms.

133]   *body's deference*   The minister, having announced that he is "mouthpiece" for the king (l. 129) and banished all the company at the banquet, reassures them that he means no violation of the duke's or the lady's honor; see ll. 40-41n.

150]   *footstool*   The image is used repeatedly in the Bible. Isa. 66:1 is representative: "Thus saith the Lord, The heaven is my throne, and the earth is my footstool. " The minister reminds Marianne of the principle of divine right.

156]   *for the nonce*   For the specific purpose (of showing good faith in valuing his marriage over worldly goods).

157]   *prevent . . . slip*   The minister slyly implies a double meaning, one polite and one imperious: "Let us not let slip by an occasion so propitious," and "Let us forestall a potential heir's claim on the dukedoms."

158] *actual* Present.

161] *down . . . bar* All hindrances and social distinctions are removed.

163] *druggist's daughter* See above, l. 24n.

166] *heaven . . . poet-sort* A stock line in a generic poem of praise to a generous patron. The glories of Louis XIV and his court were widely sung.

172-75] *Companionless . . . seclusion* Marianne will be shut up in a convent.

176] *scepter threats* Marianne is reminded again of the king's absolute power (*threats*: threatens).

182, 184] *his spouse . . . your duchess* The ceremony has not yet been performed, but the wedding day marks the beginning of Marianne's role as wife.

186-88] *myself . . . potency* Marianne paraphrases the marriage vows. She, like the duke, would sacrifice anything for love, from *pelf* (property) to power.

188-90] *What . . . now* Hypothetical future misfortune (*fortune*: fate) and choice have become a present reality.

194-95] *Never . . . him* These lines and this moment are the realization of Marianne's sainthood in the poem, as promised above l. 3. Marianne's unhesitating rejection of the minister's proposal paraphrases a lesson familiar in the New Testament, that to save one's soul one must renounce the temptations of the world. "For whosoever will save his life shall lose it. . . . For what is a man profited, if he shall gain the whole world, and lose his own soul?" (Matt. 16:25-26) The Christian paradox is further strained by the duke's circumstances: his honor and good name now depend, not on his renouncing his dukedoms, but on his not renouncing them. Now it is Marianne's youth and beauty which represent the temptation to sell his soul, and she is quick to recognize and reject the analogy between the two modes of possession.

201] *yet . . . yet* B sharpened the contrast between the form and meaning of the marriage ceremony by revising MS *late my husband* to *still* and finally to *yet*. Both yets mean "still," but the repetition reinforces the irony of the line: he is still her husband as long as he is still the man she loves.

211-12] *Husband . . . duke* As above, Marianne emphasizes the fall from the meaning of one title to the mere form of the other.

221-29] *boy . . . wed* The Marquis de Lassay, whose *Memoires* were a primary source for this parleying (see *Sources* above), was fifteen years old in the *Biographie Universelle* version of the story and in his own

Memoires; he is ten in Saint-Beuve's *Causeries*. The couple were *wed* in 1673, more than ten years after the story takes place.

233-34]   *exquisite* . . . *obscurity*   De Lassay's obscurity was not so complete as the passage implies; he remained a soldier and completed a campaign during the five years that he and Marianne were married; she died in 1678. But this account of exile, obscurity, and happiness well characterizes B's own experience of marriage. On 24 November 1846, during the early months of marriage to EBB, he wrote from Pisa, "I cannot imagine any condition of life, however full of hardship, which her presence would not render not merely supportable but delicious. It is nothing to say that my whole life shall be devoted to such a woman,—its only happiness will consist in such devotion." EBB's version of their seclusion during that period was wryly different. She wrote on 26 December 1846, "I might as well almost . . . be shut up in my old room—so very, very quiet we are" (*Correspondence*, 14.57, 92).

236]   *as sun, so moon*   The king was the sun, Marianne the moon.

238-44]   *saintship* . . . *game*   A *trick* is a fashion of dress; *scourge* signifies a flagellant style of religious self-discipline. The bereaved husband first tries *monkhood* and a religious conversion, then converts back to the world. Saul's conversion on the road to Damascus is described in Acts 9:5: "And the Lord said, I am Jesus whom thou persecutest: it is hard for thee to kick against the pricks" (i.e., to resist your fate). De Lassay tried the *scourge* but left it for the *pricks perverse* of *Life's game*—*perverse* in the sense of "turning away"; pricks are goads for animals. B again suggests the inferiority of Bartoli's brand of *saintship* to the worldly *sort.*

245]   *Saint Scholastica*   There is no saint by this name in Bartoli. B probably chose the name *Scholastica* because it suggested the pedantry of Bartoli's learning. In MS the name is crowded into a space too small for it, apparently added in revision.

246, 249]   *Paynimrie* . . . *Soldan*   Non-Christian (especially Mohammedan), or pagan, lands; Sultan. The quaint diction further emphasizes the stuffy learning of the invented anecdote.

248-49]   *girdle* . . . *leashed*   "My God hath sent his angel, and hath shut the lion's mouth" (Dan. 6:22). The anecdote parallels Marianne's refusal to be tamed, silenced or led by the Duke's collar of jewels at ll. 215-18; the girdle and necklace are details symbolizing the difference between legend and chronicle (see ll. 260 and l. 5n.).

254]   *dance the hays*   An expression meaning "to live merrily, energetically"; the hay or hays was a lively rustic dance.

256]   *sun's*   The king's.

271]   *doat*   variant of "dote."

273]   *Trogalia . . . Greeks*   The word is Greek for after-dinner fruits or nuts; as used in Aristophanes it connotes fastidious appetite.

276-342]   *"Who bade you . . . the cock's crow."*   The last two sections (XVII-XVIII) of the poem are obliquely confessional on B's part. The Duke's romantic history after Marianne left him, and the Duke's mocking epitaph ("Here lies he among the false to Love—" l. 295), evoke B's own ill-fated consideration of marriage to Lady Ashburton; see *Sources,* above. Although the unfortunate proposal took place in 1869, some sixteen years before this passage was written, the tone of the thinly veiled reference suggests that the mixed guilt and accusatory scorn felt by B over the episode had not dimmed. The idealization of Marianne and, implicitly, of EBB is also clear. B called EBB "my moon of poets" and often used this image to evoke her "effulgence" (l. 286).

290-92]   *coils . . . trophy*   The description of the triumphant "she-shape" evokes the iconography of the engraving of Carravaggio's Perseus and Andromeda which hung over B's desk throughout his early career (Orr, 21; see Plate 2). The picture is both invoked and inverted; the coiling serpent does not cower under Perseus' lance and foot, but towers over him and tramples her victim.

295-320]   *'Here . . . defender'*   The speech imagines the mocking epitaph and infamy left behind by the shamed duke. Described in the imagery of chivalric combat, the passage casts the duke as a champion defending his faith against a false challenger who *picked up our giant's glove* (signal of challenge to a knight). Although he was a giant and an eagle (in Christian art and in heraldry the eagle is symbolic of honor and strength), he was easily felled in this unfair fencing match, not by the *old pretence* (in the sense of all-too-familiar pretension, claim to power) of *virtue, wisdom, beauty,* but by the concealed weapon of impudence. Lady Ashburton, like the Duke's wooer, was an *iconoclast,* a breaker of sacred images on the *altar* of his *Past* because she perhaps wished or hoped to replace them with her own image. Despite the temptation, the duke would have been above male susceptibility; he would have been *his kind's superior* in resisting her, but for her *impudence.* The convoluted syntax of the long first sentence of this embedded dialogue, with its central conditional clause (*had it chanced . . .*) and ensuing negative and positive subjunctives (*hardly had he purged . . . ; Promptly had he abjured . . .*) mirrors the rationalization and self-deception of the fickle duke, and the self-accusatory irony of the speaker.

317-24]   *imperious stature . . . black*   Lady Ashburton was tall and dark.

332-33]   *match . . . Venus*   The myth of the birth of Venus from *sea-foam* is most famously depicted by Botticelli, where innocence and modesty accompany blond beauty in a way opposite to the other woman's looks and tactics here. *match* has the double sense of adversary, and mate. B would have seen Botticelli's painting in the Uffizi Gallery in Florence.

335]   *Samson*   The story of Samson, one of the judges of Israel, is found in Judg. 13-16. Samson's great strength lay in his long hair, a secret which God required that he divulge to no one. Beguiled by the beautiful Delilah, a "she-shape," he revealed the source of his strength, whereupon she cut his hair while he slept. When he awakened he found that God had departed from him. Nevertheless, when the crucial time came, his strength returned to destroy his oppressors.

341-42]   *Morn-star . . . cock's crow*   In Christian tradition the morning star is associated with regeneration and with the Divinity: "I Jesus have sent mine angel to testify unto you these things in the Churches. I am the root, and the offspring of David, and the bright and morning star" (Rev. 22:16). In popular belief ghosts were obliged to disappear at dawn, at *cock's crow*, following the appearance of the morning star. The duke's ghost awaits resurrection rather than banishment.

WITH CHRISTOPHER SMART

Sources and Backgrounds]   The eighteenth-century English poet Christopher Smart (1722-71) is best known for two works, "A Song to David" and "Jubilate Agno," and for the unhappy circumstances of poverty and mental unbalance in which he produced them. "Jubilate Agno" was not published until 1939 and was thus unknown to B. "A Song to David" was published in two editions in Smart's lifetime, in 1763 and 1765, but was suppressed in the collected edition of his work in 1791, and did not appear again until 1819, in a pamphlet publication accompanied by notes incorporating the legend which began with its first reviewer in 1765, that Smart scratched the poem on the wall of his asylum with a key. It was in a second edition (1827) of this pamphlet publication that B first read "A Song to David." B subsequently sought out other works of the poet, with great disappointment and mystification at the stark contrast between the inspiration and style of "Song" and Smart's other work. This incongruity, with B's analysis of its causes and proposed resolution, became the prevailing theme of his parleying with Smart.

The facts of the life and work of Smart correspond roughly to B's version in this parleying. After a precocious and promising youth and education at Cambridge, Smart declined into mediocrity, deep unhappiness, impoverishment, and finally madness in the last two decades of his life. Yet it was during a period of confinement in Bethnal Green asylum in 1763 that Smart wrote his greatest work, "A Song to David." The poem consists of 516 lines in 86 stanzas celebrating and imitating the Biblical Psalms, their catalogue of God's creation, and the wonder that their author King David inspires towards the created world. The historical context of Smart's major poem illuminates its tone and theme. "A Song to David" is in part a response to a Davidian controversy cresting in the early 1760s between denigrators and defenders of David's personal character and life. In his biography of Smart, Arthur Sherbo usefully summarizes the controversy and agrees with other scholars that "A Song to David" derives from this active and widely voiced polemic (*Christopher Smart: Scholar of the University*, [Ann Arbor, 1967], 172-74).

From the beginning "A Song to David" left a strong impression on B, and it confirms the strength of this impression that he seems to have returned to Smart's poem in the earliest stages of courtship of EBB. He had by 1844 lost track of his own copy and reread the poem in *Chambers's Encyclopædia*, a newly published and popular compendium of the time. Writing to Furnivall after the publication of *Parleyings*, B remembered two telling associations with this rereading, that he "was struck by more than one gross blunder" in the editing and that he "discovered it there on an occasion that would excuse much mistiness in my memory" (2 and 4 March 1887). The simultaneous clarity and mistiness of B's memory of his rereading of "A Song to David" are not so inconsistent as might appear; both associations reveal B's early and deep emotional response to the poem. DeVane links the similar images of a suddenly revealed chapel in the first of the courtship letters (10 January 1845), and in the parleying (Section III) written 45 years later, as evidence of the deep and persisting effect that "A Song to David" had on B (*B's Parleyings*, 105-6).

In view of his enduring reverence for "A Song to David," it is not remarkable that B's memory of the poem remained sharp without a copy at hand. After the publication of *Parleyings*, in a letter of 2 March 1887, B asks Furnivall to locate a copy of "Song" in the British Museum Library, suggesting to him that the Browning Society reprint the poem. For the writing of the parleying, however, B could rely on a memory strong enough in the 1880s to recite it: whole "stanzas I could repeat— as I did—with all the effect I supposed would follow—to people of authority enough—Tennyson, the present Bishop of London—and—last year to Wendell Holmes." We do not know which stanzas these were, but perhaps they were among the concluding ones of the poem, to which reference seems to be made in this parleying (see ll. 195-96 and n.) and in an earlier poem, "Abt Vogler" (l. 95).

LXXVI
Strong is the lion—like a coal
His eye-ball—like a bastion's mole
    His chest against the foes:
Strong, the gier-eagle on his sail
Strong against tide, th'enormous whale
    Emerges as he goes.

                    .   .   .

LXXXVI
Glorious—more glorious is the crown
Of Him that brought salvation down
    By meekness, call'd thy Son;
Thou at stupendous truth believ'd,
And now the matchless deed's atchiev'd,
    DETERMINED, DARED, and DONE.

The isolation of "A Song to David" in Smart's career, and Smart's own isolation in his literary generation, are the larger themes of B's parleying and the link that B forged between Smart's and his own time. For B, Smart offered a perspective on a period of history and intellectual transformation that B construed as transferable from the eighteenth to the nineteenth century, a perspective that was the more reliable to him for being unacceptable to his own generation. Perhaps B felt some potential affinity with Smart's lone voice raving to the madhouse walls of his all-too-sane century, writing, with a key to freedom in his grasp, a message illegible to his contemporaries. Perhaps B felt his own esthetic and philosophic position between the estheticism and scientific positivism of his own generation to be comparable to Smart's mismatch with the Enlightenment and its art. The Browning Societies may have cast him as their prophet, but B draws a parallel between his situation and Smart's in Section IX of the parleying.

4-6] *soul's . . . fancy* B prepares for his exploration of Smart's visionary masterwork "A Song to David" and of its singularity in Smart's career by evoking B's own youthful discovery of Smart, before his full judgment and appreciation were formed: both poets were led by a form of divine revelation.

7] *Song* Smart's "A Song to David." The word *Song* has implications of pure lyric, inspired and inspirational poetry, beside which other poetry, including B's own, is "prose."

11] *boyishness* B is writing nearly fifty years after first reading "A Song to David."

18] *complacently* With pleasure (*OED*).

22-23] *Golden . . . rule* The Latin poet Horace's "aurea mediocritas" or Golden Mean (*Odes*, 2.10.5) is a rule of order and moderation. Horace was taught and held as a model in the eighteenth century; although Smart translated Horace (see l. 181n. below), his own work violated Horace's rule and outraged his eighteenth century audience. B first knew Smart through his translation of Horace, a book he owned (*Reconstruction*, A2147)— an ironic introduction, in view of the contrast that B dramatizes here.

brave In two senses, "colorful," and "courageous."

26] *mediocrity* In the sense of the "aurea mediocritas" above; not pejorative in the usual sense.

36] *Chapel* A great house built before the Reformation would have included a private chapel. Here the description to follow seems to owe more to a model such as the Sistine chapel than to a simple altar for family worship. George Ridenour proposed that the chapel passage drew inspiration from Byron's "Childe Harold's Pilgrimage," 4.155-63, in which a similar effect of wonder toward the Sistine chapel is developed ("Browning's Music Poems: Fancy and Fact," *PMLA*, 68 [1963], 370). As John Maynard has argued, the influence of B's "most serious boyhood idol, Byron" has been underrated (*B's Youth*, 175).

40-60] *Rafael . . . theirs* The setting is a shrine to the Madonna, its centerpiece a painting by Raphael (1483-1520), held by many to be the greatest painter of the High Renaissance.

fronted Confronted.

Art's divine Art's divining, divination.

shapes never wed . . . earth's despair Art's ability to redeem disillusion by marrying its idealizing vision to *earth's despair.*

Raphael's painting here signals the narrator's sudden emergence from the eighteenth century into the sixteenth, and the lesson of Raphael and of Smart that great genius is transhistorical, belonging to no one era. B's invocation of Raphael may also suggest his dislike of the Pre-Raphaelite movement and its rejection of esthetic traditions represented in Victorian England by the Royal Academy (where Pen had had a painting accepted for exhibition) and the Academy's reverence for Renaissance conventions as embodied in Raphael. B's reverence for Raphael is expressed elsewhere as well, notably in Caponsacchi's visionary discovery of his mission to rescue Pompilia in *The Ring and the Book*, 8.396-402. B would have known well two of Raphael's madonnas in the Pitti Palace in Florence, the "Madonna del Baldacchino" and the "Madonna del Gran Duca." See also the poems "Andrea del Sarto" and "One Word More" in Vol. 6 of this edition, 7, 141, and nn. 379, 418-19.

74] *placid* Pleasing (*OED*).

78-84] *smoke . . . untransfigured man* Without direct allusion, the imagery and language of this passage is strongly reminiscent of Biblical accounts of miraculous human ascent to heaven or divine manifestation on earth. Fire is often a symbol of divine inspiration and visitation in the Bible. See especially God's voice in the burning bush to Moses (Exod. 3.2); the chariot of fire and whirlwind which took Elijah to heaven (2 Kings 2.11); the descent of the Holy Spirit on the disciples as tongues of fire (Acts 2.2-3); and the transfiguration of Christ, who after a brief period of glory returned to his human state, descended the mountain, and turned toward Jerusalem, where he was to meet his death (Matt. 17.2).

87-103] *Now . . . poet-pair* In response to an inquiry by John Nettleship, B revised this passage slightly in a letter of Aug. 31, 1889 (*N&Q*, NS 17 [Jan. 1970], 23).

90-91] *Rafael . . . Watts* With Raphael, Michelangelo (1475-1564) exemplified the highest achievement of the Renaissance. Frederick Leighton (1830-96) and George Watts (1817-1904) were English painters and sculptors, and also friends of B's; they were not associated with the pre-Raphaelite movement. Leighton was elected president of the Royal Academy in 1878. He had painted B's portrait in 1859 and designed EBB's tomb in Florence.

94] *flute-breath . . . trumpet-clang* The trumpet and flute are traditionally contrasted as naturally expressive of differing kinds of emotion; see, for example, Dryden's "A Song for St. Cecilia's Day": "The trumpet's loud clangor/Excites us to arms,/With shrill notes of anger/And mortal alarms . . . . The soft complaining flute/In dying notes discovers/The woes of hopeless lovers" (3,4). Here Milton's oratorical strength and Keats' lyric intensity seem to be the referents.

96-97] *Milton . . . point* Presented as the link and sole bright spot between John Milton (1608-74) and John Keats (1795-1821), Smart here is made to reflect a belief common among critics of B's time about the inferiority of the poetry of the eighteenth century.

affinity on just one point: connection through Smart's one peak of achievement. Despite B's praise, "A Song to David" is not Miltonic except for its theme; Smart's deliberately Miltonic verse, written after the

"Song," is generally held to be among his inferior work. Toward Keats B felt from an early age "a lifelong interest" and a kinship closer even than with Shelley (*B's Youth*, 195). Writing to EBB in May 1846, B spoke of meeting Severn, who was with Keats during his final journey to Rome and death there. "Severn, I saw . . . Keats' Severn, who brought his own posthumous picture of Keats, and talked pleasantly about him" (*Correspondence*, 12.325). B's construction of a poetic archetype in "Popularity" is his best known comment on Keats (see Vol. 6.119 of this edition).

106-10] *sphere . . . superimposure* In poetic usage the word *sphere* is often a synonym for heaven, and the passage appears to refer to the rare and difficult contact between poetry and divinity. The enigmatic imagery of cube and sphere may derive from the well-known Euclidian proof of the impossibility of squaring the circle, or here, the impossibility of cubing the sphere.

110-12] *success . . . singing-dress* See 96-97n.

113-17] *screen . . . truth* The thought and imagery of this passage are Shelleyan. Cf. "A Defence of Poetry": "A poem is the very image of life expressed in its eternal truth." "The mind in creation is as a fading coal which some invisible influence, like an inconstant wind, awakens to transitory brightness: the power arises from within . . . ." See also Isa. 6.6: "Then flew one of the seraphim unto me, having a live coal in his hand, which he had taken with the tongs from off the altar."

119-20] *blaze . . . Hayley* The poet and biographer William Hayley (1745-1820), whose works were called by Byron, "for ever feeble and for ever tame." Hayley was a patron of Blake's, who illustrated a volume of Hayley's ballads, but Hayley failed utterly to understand Blake's visionary works. Of Hayley Blake wrote, "Thy friendship oft has made my heart to ache; / Do be my Enemy for Friendship's sake." Smart's best work was similarly misunderstood by even his best friends. The depiction of Smart as meteor-like against the darkness of eighteenth-century poetry as personified by Hayley may be an ironically punning reference to Halley's comet, a celebrated observation by the eighteenth-century astronomer William Halley.

121-22] *dead . . . dead* "Let their dead bury their dead" (Matt. 8:22).

124-39] *suppose . . . explained* "Let us assume for the moment that I might chance to be unaware of the common diagnosis that the 'Song' was a dangerous aberration of an unhealthy brain; how else might we explain the singularity of this poem in Smart's career?" The point of the passage is the facile dismissal of genius by ordinary minds. Smart's doctors' view was held in common even by Smart's supporters.

Christopher Hunter, Smart's nephew, published a collection of Smart's poems in 1791, lamenting in the preface, "These [poems after 1763] were written after his confinement and bear for the most part melancholy proof of the recent estrangement of his mind." "A Song to David" was suppressed in the collection.

135]   *prose*   Smart wrote essays and reviews as well as poetry, but here the reference may be to pedestrian versifying, as opposed to the lyric fire of "A Song to David."

147-51]   *revealed . . . language*   "And he that sat upon the throne said, Behold, I make all things new. And he said unto me, Write: for these words are true and faithful" (Rev. 21:5). The section containing this allusion has as a whole the prophetic tone of the book of Revelation.

151-56]   *heaven's vault . . . below*   The panoramic view of heaven and earth and the sharp particularity of the images in these lines echo Smart's language in the "Song to David."

    pompous: magnificent. Smart uses the word in the same sense: "The Pheasant shows his pompous neck" (l. 367).

153]   *swilled*   Drenched.

156-62]   *name . . . dissident*   "And out of the ground the Lord God formed every beast of the field, and every fowl of the air; and brought them unto Adam to see what he would call them: and whatsoever Adam called every living creature, that was the name thereof" (Gen. 2:19). Man, in his function as the crown of ordered creation, is the namer. *Design* is here the manifestation of the Creator. The argument from design is one of the arguments for a divine creator, and was used both against eighteenth-century skeptical rationalists, and against nineteenth-century Darwinian evolutionists. B would have included among *the many dissident* a wide range of doubters and unbelievers, against whom Smart and B ("your thought and mine") both as believers and as artists are ranged.

175-77]   *scribble . . . wainscot*   The legend that Smart scratched the "Song" on the wainscot of his cell began with the first review of the poem, by John Lanhorne in the *Monthly Review* of April 1763. The review calls the poem "irregularly great" and ends with the famous reference to Smart's madness: "It would be cruel, however, to insist on the slight defects and singularities of this piece, for many reasons; and more especially, if it be true, as we are informed, that it was written when the Author was denied the use of pen, ink, and paper, and was obliged to indent his lines, with the end of a key, upon the wainscot" (Sherbo, *Christopher Smart,* [1967], 168-69). The legend made its way verbatim into notes in later editions of "A Song to David," including the edition of 1827 in which B first read the poem. The generally positive tone of Lanhorne's review may lend credibility to the legend, since it is not used to dismiss the poem out of hand, as the speaker in B's lines does.

179-81]   *lopped . . . Horace*   From classical times the crown of bay leaves has symbolized genius; the symbolism derives from the legend that Apollo, god of music and poetry, transformed Daphne into a bay tree when she rejected him. Here the reference is to the eighteenth century's reverence for the classics and for Horace's esthetics, and to Hunter's omission of "A Song to David" from the collected edition of Smart's works in 1791 (see *Sources* above). B was given Smart's translation of Horace's works by his uncle in 1824 (*Reconstruction*, A2147).

182-83]   *never . . . line*   Smart continued to write and publish both prose and poetry after 1763 until his death in 1771, and it was mainly this later work which B first knew and describes in the opening of this parleying. See ll. 23-24 and n.

183 *paced the sward*   I.e., as a free man.

185-86]   *judged . . . fancy*   The words *judged* and *fancy*, commonly contrasted in sense and connotation, are here used more or less synonymously and pejoratively; *fancy* has the sense of "notion." The terms introduce a rhetorical question ending l. 195, to which the answer is, *I know / Full well you never had the fancy*.

185-265]   *Was . . . concern*   Section IX develops a rationale for Smart's lapse from the inspired poetry of the "Song," proposing a progression from his lyric achievement to the narrowly religious works after "A Song to David." Two contrasting hypotheses are introduced by the parallel structure of ll. 185 and 201, the first false and the second true: "Was it because you judged that merely (*thus ever and thus only*, l. 188) cataloguing and describing each strength and beauty of creation was sufficient?" (No) "Or was it because you judged that strength and beauty are means and that teaching should complete their lesson?" (Yes).

195-200]   *So . . . purpling*   Strength and beauty are particularized in the images of leviathan, in the Bible a symbol of the majesty of creation, and of the purple clematis, a climbing plant called Virgin's Bower which has a star-shaped flower and whose seeds are propelled by feathery vessels.

faint off   Fade before producing seed. Cf. "Song," ll. 155-56, "Strong against tide, th'enormous whale / Emerges as he goes" and "there is that leviathan, whom thou hast made to play therein" (Ps. 104:26). B's garden at Warwick Crescent was transformed in the early 1880s with the help of his friend Mrs. Thomas Fitzgerald, and his writing desk overlooked the garden. He wrote to her 3 June 1882, "I wish you could see our little glory of a garden: I never thought that so much display could come out of shrubs planted a few months ago . . . it is amusing to hear S[arianna] and myself agree that we shall miss nothing so much in any new abode as that garden which, for so many years, we ignored the possibility of getting any good out of" (*Learned Lady: Letters from Robert Browning to Mrs. Thomas Fitzgerald*, ed. Edward McAleer [Cambridge, MA, 1966], 135-36).

199] *prose* The word choice reflects both self-deprecation by B and a Victorian sense of the eighteenth century as an age of reason and prose; prose should be taken in the sense of "prosy discourse" (*OED*), commonplace utterance, which by comparison with "Song" B designates both his poem and Smart's later writing, much of which was verse.

207] *proseman* See l. 199n. above.

211] *teaching* Among Smart's published works after "A Song to David" were odes, oratorios, translations of the Psalms and of Horace, and verse settings of parables for children, none more overtly didactic than "Song." B departs from the biographical evidence to make his point about the moral progression of the soul from strength and beauty to truth.

214-15] *Man . . . little* The double negatives connote evasion of immediate reality in the search for knowledge. Smart's lyric vision is presented as a corrective to this evasion.

240-47] *other . . . ladder-top* Here B turns from what he seems to have regarded categorically (and mistakenly) as the pagan estheticism of the Pre-Raphaelites to the other extreme of the Victorian age, its transferal of faith from religion to science. While this passage makes no direct reference to spokesmen for scientific progress and religious skepticism, it bears on a large company of influential figures whom B had read and many of whom he knew personally. B's biographers evoke the immersion in controversy which his return to London after the years in Florence effected: "Now after many years, he was steadily experiencing the discussion which makes contemporary intellectual history . . . . People were bewildered, terrified, enraged by the new theory in biology. They were alarmed and dismayed by a whole series of new books that put religious beliefs and traditional dogma into question: Darwin's *Origin of Species* was published in 1859; the multiauthored, skeptical *Essays and Reviews* in 1860, Colenso's *Critical Examination of the Pentateuch* in 1862, Renan's *Vie de Jesus* in 1863, and Strauss's *New Life of Jesus* in 1874" (Irvine and Honan, 390-91). A peroration by John Tyndall, a member of B's circle and an influential scientist, focuses the climate of Victorian controversy and the argument of the concluding lines of "With Christopher Smart": "We claim, and we shall wrest, from theology, the entire domain of cosmological theory. All schemes and systems which thus infringe upon the domain of science must . . . submit to its control, and relinquish all thought of controlling it" (address in Belfast, 1874, quoted in *B's Parleyings*, 197). It is this dogmatic tone to which B objects, and to the failure of imagination behind it. B disclaimed resistance to science, and asserted not only interest and sympathy with the exciting new discoveries, but his own earlier anticipation of evolution: "Last, about my being 'strongly against Darwi, rejecting the truths of science and regretting its advance'—you only do as I should hope and expect in disbelieving *that*. . . . In reality, all that seems *proved* in Darwin's scheme was a conception familiar to me from the beginning: see in Paracelsus the progressive development from senseless matter to organized" (B to Furnivall, 11 October 1881, *B's Trumpeter*, 34). Smart felt ambivalent admiration and dismay at Isaac Newton's influence in the eighteenth century. Similarly, B felt a kinship with evolutionary theory, but felt also that to mount an evolutionary ladder without regard for the mystery of creation was to misapply law and to misread the evidence (the pun on *rose* and *rows* ll. 244-45 embodies the parallelism).

241]   *as . . . may*   As if you might.
255]   *Offuscate*   Obfuscate; obscure (*OED*).

WITH GEORGE BUBB DODINGTON

Sources and Backgrounds]   The career of George Bubb Dodington (1691-1762) spanned the reigns of all three Hanoverian Georges. He was a member of parliament and a public figure in the major branches of government—foreign affairs, finance, the navy—from 1714 until his death. He was, however, far more ambitious than successful during much of his career, and at the time he began his diary at the age of 57 he was mainly concerned both to document what he hoped was a turning point in his flagging professional life, and to establish his reputation with the public and with posterity. The diary, published in 1784, had the opposite effect: it was read as an exposé of political corruption and an argument for electoral and parliamentary reform, rather than as a record of the career of a tireless public servant. Dodington did, however, accomplish one purpose, to record a new rise to power. He was returned to favor under George III, whose supporter he had long been, given a peerage, and returned to the cabinet as First Lord of the

Admiralty. Two copies of the 1784 edition of Dodington's Diary were in B's library. One was Robert Browning Sr.'s; B was probably introduced to it at a young age by his father. The other was bought by B, apparently to assist in the composition of this parleying, which, however, evidences no greater fidelity to its source than the other poems in the series. This latter copy is signed and dated Jan. 20. '86 on the flyleaf (*Reconstruction*, A1581).

The *Diary* begins with a lament about the onset of gout; it ends, six weeks before Dodington's death, on a wave of triumph over the cabinet appointment: "In the beginning of this year [1749] I was grievously afflicted with the first fit of the gout I ever had . . . ." "Joy Joy Joy to my Dearest Lord, this is the greatest happyness I could wish for in this life" (*The Political Journal of George Bubb Dodington*, ed. John Carswell and Lewis Dralle [Oxford, 1965], 3.441).

The fourteen years between these two entries trace highs and lows of political survival and daily life among a social and literary as well as political circle which included Henry Fielding (who dedicated the novel *Jonathan Wild the Great* [1743] to Dodington), Voltaire, Horace Walpole, Samuel Johnson, the great Whig leader William Pitt (in whose ascendancy the Tory Dodington was forced into temporary retirement), and such lesser known but illuminating presences as Dodington's American expatriate secretary James Ralph, who travelled to London with Benjamin Franklin and features conspicuously, and invidiously, in Franklin's *Autobiography*.

Many of Dodington's contemporaries found him ridiculous or dangerous or both. Lord Chesterfield, Horace Walpole, and Alexander Pope in the "Epistle to Doctor Arbuthnot," among others, made Dodington an object lesson in vanity, display, habits of intrigue, and gross physical indulgence, all of which can find confirmation in the *Diary*. But as time will have it, attention and interest have in our own time returned to the *Diary* as a rare and valuable eighteenth-century document, with the abuses it records regarded less as a mirror of the personal failings of the author than as a mirror of an age when patronage, personal alliances, and intrigue, not the electoral process, were the mainspring of politics.

It is the electoral process of his own time and its abuses which more concern B in this parleying than those of Dodington and the eighteenth century. After three Reform Bills, in 1832, 1867, and 1882, parliamentary representation and function had been transformed. In returning to Dodington and his diary, B sought a historical parallel to a portrait of Victorian political intrigue and false leadership in the person of the Tory leader Benjamin Disraeli. The reader becomes clearly aware that Dodington is but a stalking-horse, yet the real target of the satire remains unnamed. This anonymity of the primary target of the parleying lends it an odd effect of intensity combined with obscurity, and the anachronistic dialogue between Disraeli and Dodington in section V and after is confusing in more than one way, both as convoluted quotation-within-quotation, and as the superimposition of one political exercise on another.

B apparently told Mrs. Orr that Disraeli was the elusive target of his parleying, but she does not elaborate beyond the following comment: "he finds the natural contrast to the half-successful schemer in the wholly triumphant one: and the second picture, like the first, has been drawn from life. It is that of the late Lord Beaconsfield—as Mr. Browning sees him" (Orr, 351).

Furnivall had encouraged B as early as March, 1879 to make poetic use of Disraeli: "When you have time, I *do* hope that you'll read O'Connor's *Life of Lord Beaconsfield*. It is most admirable material for a poem" (*B's Trumpeter*, 14). Reflecting on this advice in an article in the *Pall Mall Gazette* written shortly after B's death (and apparently unaware that B had indeed followed it), Furnivall wrote, "After Mr. Disraeli's death, I was very anxious that Browning should vivisect him in a Blowgram [sic] poem. He admitted that the subject would suit him; but he had kept aloof from English politics; and how could he treat such a character without offending almost all his Tory friends, many of whom he valued" (*B's Trumpeter*, 201). Perhaps the device of anonymity in the parleying was designed to protect B's Tory readers; it apparently all too effectively protected even the originator of the subject of the poem from knowledge of his success.

If B consulted the O'Connor biography, he read a sustained exercise in character assassination unrelieved even by irony. A typical passage runs: "That whole character is complete in its selfishness, that whole career is uniform in its dishonesty . . . . His maturity without virtues is the natural sequel to his youth without generous illusions. There is throughout the same selfishness—calm, patient, unhasting, unresting . . . . for such a man millions of pure hearts beat with genuine emotion . . . . Which shall a near posterity most wonder at— the audacity of the impostor, or the blindness of the dupe?" (T.P. O'Connor, *Lord Beaconsfield: A Biography* [London, 1879], 675).

And yet, despite B's settled dislike of Disraeli the man and politician during his lifetime, it may have been a different set of circumstances which finally sparked the portrait in this parleying of the "statesman shape / I fancy standing with our world agape," whose ability to manipulate an elite Sacred Band (ll. 244-45, 267) was the secret of his power. After Disraeli's death in 1881 a powerful movement calling itself the Primrose League (after Disraeli's supposed favorite flower) emerged. It was designed both to conserve the image of the charismatic, exotic leader, and to consolidate his conservative legacy against the popular liberal William Gladstone. Richard Shannon, author of *The Age of Disraeli, 1868-1881* (London, 1992), writes of the Primrose League: "No personality cult in British politics has ever matched the Primrose League. This had much to do with Disraeli's exotic origins and the romantic quirkiness of his career. Things held against him by his party in his lifetime became, in the distant glow of folk-memory, materials of politically nutritious myth." It is this fanatical aspect of Disraeli's leadership and following that B explores in his parleying, by associating the irrational and obsessive quality of the Disraeli cult with Spiritualist cults. Perhaps there was a further dimension to B's repugnance toward the Primrose League, revealed in his occasional asperity toward the cultish tendencies of his own literary followers. The Browning Society was founded close in time (1881) to the formation of the Primrose League (1883) and may have seemed to him to bear other resemblances as well. To questions of doctrine and interpretation of his works from the Browning Society, B came to respond, "I've said what I want to say, in my works. You must take them and make what you can of them; you get no more out of me" (*B's Trumpeter*, Appendix B, 201). B's distrust of the motives of his own followers may have lent immediacy to the portrait of a cult leader and his followers in this parleying. For the tone of the Browning Society and its proceedings as perceived by some of the more irreverent late Victorians, see Max Beerbohm's cartoon, Plate 3.

1] *George . . . Melcombe* To B and to Dodington's own contemporaries his name alone suggested his rise from obscurity to the peerage through self-promotion. Dodington changed his name from Bubb to his mother's family name (Dodington) after the death of a patron-uncle in 1720, dropping his father's name altogether. But Bubb remained the name most commonly used by Dodington's enemies. Dodington received the peerage that he had long sought late in his life, in 1760, when George III succeeded to the throne.

2] *wrong way* Inexpedient, ineffective; not wrong in the sense of immoral; hypocrisy is assumed here.

10] *right reason* The phrase is here used ironically, with the imputation of rationalization; perhaps a nineteenth-century slur on the eighteenth century's faith in reason.

16]   *Labourers . . . hire*   "for the labourer is worthy of his hire" (Luke 10:7).

17-18]   *bears . . . infidel*   A conflation of proverb and scripture. *Bears the bell* is from an old saying meaning to win the prize, be first fiddle. "But if any provide not for his own, and specially for those of his own house, he hath denied the faith, and is worse than an infidel" (1 Tim. 5:8).

24]   *downy fluff*   An allusion to "feather his own nest."

32]   *volatile*   Bird (*OED*).

32]   *pelf*   Gain, spoils.

33]   *mudlark*   British colloquialism for street urchin. A mudlark is a species of lark that makes mud nests.

36-37]   *rook . . . crow*   Rooks nest in colonies; crows do not.

40]   *Darwin . . . bower*   Charles Darwin (1809-20), great naturalist and author of *On the Origin of Species by means of Natural Selection* (1859) and *The Descent of Man* (1871). The latter describes the male bower bird, which builds an elaborate display to attract a mate, as an example of natural selection: "the bowers, which . . . are decorated with feathers, shells, bones, and leaves, are built on the ground for the sole purpose of courtship, for their nests are formed in trees . . . . The bower . . . of the Fawn-breasted species . . . is raised on a thick platform of sticks" (1874 ed., 432-34).

49]   *sourish smile*   Reluctant or involuntary favorable response; parallel with the coy "female simper" in l. 54.

   Sage   Darwin.

69]   *a lump*   A heart.

83-84]   *Fates . . . lot*   The humble public servant on the one hand deprecates his self-sacrifice, and on the other anticipates glory and reward; such has been the fate (*lot*) of some crafty fellows.

87-89]   *rabble-rout . . . populace*   For the politician, the ignorant masses include everyone; they are all dupes.

110]   *sham . . . persuade*   "Call it sham, if you insist on calling a spade a spade, or use other words: preach and teach, persuade." The word *sham* refers back to the same word in l. 66, where the same issues of euphemism and hypocrisy are emphasized.

120-85]   *Yes— . . . your nature*   Section IV answers George's defense of his hypocrisy and its mask of love by saying he is behind the times. Progress in knavery since the early rule of might-makes-right requires new definitions of leadership and new strategies of deception and manipulation.

129-30]   *smiles . . . swine*   "neither cast ye your pearls before swine, lest they trample them under their feet, and turn again and rend you" (Matt. 7:6).

136] *succeeds* Follows.

145] *rule the roast* Preside, dominate. An older version by several centuries of the proverbial expression "to rule the roost." The phrase, whether *roast* or *roost*, seems originally to have had a domestic context: the head cook is in charge of the roast; the cock's favored hen roosts next to the cock.

161] *mixtures . . . composite* A rhetorical question: are mixtures made of single components? No one quality suffices for leadership. cf. ll. 174, 175.

168] *Why . . . beside* Since Dodington's mix of aggression, guile, and hypocrisy is all too typical of mankind in general, why not summon a more striking example of political success? The line signals the transition in Section V to the unnamed successor to Dodington in B's own time, who represents the refinement of political skills that Dodington lacked.

170] *conquering . . . conquer* "And a crown was given unto him: and he went forth conquering and to conquer" (Rev. 6:2).

171] *last expedient* latest ruse.

185-86] *"State . . . I pretend* The new voice here is the narrator role-playing the persona that Dodington should have assumed. The fresh example sought in l. 168 has been launched. The conspicuously unidentified speaker is almost certainly Disraeli, whom B considered thoroughly unscrupulous.

191-211] *owns . . . trickster* The hunger for spiritual life persists (*owns*: acknowledges, admits) in a doubting age. Victorians were disturbed by the impact of the "Higher Criticism," which questioned previous assumptions about the historical accuracy of the Bible; by changing social and economic conditions that challenged the entrenched class system in Britain; and by the "new science" of Charles Darwin and others. The suggestion that religion has become equated with superstition and outworn ceremonies caricatures the *doubting age*. The phrase *rapt gazers* connotes fortune-telling: a crystal-ball gazer in a trance-like state stares fixedly into a crystal ball and reports what she sees. Here the gaze is on the *master of the minute*, a politician claiming the gift of prophecy. B was vehemently opposed to the phony claims of spiritualists and to the increased appeal, as B feared, that exotic figures such as Disraeli drew from that popular movement. EBB was drawn to spiritualism, which became a sore subject between the Bs. B satirized both medium and audience in "Mr. Sludge, 'The Medium'" (see the pre-

sent edition, 6.285-351 and nn.). The detail of these lines in the par-
leying attest to B's close observation of Home's methods and power of
incorporating his audience's skepticism as well as credulity into his
performance.

   the adept's / Supremacy   The occult initiate's superhuman powers.
   yields up   Believes.
207-11]   *Professor . . . trickster*   Disraeli's political opponents called
him "The Professor" to satirize his literary avocation, and *Punch* and
other journals of the day referred to him as "Professor of Mystery."
215]   *Confederate potency*   Occult assistance; the phrase expresses the
supernatural contacts which the term "medium" literally denotes.
219-20]   *Bard . . . heart*   Annotators have speculated that the refer-
ence is to the line "One touch of nature makes the whole world kin"
(*Troilus and Cressida*, 3.3.175). The more likely allusion would seem to
be to Shylock's speech about a Jew's common humanity: "Hath not a
Jew eyes? . . . If you prick us, do we not bleed?" (*The Merchant of
Venice*, 3.1.61,66). Disraeli's father had changed the family name from
D'Israeli to Disraeli, and Disraeli had converted to Christianity. B's line
carries heavy irony, as of course does Shylock's speech.
224]   *qualify*   Describe.
228-31]   *year . . . accursed*   Disraeli had died in 1881; the reference
to a *year ago* is a relative measure of a political turnaround. Probably
the *thunder at the thing which, lo, / To-day he vaunts for unscathed* is also a
generalized swipe at Disraeli's notorious legacy of political ambiguity,
his ability to protect Tory principles while seeming to make conces-
sions. But whatever the actualities or specifics of Disraeli's political
double-dealing in his lifetime, the personality cult established after
Disraeli's death, which idealized him and glossed over inconsistencies
in his career, probably suggested this passage and the profile generally
in this parleying (see *Sources* above). B also had direct personal experi-
ence of Disraeli's facile hypocrisy; Allingham records in his diary an
expostulation from B in 1876:

> "What a humbug he is! Won't I give it him one of these days!"
> Royal Academy dinner. Dizzy's speech. "What struck him most was
> 'the *imagination* of the British School of Art, amid ugly streets and
> dull skies, etc. etc.'"
>
> Afterwards Disraeli came up to Browning and said, "What do
> you think of this Exhibition?"
>
> Browning wished to hear Disraeli's opinion. Disraeli said—
> "What strikes me is the utter and hopeless want of imagination"

(as much as to say, you didn't think me such a fool as I seemed in my speech!)

Browning told this to Gladstone, who said pungently, "It's hellish! He is like that in the house too—it's hellish!"

"And so it is," added Browning. (Allingham, *Diary*, 246)

234] *aes triplex* Triple bronze; Horace likens a hero's courage to being encased in triple-strength armor (*Odes* 1.3.9). The implicit pun on "brazen liar" becomes explicit at l. 277. Cf. "O coward visage!" l. 243.

241] *uncouth* Involuntary.

246] *conscience . . . conscience* Ability to justify falsehood.

249] *Mendacious intrepidity* A (Disraeliesque) euphemism for "bold-faced lying."

249] *quid vis?* "What (more) do you want?" The Latin, as with the Latinate polysyllabics of *mendacious intrepidity*, has a euphemistic effect on the villainy it refers to.

250-58] *Besides . . . guile* The passage develops an important distinction between the transparent lying of "mendacious intrepidity" above, and more conventional imposture and guile, with its emphasis on *earnestness* (ll. 255, 56, 57), a word of which Victorian moralists were overfond.

film-work Cover story.

259] *wants* Lacks.

261] *our chief* As Prime Minister (1867-68, 1874-80) Disraeli was often called "Chief" by his friends.

267] *Sacred Band* Probably a reference to the personality cult called The Primrose League which formed around Disraeli and his legacy after his death; see *Sources* above. The original Sacred Band consisted of elect Theban warriors who fought against Sparta in 406 B.C.

269] *subintelligential . . . wink* Signals imperceptible to the general public but not unintelligible among initiates. The Primrose League elevated Disraeli's elusive and exotic style and personality into conservative political myth.

277] *triply . . . brass* A reference back to l. 234 and a pun on the brazen effrontery of using flattery, sneers, and scorn (ll. 270, 274, 276) to accomplish his end.

284] *Did he say* If he said.

302-5] *tread . . . soul* The language and reference here are obliquely Biblical. Disraeli is associated with the Prince of Darkness through his power of the lie, which can not only subvert but invert the

Biblical injunction to love truth. It is man who in Gen. 3:15 is ordained to tread upon the snake, not vice versa. The message of the first book of the Bible is repeated in the last, where in the vision of the new Paradise it is said that outside the gates "are dogs and sorcerers . . . and whosoever loveth and maketh a lie" (Rev. 22:15). The *Something inside us all and each, that stands / Somehow instead of somewhat* repeats the groping language and moral affirmation of other significant lines in this parleying: ll. 69, 220, 223, 246.

308] *portent . . . influence* The words *portent* and *influence* refer to astral signs. B contrasts these astrological terms suggestive of superstition with the Biblical language of ll. 302-5.

316] *make acquist* Acquire.

319-20] *Hearth . . . Rome* Disraeli was a famous phrase-maker, and nationalism, empire, and Christian faith were his great themes, as they were also the declared aims of the Primrose League, namely "the maintenance of religion, of the estates of the realm, and of the imperial ascendance." Disraeli was known to appeal to anti-Catholic sentiment upon occasion.

327] *Ventum . . . triarios* "It has come to the third line" (cf. Livy, *History of Rome from its Foundation*, 8.8). A military expression signifying trying a last resort.

WITH FRANCIS FURINI

Sources and Backgrounds] Francesco Furini, c.1600-1649, was a painter in Florence for the first forty years of his life, and a priest in Mugello, a village near Florence, for the last nine. Furini was not highly regarded as a painter either in his own lifetime or later, although he enjoyed some popularity as a painter of the female nude. As one twentieth-century critic has felicitously characterized his work, "Furini . . . produced paintings of a morbid sensuality . . . but nobody can deny that he had a special gift for rendering the melodious calligraphy of the female body" (Rudolf Wittkower, *Art and Architecture in Italy, 1600-1750* [London, 1958], 244). Most of Furini's surviving paintings remain in Florence, where B saw them for the first time after he moved to Florence in 1847. Thus the parleying "With Francis Furini" is alone in the collection in reflecting B's mature rather than youthful attraction to his subject.

What attracted B to Furini was less the merit of his painting than a combination of circumstances that made Furini's work relevant to nineteenth-century experience, to B's own and to his generation's: Furini's mid-life change of vocation from painter to priest, and the claim of his biographer Baldinucci that on his death bed Furini repudiated his paintings of nudes. These events coalesce in the parleying "With Francis Furini" with the threat posed by evolutionary theory to religious faith; with the fondness of Pen Browning for the female nude as subject; and with the failure of the Royal Academy of Art to approve either Pen's artistry or his subject matter. For B, the common factor in these distant and disparate events was the significance of the naked human body in connection with Victorian controversies over moral values.

In view of the powerful synthesis of personal, cultural, religious, and esthetic forces in "Furini," it is not surprising that the talismanic myth which plays its part in B's work throughout his career, the Perseus and Andromeda myth, plays its part in the rescue of meaning in this poem. (See DeVane's "The Virgin and the Dragon," *Yale Review* 37 [1947], 33-46). In "Furini" the Caravaggio painting of Andromeda, an etching of which hung in view of B's desk from the time of his earliest work (see Plate 2), becomes interchangeable with Pen's "Joan of Arc and the Kingfisher," and with a painting of Andromeda by Furini.

B's source for the biographical facts about Furini was a twenty-volume history of painting by Filippo Baldinucci (1624-96). B had earlier used Baldinucci's *Notizie De' Professori del Disegno da Cimabue in Qua* (*Comments on Leaders in Painting from Cimabue to the Present*) to supplement Vasari, in writing both "Fra Lippo Lippi" and "Andrea del Sarto" (1855) and *Pacchiarotto* (1876). In the latter collection Baldinucci was the object of satire in "Filippo Baldinucci on the Privilege of Burial. " See this edition, 5.183, 6.7, 13.242 and nn. In this parleying, Baldinucci's censorious judgment of Furini's "lascivious" nudes anachronistically joins forces with the views of the Victorian critic John Callcot Horsley, treasurer of the Royal Academy 1882-1897, who in 1886 rejected Pen Browning's "Joan of Arc and the Kingfisher" on similar grounds. In his zeal Horsley went so far as to initiate in *The Times* a campaign against nudes in general, citing Watts, Leighton, and other painter friends of B's as offenders. Letters to *The Times* filled editorial columns for a month in May 1885 (see *B's Parleyings*, 184), one proposal for the organization of a society for the prevention of nudes in painting being actually undertaken. B meanwhile lent absurdities of his own to the fracas, appealing emotionally to the Grovesnor Gallery to take Pen's "Joan" after its rejection by the Royal Academy. "The tears coursing down his cheeks moved the authorities so much that they bypassed their own rule" of not accepting Royal Academy rejects (Maisie Ward, *The Tragi-Comedy of Pen Browning* [New York, 1972], 66).

Perhaps the most problematic of the problematic *Parleyings*, and at the same time the closest to the bone and nerve of B's experience and belief and the boldest in its expression of his thought and feeling, the parleying "With Francis Furini" is an uneasy balance of text and subtext. But for these very reasons, a map of the uneven terrain and deceptive strata of this parleying is also a guide to the collection.

1] *that* Opening *in medias res*, B shows his impatience to introduce the main issue of this parleying, that of the female nude in painting. B takes his facts from Baldinucci's life of Furini (see *Sources*, above), but draws the line at accepting Baldinucci's version of Furini's deathbed recantation of his paintings. B's version of the death scene is given ll. 134-43.

3] *Tuscan . . . painter-priest* Tuscany is a central region of Italy of which Florence is the chief city. Furini had separate careers as painter and priest.

6-7] *Saint . . . Mugello* St. Ansano's Church, in Mugello, a poor peasant region N of Florence.

10-14] *Bounty . . . tickled* According to Baldinucci, Furini was known for a generosity often beyond his means, and he became a priest partly in an attempt to overcome his spendthrift habits.

17-22] *prompt . . . masterpiece* Furini continued to paint after he became a priest, but for charity, not for the commissions he had earlier received from wealthy nobility (*princes*).

Don See "With Daniel Bartoli" l. 1n.

23] *wine and oil* Wine of communion and oil of unction.

27] *scan* Find after close examination.

33] *blazon* Show, publication (Samuel Johnson's *Dictionary*).

35-42] *modern . . . impotency* Here B initiates a contrast between poetry and painting, the skills necessary to each, and between idea and image, head and hand, that will be a consistent framework for his development of Furini's place in *Parleyings*. The passage elevates the disciplined training necessary in painting over the poet's ability to allow *Fancy's free passage by the pen*, and suggests that Furini's *precision of the brush* might be a model for *modern art*. B had many friends among the Pre-Raphaelites, whose commitment to exact truth to nature was their ruling principle, according W.M. Rossetti in the short-lived journal *The Germ* (1850), which was the impetus to the movement. A favorable parallel is made here between modern art and Furini. Inquiring, does not modern art support my judgment about the importance of technique, and what good is inspiration joined to lack of technical skill? (*painter's impotency*). B defends in Furini, and implicitly in Pen, the very skill that

Andrea del Sarto disparages in "This low-pulsed craftsman's hand of mine" (l. 82). In the 80s, Pen Browning (whom his father now called Robert), after a period of concentrated study in Antwerp with a teacher recommended by Millais, and a briefer period of study under the sculptor Auguste Rodin in Paris, was finding an audience for his exhibits and even buyers for his paintings, largely through his father's insistent and persistent loyal sponsorship.

42-43] *Agnolo . . . hand* Michelangelo (1475-1564), great Florentine painter and sculptor, known for his exact rendering of anatomy as well as for his inspired depiction of character.

44-49] *Who . . . unhurt* "A deficiency of technical skill can wreck an otherwise inspired painting, whereas a poet needs only inspiration."

Film-wings The muse, figured as a fragile winged creature.

51-58] *But . . . earth* These lines are addressed again to Furini, not Michaelangelo.

house of life Church; a loose allusion to the many references to Christ as the giver of life. "I am the way, the truth, and the life" (John 14:6).

54] *Poured forth by pencil* Sketched hastily; see ll. 15-18 above.

56] *Fleshly perfection* In the nude. This was the controversial issue of Furini's painting, and the relevant one for B; see *Sources*, above.

59-60] *ape . . . pen-creation* To rely on inspiration without craft.

71-75] *chronicler . . . nudity* Filippo Baldinucci; see *Sources*, above, and l. 1n. *fame:* rumor, evil repute (*OED*).

76-119] *Yes . . . Baldinucci* The lines restate Baldinucci's case against Furini and suggest more clearly the parallels between Furini's and Pen Browning's paintings of nudes, and Baldinucci's and Horsley's condemnation of them (see *Sources*, above). The subjects Eve, nymphs, Diana, and Venus are generic nude subjects, but Pen did sculpt an "Eve after Temptation" (1882; *Reconstruction*, K75). He painted "A Faun Playing the Pipe to Two Nymphs by a River" (1884), and there is an 1899 "Diana" (*Reconstruction*, K137, K56).

80] *Naked and unashamed* "And they were both naked, the man and his wife, and were not ashamed" (Gen. 2:25). The conspicuous omissions here are Furini's Andromeda and Pen's "Joan of Arc and the Kingfisher." See *Sources*, above, and ll. 594-614.

86] *lymph* "pure water . . . a stream" (*OED*).

102] *Philip* Filippo Baldinucci.

104-6] *excuse . . . his very words* Baldinucci did not know Furini and Furini gave no such defense of himself. The tone and address are B's to Horsley. DeVane argues that B frequently suggested subjects to Pen (*B's Parleyings*, 182 n.45), and thus that his indignation at Horsley's prudishness is personal as well as paternal.

110-11] *elf . . . Him* The best artist is a dwarf (*elf*) beside the lord of creation. The finger of God is a recurrent figure in the Bible for God's will or power (see Exod. 8:18-19 for example), and Michelangelo's Sistine Chapel puts the finger of God touching the nude Adam's at its center.

115] *idle fancy* Lust.

125] *bid them burn* "as to" is understood, parallel with "as to grope" l. 122.

133] *seal God set* "in the image of God created he him; male and female created he them" (Gen. 1:27).

134] *supremest work* In a double sense: last, final (*OED*), and best.

140-41] *star-device . . . Andromeda* The northern constellation. The figure of Andromeda symbolized for B an essence both of earthly beauty and of its vulnerability to evil uses or conceptions. DeVane, who has written the seminal study of the Andromeda myth in B's works (see *Sources*, above) argues that Baldinucci's mention of an Andromeda by Furini gave B the link that he sought among Pen's nudes, Furini, and the evolutionists (*B's Parleyings*, 190).

145-46] *critic . . . artist* Baldinucci and Horsley were both painters as well as critics.

146-47] *Ossa . . . Olympus* The proverbial expression, based on the passage in the *Odyssey* (11.315) in which the Titans attempted to scale the heavens by piling Mt. Pelion on Mt. Ossa, means adding difficulty to difficulty. B revises the expression to signify putting difficulty in the way of perfection; Olympus is the sacred dwelling of the gods.

154-55] *satyr . . . instinct* A blue-fly, also known as blow-fly, blue-bottle, and flesh-fly, deposits its eggs in carrion flesh. Among the letters to the editor in a lively series in *The Times* in May, 1885, about the issue of the female nude in painting was one signed "A British Matron," which, DeVane argues, B took for a pseudonym of Horsley's (*B's Parleyings*, 184).

159] *fly-blow* Lay eggs in; see 154-55n.

165] *Michael . . . Rafael* Michelangelo (1475-1564), Leonardo da Vinci (1452-1519), and Raphael (1483-1520), the great names of the Italian Renaissance.

173-76] *Correggio . . . Virtue* A Renaissance artist named for his birthplace of Correggio, near Parma in the N of Italy, Antonio Correggio (1494-1534) showed in his work the influences of Michelangelo, Leonardo, and Raphael, and is alluded to for here for both his exemplary qualities as a student and the features of his work which became a lesson for other painters. He was founder of what became known as the School of Parma. EBB spoke admiringly of Correggio's "Virgin of St. Jerome" in Parma: "Correggio . . . is sublime at Parma; he is wonderful" (*Letters of EBB*, 2.9). B makes reference in "Bishop Blougram's Apology" to "Correggio's fleeting glow" (l. 114). Lairesse used Correggio as an example of classicism in painting; see "With Gerard de Lairesse," *Sources*. In Italian (*Correggio's tongue*) the word *virtu* signifies artistic strength or skill, as in "virtuoso"; here of course *Virtue* has both the Italian and the common English senses.

177-182] *artist . . . flame* The *artist* is Michaelangelo. His allegorical female nudes were sculpted for the tomb of Giuliano de' Medici in the New Sacristy in the Church of San Lorenzo, Florence. His "Creation of Eve" is part of the ceiling fresco in the Sistine Chapel in Rome.

183] *recreant* Religious traitor, heretic.

187-88] *Art's . . . Sacred* Perhaps because they grow at heights inhospitable to other trees, *pine-trees* are classically associated with the gods. A *pale* is a boundary or fence. *Pignuts* are ground nuts or tubers, suitable for pigs like Baldinucci. The *Sacred* are the great painters who dwell inside *Art's pale*.

188-211] *If . . . Philistine* The oddly assorted, groping imagery in this section, of head and hand, sky and earth, spirit and flesh, vapor and star, is obscure and perhaps deliberately so, in view of the embedded message that it conjures the artist to deliver. The passage serves as prelude and invocation to Furini's prayer beginning l. 232, and his sermon beginning l. 265, which answer the call for *warning* l. 202, *scruple of the better sense* l. 204, and smite *the Philistine* l. 211. As revenge on the heathen Philistines for burning his wife, Samson "smote them hip and thigh with a great slaughter" (Judg. 15:8). B surely had in mind also Matthew Arnold's use of *Philistines* in *Culture and Anarchy* (1869) to mean bourgeois enemies of art.

192] *portion* Dowry, legacy; an extension of *dower*, l. 189.

211] *You* Baldinucci.

233] *Deviser . . . gifts* "Every good gift and every perfect gift is from above, and cometh down from the Father of light" (Jas. 1:17).

235] *measuring rod* "And he that talked with me had a golden reed to measure the city, and the gates thereof, and the wall thereof" (Rev. 21:15).

237-39] *hands . . . divine* "And God said, Let us make man in our image, after our likeness (Gen. 1:26). And the Lord God formed man of the dust of the ground, and breathed into his nostrils the breath of life, and man became a living soul" (Gen. 2:7).

261-64] *she . . . knowledge* Such open-mindedness on the part of science was not always the case. B's friend John Tyndall, for instance, militantly stated, "We claim, and we shall wrest from theology, the entire domain of cosmological theory. All schemes and systems which thus infringe upon the domain of science must, *in so far as they do this*, submit to its control, and relinquish all thought of controlling it" (address in Belfast, 1874, quoted in Devane, *B's Parleyings*, 197).

265-80]   *Evolutionists . . . progress*   The passage suggests both the common ground and the conflict between faith and evolutionary thought, as envisioned by B through Furini. Holding that his own work and beliefs had anticipated Darwin, B protested to Furnivall, "Last, about my being 'strongly against Darwin, rejecting the truths of science and regretting its advance'—you only do as I should hope and expect in disbelieving *that* . . . . In reality, all that seems *proved* in Darwin's scheme was a conception familiar to me from the beginning: see in *Paracelsus* the progressive development from senseless matter to organized, until man's appearance (*Part V*). Also in *Cleon*, see the order of 'life's mechanics,'—and I daresay in many passages of my poetry" (11 October 1881, *B's Trumpeter*, 34). But B felt decided conflict between the ascendant, upward perspective of an optimism like his own, grounded in moral struggle and development, and the pessimism of a mechanistic scheme of human evolution. Furini derives his premise of opposite high and low *stations for discovery*, and his language, *Have you done / Descending?* from the title of Darwin's second influential book, *The Descent of Man* (1871).

271]   *spasm*   Mechanistic version of religion's First Cause, or God.

280]   *being's progress*   In assuming that faith and science agree that evolution implies progress, Furini and B adopt a misconception common to non-scientists in the Victorian age.

294-96]   *millionth . . . star*   The millionth thing is a figure for the smallest microscopic part, which, like the infinite moment in B's philosophy, can hold microcosmic perfection. In a letter to EBB of 11 January 1846, he analyzed his happiness: "Now, here is one sign of what I said: that I must love you more than at first . . a little sign, and to be looked narrowly for or it escapes me, but then the increase it shows *can* only be little, so very little now—and as the fine French Chemical Analysts bring themselves to appreciate matter in its refined stages by *millionths*, so—!" (Kintner, 378).

301]   *initiator-spasm*   See l. 271n.

385]   *righteousness*   The moral sense, consciousness (l. 299), in contrast to power l. 282 and reason l. 290.

323-26]   *mere . . . intuition*   The lines contrast the gradualism assumed in early evolutionary thought with the transformative and unpredictable nature of spiritual change. Writing to Furnivall, B contrasted scientific and metaphysical ways of thinking: "When one is taunted . . . with thinking successive acts of creation credible, metaphysics have been stopped short at, however physics may fare: time and space being purely conceptions of our own, wholly inapplicable to intelligence of another kind—with whom, as I made Luria say, there is an 'everlasting moment of creation' if one at all,—past, present, future, one and the same state" (Oct. 11, 1881, *B's Trumpeter*, 34).

330]   *Prime Mind*   The phrase can mean the original creator, or God; here it seems to adapt the biological classification of man, *homo sapiens*, to a designation of mind as the primary feature of the species.

334]   *qualifying*   Defining.

349]   *at the bottom*   From a perspective directed upward, opposite to that of the evolutionists, ll. 366-67.

352]   *enisled*   The figure prepares for the personification of revelation as a female nude surrounded by an ocean of doubt. See the images of Andromeda, ll. 490. 529, and of Joan of Arc, l. 368. The word *enisled* also recalls the first l. of Arnold's "To Marguerite—Continued" (1852), a poem B loved.

385]   *save . . . face*   Readings of the line vary widely. It seems probable that the poet has in mind the painting toward which he is moving his defense, Pen's "Joan of Arc and the Kingfisher" (see ll. 568-72 and n.) and in which the nude is seen from behind, her face averted (see Plate 4).

389-93]   *Were . . . flesh-perfection*   The *underground* (that which is hidden: soul, l. 379) will answer that no *labour* to depict worldly beauty is *lavished vainly*, that *flesh-perfection* is the beginning of the search for God.

401]   *hundred pictures*   A round count, implying that Furini was a prolific painter, which he was; see *Sources*, above. Few of his paintings were accessible to B, however.

407-10]   *dip . . . rock-spit*   Though not specified by name until l. 490, the Andromeda myth and Caravaggio's "Perseus and Andromeda," both central to B's poetics, are implicit in Furini's evocation of the posture of faith surrounded by doubt; see *Sources*, above. In the etching Andromeda is standing on a rocky spur against which waves are dashing. See Plate 2.

417-20]   *Evil . . . Cause*   The argument goes back to St. Augustine (354-430), who in his *Confessions* wrote "In my ignorance I was much troubled, and departing from the truth seemed to myself to be making toward it; because as yet I knew not that evil was nothing but a privation of good" (Book 3). See also ll. 454-60.

424-67]   *Look . . . evil*   Furini's rapturous credo answering the forces of doubt is also B's. Furini tracks the range of visionary and passionate experience available to soul and body, but recognizes the persistence of *doubts* and *strife . . . —for why?* Answering his own question, he proposes that the challenge of the evolutionists, who would name the *Cause* a mere mechanical *protoplast*, is itself a part of the grand design to reinforce faith through opposition.

429]   *stings*   Prompts.

446-48]   *sealing . . . Perfection*   "Son of man, take up a lamentation on the king of Tyrus, and say unto him, Thus saith the Lord God: Thou sealest up the sum, full of wisdom, and perfect in beauty" (Ez. 28:12).

473]   *trench on*   Step on, put full weight on, enter into.

483]   *Type . . . antitype*   Mrs. Orr emphasizes this language in her summary of the parleying "With Francis Furini," probably echoing B's explication of the poem to her (Orr, 354).

486-91]   *Make . . . monster*   The analogy between the illusion of evil and the illusion of art is a leap not easily explained even by the intuitiveness of Furini's reasoning here. But given the deep connections between the Perseus and Andromeda myth and B's art and philosophy, the leap is a necessary and natural one. Baldinucci mentions that Furini painted an Andromeda, but the reference here is clearly to the etching by Giovanni Volpato of the fresco by Caravaggio which hung beside B's desk. See Plate 2.

501-3]   *artificer . . . make-believe*   For the reference of these lines B apparently directed Mrs. Orr to the famous story of the Greek painter Zeuxis, whose paintings were so realistic that birds swooped down to peck at his grapes (Orr, 355).

521]   *Contrariwise . . . told*   I.e., "On the other hand, if you must have some answer, here it is."

526]   *retrocede*   Go back, recede.

532]   *ministrate*   Minister. *OED* cites B for the usage.

539]   *messuage*   A legal term for house and lands.

544-45]   *uncouth . . . mouth*   The ancient pagan (*uncouth*) symbol of eternity was the ouroburos, a snake with its tail in its mouth. Adrienne Munich reads this startling image as Furini's and B's visionary conquest and conversion of sea monster-as-evil: "It is that ability to transform evil into a sign of transcendent good that proves the emblem maker's power over the evolutionist's" (*Andromeda's Chains* [New York, 1989], 137. Munich's illustrations include a seventeenth-century print of the ouroburos, 136.

548]   *psalmody*   Singing.

549] *pencil . . . attaint* The word *pencil* can mean an artist's fine brush (*OED*).

attaint Disparage.

555] *self-scathed* Self-punishing.

567] *healing . . . nations* "and the leaves of the tree were for the healing of the nations" (Rev. 22:2).

568-72] *Burn . . . astir* The peasant girl Joan of Arc (c.1412-31) was guided by voices and visions to lead the French army against the English in the siege of Orleans (1429) in the Hundred Years' War. She was burned at the stake as a heretic. The painting that B invokes was one of Pen Browning's, titled "Joan of Arc and the Kingfisher" and represents the heroine before she went to war. See Plate 4.

577-78] *king . . . corner* In 1428 when Joan undertook to advance from Orleans to Reims to crown the Dauphin, the English and their French allies occupied almost all the northern part of the kingdom.

581-87] *Memorize . . . fiction* Furini can *memorize* (make memorable) the moment of Joan's heroic decision better than any writer. Two well-known French men of letters of B's generation are here compared to Furini as inferior seekers of truth. To paraphrase, "the *wise* know that painting is much better than writing at piercing through *fancy's film-work*; otherwise you might as well ask Sainte-Beuve or Quicherat." Charles Augustin *Sainte-Beuve* (1804-69) was an influential literary critic whose popular series of literary columns published in newspapers in Paris 1849-69 would have been familiar to B during his extended visits to Paris during that period. Jules *Quicherat* (1814-82) is more directly connected with the facts of Joan's history. He edited five volumes of archival documents, *Proces de condamnation et de rehabilitation de Jeanne d'Arc* (*Proceedings in the sentencing and rehabilitation of Joan of Arc*), on the trial of Joan of Arc and the later conferral of her sainthood.

588-93] *prudishness . . . thought* The Duc d'Alencon was lieutenant general of the French armies and a close comrade-in-arms of Joan. His testimony to her good character is included in the records in Quicherat's *Proces*, 4.4-5. B mentions this passage (which was in Latin, the language of legal proceedings) in a letter to Furnivall, in context with Pen's painting of Joan: "I am amused at the objection taken by some of the critics to the Eve-like simplicity of Pen's peasant-girl, who before going on to saintliness . . . was satisfied with the proverbially next step to it—cleanliness. If they knew anything of Joan's habits even when advanced in her saintly career, they would remember she was no prude by any means: her favoured young cavalier, the Duc d'Alencon, mentions that he had frequently seen her undress, and that 'aliquando videbat ejus mammas quae pulchrae erant'" ['Sometimes he had seen her breasts, which were beautiful'] (*B's Trumpeter*, 132). The long background to B's involvement with this painting of Pen's tends to confirm DeVane's theory that B often suggested subjects to Pen (*B's Parleyings*, 182 n.45).

601-607] *Now . . . blue bird* The italicized lines were composed by B for the exhibition of Pen's "Joan of Arc and the Kingfisher" at the Grosvenor Gallery and were shown with the painting. B wrote several poetic inscriptions for the paintings of friends, among them John Woolner and Frederick Leighton.

Fisher-king The European Kingfisher (*Alcedo atthis*) is a brilliantly colored bird with an iridescent blue back. The poetic inscription suggests a pun on the bird; Joan is likewise a king-fisher, a dauphin-fisher and a king-maker.

608-11] *Martin-fisher . . . Martin* The name is applied in French to various birds, as in *martin-chasseur*, the hen-harrier; *martin-pecheur*, the kingfisher.

611-12] *turn . . . away* In Pen's painting Joan's figure is seen from the back; see l. 385 and n., and Plate 4.

616] *Omnia . . . meant* "All is not for all," an abbreviated form of the proverbial "Omnia non pariter sunt omnibus apta" (All things are not alike for all men"). *No harm is meant* is a sardonic paraphrase of a comment made in the extended debate in *The Times* in May 1885 over the immoral effect of nudes in paintings. See *B's Parleyings*, 184.

WITH GERARD DE LAIRESSE

Sources and Background] Gerard de Lairesse (1640-1711) was born in Belgium but studied and lived most of his life in Amsterdam, where he was well-known as a Dutch painter. He was an admirer and follower of the French painter Nicolas Poussin (1594-1655) and Poussin's neoclassical style of painting. Lairesse suffered from syphilis and lost his sight from the disease at about the age of fifty, when he turned his talents to instruction in the technique, theory, and history of painting. His *The Art of Painting in All Its Branches* (*Het Groot Schilderboek*, [Amsterdam 1707]) was very popular and went through several editions and translations into French, German, and English during the eighteenth century. B read the second English edition (1778), translated by J.F. Fritch. Its date of purchase is indicated by Robert Browning Sr. on the title page as 1804, and on the fly-leaf is an inscription by B dated 13 February 1874: "I read this book more often and with greater delight, when I was a child, than any other: and still remember the main of it most gratefully for the good I seem to have got by the prints, and wondrous text" (*Reconstruction*, A1379).

The chord which Lairesse struck in the very young B—who had produced recognizable subjects on paper when he was just over two years old, according to his father—was an emphasis on landscape. According to Lairesse, the greatest pleasure in art is afforded by landscape. Understanding what is beautiful or ugly in scenery and its tones of light, and coordinating a painterly subject with an appropriate landscape and time of day, are the primary duties of the artist. Lairesse is specific about what is beautiful and appropriate, and what is not. In order to illustrate his criteria, he takes the reader on a "Walk" through a landscape "Of Painter-like Beauty in the open Air," and then through a landscape "Of Things deformed and broken, falsely called Painter-like" (headings for chapters 16 and 17 of *The Art of Painting*; chapter 17 was the main source for "'Childe Roland to the Dark Tower Came'"). Lairesse's exercise-model appealed naturally to B's own love of landscape and of extended walks. His well-documented eight-mile walks between his home in Hatcham and the Barrett household in Wimpole Street in the 1840s, and the three hour walks before breakfast in the 1880s with Sarianna in the Italian Alps, were typical of his lifelong habits.

Paintings then attributed to Lairesse were readily accessible in the charming Dulwich College Picture Gallery, opened in 1817 and the first public gallery in all of London, just a two-mile walk from B's home in Camberwell. Likening his affection for the gallery to his love for EBB, the poet wrote to her on 3 March 1846, "of that Gallery I so love and so am grateful to—having been used to go there when a child, far under the age allowed by the regulations . . . . I have sate before one, some *one* of those pictures I had predetermined to see,—a good hour and then gone away. . it used to be a green half-hour's walk over the fields" (Kintner, 509; *Correspondence*, 12.124). (See ll. 31-35 and n. for more specific reference to these pictures, and for corrections of their attribution to Lairesse.)

The lessons pointed by Lairesse held less appeal for the poet in his maturity. Even as a young man, as this parleying makes clear, B felt disappointment at Lairesse's classicism in practice. The latter's insistence on the superiority of Greek myth over modern subjects provoked in the mature B a more thoroughgoing protest against this investment in the past both by Lairesse and by such contemporaries as Arnold, Tennyson, and the pre-Raphaelites. In defense of poetic change, B invokes as strengths of modernity features of his own poetry such as psychological depth, and alludes to the innovative use of classical sources by such poets as Shelley; see ll. 181-209n., 210-61n., and 262-307n. Among all the parleyings, the tension between resuscitation of the revered dead and rivalry with them is perhaps clearest in "With Gerard de Lairesse." Indeed the "Walk" becomes a race and a contest at ll. 174-76, and B's defense of modernism against what he felt as a false and pessimistic nostalgia for the past in Victorian art emerges in full voice.

1]   *struck blind*   Lairesse went blind at about the age of fifty.
8-9]   *pageantry . . . brain*   Mrs. Orr reflects B's judgment of Lairesse's paintings in her description of their subjects: "he was saturated with the pseudo-classical spirit of the later period of the renaissance; and landscape itself scarcely existed for him but as a setting for mythological incident or a subject for embellishment by it" (Orr, 355).
14-15]   *gay . . . serene*   That is, in the many escapades involving gods and mortals.
   serene   Air of the heights of Mt. Olympus; compare Keats on the "demesne" of Homer: "Yet did I never breathe its pure serene / Till I heard Chapman speak out loud and bold" ("On First Looking into Chapman's Homer," ll. 7-8).
22]   *pencil*   Fine artist's brush; see "Furini," l. 549.
26-30]   *mouth . . . veritable*   Lairesse's descriptive powers in words took the place of his actual (*veritable*) paintings.
31-35]   *myself . . . artist-work*   The Dulwich Gallery, S of London, where the young B was a frequent visitor, owned three paintings then attributed to Lairesse. All have since been reassigned to other painters. There are paintings by Lairesse in Paris, where B might have seen them later in his life. B read Lairesse's *The Art of Painting in All Its Branches* when he was still a child and sought out the author's work in the Gallery.
46]   *"Walk"*   Lairesse's instruction in The Art of Painting took the form of a guided walk through various landscapes.
50-58]   *Faustus' . . . actual*   The robe and cap are examples of magically enhanced, and dangerous, powers over nature, in contrast to Lairesse's emphasis on *worth/ In trivial commonplace . . . Beyond / The ugly actual*. With the help of the devil and a magic robe, the *Faustus* of medieval legend was able to fly through the air. *Fortunatus*, hero of medieval German and Dutch legends, gains a magic cap which proves the destruction of his sons. Carlyle uses Fortunatus and his hat to illustrate the illusion of space and time in *Sartor Resartus* 3.1, "Natural Supernaturalism." Despite his counsel to infuse real landscape with mythical narrative, Lairesse also advised simplicity and naturalism in painting, values consonant with B's own criteria in poetry and with his complex fascination with the grotesque, the *ugly actual*.

71-80] *sepulchre . . . tome* Lairesse's favorite subjects were from Ovid. The story of Phaeton, given permission by his father Helios to drive the chariot of the Sun, and Phaeton's destruction by a thunderbolt from Jove when the chariot threatened to incinerate the earth, is told in *Metamorphoses* 1.748-2.339. Lairesse describes an appropriate setting for Phaeton's tomb in *The Art of Painting*, 255.

84] *choke-full* Variant of "chock-full. "

86] *Us . . . seeing* "Having eyes, see ye not?" (Mark 8:18).

100] *antique song* Greek poetry.

105-6] *men . . . apprehend* The phrase and title of B's most celebrated collection of poems *Men and Women* is a cue that while this judgment may be what some *poets apprehend,* it is not B's judgment. The reference is broad, and may include many of B's contemporaries who turned to the past for inspiration: Arnold, Tennyson, Swinburne, Meredith, and the Rossettis. Of Tennyson's *The Holy Grail and Other Poems,* B wrote, "We look at the subject of art in poetry so differently! Here is an Idyll about a knight being untrue to his friend and yielding to the temptation of that friend's mistress . . . . I should judge the knight's soul the proper object to describe. Tennyson thinks he should describe the castle and the effect of the moon on its towers and anything but the soul" (Hood, 134).

108] *painters turn* Such painters as D.G. Rossetti, Burne-Jones, Holman Hunt, and Millais, who in addition to painting classical subjects, illustrated mythological poems: Tennyson's "The Lady of Shalott," Keats's "Isabella or the Pot of Basil," and others.

120-21] *Dryope . . . bled* The nymph Lotis was transformed into a lotus tree to protect her from a pursuer, and unknowingly, Dryope attempted to pluck a blossom from that tree. Dryope was punished by being turned into a lotus tree herself. Lairesse invokes Dryope's transformation as a prime subject for art (*The Art of Painting*, 239-40). But B adds a dimension of his own to the example by evoking the association of sleep and dream with the lotus plant through the assertion of his own wakeful realism (ll. 111-12, 122). The story is told in Ovid, *Metamorphoses,* 9.340-45.

133] *elder age* The ancients.

138] *composed* Resolved, harmonized.

143] *acquists* Acquisitions (obsolete); i.e., sense and soul l. 139, love and knowledge ll. 142-43.

158] *freakish* Fantastical (*OED*).

163-65] *rose . . . love* The parodic diction satirizes Lairesse's view of the necessity of mythic intervention into art's representation of reality, though in fact the example is not one of Lairesse's. The reference is to the story of Venus and Adonis. Venus, pricked in play by one of Cupid's arrows, fell in love with Adonis, who was later mortally wounded while hunting a wild boar. Venus turned the blood from his thigh into the red rose, and her own tears into the anemone (Ovid, *Metamorphoses*, 10.303-59, 708-39). Both EBB and Shelley translated *Lament for Adonis* by the Greek pastoralist Bion (born c.100 B.C.), and Shelley's "Adonais" draws on the story.

166] *we . . . all*   That is, "we (living) poets retain what you taught us."

168-70] *if . . . Protoplast*   The odd exclamation affirms progress and rejects "retrogression" (l. 165). *Protoplast* is borrowed from evolutionists' notion of an original, essential life-stuff; *blame the Protoplast* signifies "life goes on, no matter how much *this world* (the present) may lament its inferiority to the past."

174-76] *walk . . . race*   B makes a deft transition and play on Lairesse's organizational device in the two chapters on landscape in *The Art of Painting*. Lairesse's "Walk" has become a race between the present and the past, between Lairesse's and B's ability to poeticize landscape.

181-209] *Section VIII*   The first station on the "Walk" is the mountain in the Caucasus chain between the Black and Caspian seas, where Prometheus was imprisoned and tortured by Jupiter for his theft of fire from the gods, a heroic rebellion undertaken by Prometheus for the benefit of humankind. The myth was retold by Aeschylus in his *Prometheus Bound*, which was translated by EBB in 1833, and again in 1844, with B's consultation. Shelley also retold the myth in his *Prometheus Unbound*. There is some question which of these is the background for this section of "Lairesse." DeVane and Pettigrew-Collins adopt the view of Porter-Clarke that B's version of the myth echoes EBB's, largely on the ground that the epithet "winged-hound" in EBB's translation appears in "Lairesse" as *eagle-hound* l. 197.

But the tone of B's and Lairesse's "Walk" is one of test and skepticism toward the use of classical sources, and it seems more likely that Shelley is the reference here than EBB. Shelley too uses the epithet "winged hound" (*Prometheus Unbound*, 1.34), and more significantly, Shelley consistently absorbed classical sources in his work; he is a more obvious thematic target than EBB in the context of "Lairesse." Moreover, there are more specific allusions and implicit borrowings from Shelley than from Aeschylus or EBB in this section. The bird which gnaws the vitals of the hero in "Lairesse" is a vulture (see ll. 192-93, 198 and nn.), as in Shelley; it is an eagle in EBB (there is some ambiguity in historical usage of the terms). A dawn setting and a storm are important elements in Shelley and in B. Most tellingly, the distinguishing feature of Shelley's version, Prometheus' foreshadowing of Christ in his forgiveness and pity for Jupiter, is present in B's version, in the reference to Prometheus' *unconquerable smile* l. 195 and in the admonition to him to *love ever!*, l. 206.

192-93]   *heaped . . . crouching*   The hump and bent neck of the vulture sent by Jupiter to tear at Prometheus' liver.

198]   *eagle-hound*   The compound suggests a large bird of prey, not necessarily specifically an eagle.

200]   *Fate's secret*   Writing to EBB in March 1845 about a projected revision of her translation of Aeschylus' *Prometheus Bound*, B proposed an introductory drama exploring the relationship "between Jove and [Prometheus]. . he will reveal the master-secret to Jove when he shall have released him." In letters between 27 February and 11 March 1845, exchanges between B and EBB about Prometheus are central, eliciting from B revealing and categorical comments about reading and writing, as well as about the dynamics of power and moral action between Jove/Jupiter and Prometheus (Kintner, 37; 29-40). This emphasis is also Shelley's, as B indicates in the letter of 11 March. Mrs. Orr says that only ll. 208-9 were directly derived from Aeschylus and that "another version of the Promethean myth" suggested the thunderstorm (Orr, 356 n.2).

210-61]   *Section IX*   The appearance of *Artemis* (l. 245) after the Promethean storm follows Lairesse's direction to coordinate light, time of day, and action—the action of hunting, in the case of Artemis. She is seen in her functions as huntress, goddess of the moon, and patroness of young virgins. In the contest with Lairesse, B demonstrates again in this section his power both to raise a living landscape and to lend it human, psychological, and original interest. The chamois stag's perspective on Artemis at the moment of death ll. 246-53 is uniquely B's and, in terms of the contest between Lairesse and B, also uniquely "modern."

221-22]   *bull . . . sport*   A *bull* can be any large animal such as an elk or buffalo as well as a bovine. Here the comparison of a rushing stream after a storm and a bull fleeing a hunt (*formidable sport*) is an ingenious application of B's double vision (l. 119) in his competition with Lairesse.

231-33]   *garb . . . knee*   A belted or girdled (*succinct, OED*) garment protecting her modesty from the *smirch* of visibility.

234-37]   *bow . . . crescent*   The tips of an archer's bow are called horns. When the bow is bent, they resemble the arc of the crescent moon worn by the goddess of the hunt as a headdress in classical depictions of Artemis.

239]   *repugnant*   In opposition to, standing up, as the crescent moon insignia sits poised on Artemis' brow.

242] *lucid* Luminous.

246-50] *chamois . . . births* A chamois is a mountain goat, perhaps a symbol of the virility with which Artemis is at war.

255-58] *deaths . . . temple-step* Artemis enjoined her followers to reject the weakness of love, and punished infractions against their vow of perpetual maidenhood with death, dealt invisibly by moonbeam arrows dispatched from the bow of her crescent arc. Hymen is the god of marriage, represented by a young man carrying a torch and a veil.

262-307] *Section X* Lairesse's recommendations for paintings representing actions at noon, the hour of this section, are subjects connected with rest and retirement from heat and bright sunlight. Once again B contributes his own dimension to the scene while also following Lairesse. The landscape is dominated by the sun, as Lairesse prescribes, and its description leads naturally to the secluded glade where Lyda sleeps, spied on by her rejected suitor, the satyr whose panting human heart is B's revised focus and the key drama of the scene.

267] *herbless* Barren, rocky.

283-302] *Satyr . . . sake* Their upper half man, their lower half goat, satyrs were followers of Bacchus and were associated in myth with nature, music and dance, wine, and lust. The story of Lyda and the satyr whom she spurned, who was himself loved with an unrequited love by Echo, who was herself loved by Pan, is told by the Greek pastoral poet Moschus, who wrote c.150 B.C. Shelley translated Moschus' story as "Pan, Echo, and the Satyr" in his *Idyls*, 5.1-6; EBB owned an edition of Moschus and annotated its margins (*Reconstruction*, A242). Mrs. Orr indicates that Shelley's work is B's source (Orr, 356 n.3). The surface-and-depth double vision (see l. 119) of the satyr's suffering behind his mask of mirth is, however, entirely B's.

308-62] *Sections XI and XII* These two sections describe a historical rather than a mythical scene, but one that has taken on near-legendary status in painting and literature. The surrender of Darius III and the Persian empire to Alexander the Great and Greek rule in 331 B.C. marked the spread of Greek civilization into Europe, Asia, and Africa and seemed to signal the victory of Hellenism over all the civilized world—past, present, and future. The setting is the site of the great battle between Persian and Greek armies in the Euphrates valley. The time is sunset, expressive of momentary glory followed by darkness and new day (ll. 335-41). The two great adversaries see the stakes of the battle as no less than *rule in reach / Over the race of man* and see themselves as dividing the forces of the known world, *earth halved almost* between them (ll. 324-25, 327). B evokes both the glory and the vainglory of the moment, but clearly offers this scene as the capstone in the "Walk" and the final demonstration of the decline of the long day of the Hellenic golden age.

332] *Macedonian* Alexander was born in Macedonia, to the N of Greece; he conquered Greece before he went on to extend Greek power.

355-59] *journey . . . longer* The "Walk" is completed, but the journey continues, the direction unknown.

Caucasus, Arcadia References to the earlier sections of the walk, to the stories of Prometheus, the satyr, and Artemis. *Human heroes* recap the mythic and historic stages of the "Walk," but to return to the Promethean setting, or to the Arcadia belonging to Artemis and the satyr, or to the locale of even the greatest of mortal heroes such as Darius and Alexander, is impossible.

360-62] *ghost . . . hands* Mrs. Orr, DeVane and others generalize that this figure is "pagan hopelessness of the to-come" (Orr, 357), "symbolical of the emptiness of the Greek philosophy" (*B's Parleyings*, 249). It seems less likely that the ghost is a comment on antiquity and its learning than on later combative classicists and neo-classicists— here collectively personified by Lairesse and their cause dramatized by the contest enacted in the "Walk."

scarce strives No longer contends.

deprecating hands Prayerful, pleading gestures. The ghostly Lairesse, silenced and voiceless, concedes defeat.

381] *glozed* Interpreted, with an implication of specious or deceptive intent.

382-89] *Dream . . . glory* The lines are applicable to the Pre-Raphaelite poets, to Tennyson, Landor, and Arnold, all of whom were among B's circle. DeVane argues in careful detail that Arnold and his "Preface to Poems, 1853" are B's source for the satirical advice to "Dream afresh old godlike shapes . . . . Push back reality" (*B's Parleyings*, 235-39).

394-404] *best . . . indeed* The reference is to the narrative in general of Book 11 of the *Odyssey*, where Odysseus recounts his visit to Hades to receive prophecy and counsel from Tiresias for his trip home. At the appointed place Odysseus and his men conjure up the dead by pouring libations and scattering grain (*dust-heaps*), and by digging a pit to catch the blood of a sacrificial lamb and a ewe. The dead appear in throngs, wretched but eager to taste the *sip of sacrifice*, after which they may speak but must speak *truth*, which is invariably their unhappiness in the afterlife and their desire to hear about their *lost loves* left behind. Odysseus speaks with loved ones, old comrades and the heroic dead, but the specific encounter told here is with Achilles, who corrects Odysseus's impression that Achilles must be a king among the dead. Achilles tells Odysseus that it is better to be a serf among the living than a lord among the dead (*Odyssey*, 11.488-91). B adds to his source Odysseus's vivid description of the *sip of sacrifice* releasing death's desire to return to life. It is this failure of Greek thought to include any transfigured concept of the afterlife that for B was its great weakness. MS ended the quotation at the end of the section at l. 408; the 1887 and 1888-89 editions ended it after *indeed* l. 404. Given that the thought in the last sentence of the section is part of Odysseus's and Achilles's speech in the original, and that it is essential to completing the contrast introduced in the sentence before it, the present editors feel that the MS punctuation should be considered as a valid alternative reading to the punctuation of the copy text; see variants.

409]   *Be death*   A subjunctive, not an imperative, verb: If death be . . . .
423-24]   *Greek . . . us*   The *Greek Bard* is probably a generalized term here. The refrain is a common one in pastoral elegy, which typically describes the poignancy of the renewal of spring at a time of grief for the death of a loved one.
426-34]   *Dance . . . yellows*   The lyric was first published separately in 1886 (with the title "Spring Song") in *The New Amphion*, a magazine published by the Edinburgh UP. B's response to sad Greek pastoral is to reverse its sentiment by embedding a garden of celebratory lyricism in his parleying's tribute to a dead hero.

WITH CHARLES AVISON

Sources and Backgrounds   "With Charles Avison" is clearly dated in composition by internal evidence. The first section of the poem is devoted to a scene outside B's study window on a blustery March day. A small bird appears to be attempting to gather materials for a nest, and as the poet observes this little drama, he notes its resemblance to the themes of his poem: by means of puns and other verbal extensions, the March weather, the bird, and its nest-building become a fable about recurrence, change, and renewal. The precise setting and date of the scene in the poem match the chronology of production of *Parleyings* to place the writing of "With Charles Avison" almost certainly in March of 1886.

Charles Avison (c.1709-70) was born in Newcastle, where he remained for his celebrated career as church organist, composer, and theorist. His *Essay on Musical Expression* (1752) was in B's father's library. A *Grand March in C Major* frequently played by B's mother on the family piano was attributed to Avison (*Reconstruction*, A139, J93). The

Grand March is in a collection of pieces by different composers, all transcribed by Robert Browning Sr. (*Reconstruction,* J93). The march is identified in his hand as composed by Charles Avison. The piece is not, however, in Avison's characteristic florid, Baroque style, and the attribution is doubtful. According to the *Grove Dictionary of Music,* B is the only authority for Avison's authorship of the *Grand March.* The simple structure and harmony of the piece—an ABA melody of two eight-measure sections and a repeat, accompanied by an unfigured bass line—suggests that it may have been transcribed from a recollected performance and not from a written source, with the loose attribution such a circumstance might bring.

The poem's attribution of unusual depth and power to the simple composition must also be questioned. B's sense of the extraordinary depth and range possible to musical expression, his liberal and nationalistic identification with the political freedom associated with the seventeenth-century Parliamentarian movement, and the personal association of the piece with a happy and secure childhood, all converge on the fragile vehicle of the March.

Such is the power of B's emotional and intellectual associations with Avison both as composer and as writer that Avison himself is soon eclipsed as subject. Although both broad arguments and details of reference in this parleying make clear that B returned to Avison's *Essay* as he wrote—as he does not seem to have done in other parleyings—the argument of the *Essay* is never clearly engaged. In its time the *Essay* was part of an active polemic among rival factions broadly defined as partisans of Handel and younger Italian opera composers. For the poet of *Parleyings,* the interest of Addison's musical analysis was less topical and more universal: the essay's discussion of the unmediated emotional language of music and its attention to changing musical styles and tastes. B's poem develops the contrast between these topics, exploring on the one hand in some of B's loftiest and most powerful poetic language the indirect but profoundly spiritual expression and meaning in music, and its ability to retain this power through stylistic and historical change (see especially ll. 134 ff.). On the other hand, the poem dwells also on the threat that meretricious novelty and spurious complexity—as some viewed the innovative chromatic harmonies of Wagner—posed to the universal language of music, as represented by the sturdy affirmations of the unmodulated C Major key and the even march pace of Avison's march. By extension, these affirmations are linked in the poem to the steady, progressive norms of British liberal politics that the march is made to embody.

The poem follows a three-part structure roughly corresponding to three-part musical form: a narrative theme punning on the calendar month of March and the march of time, and linking biographical and contemporary references; a developmental section (VI-IX) on the nature and function of music as the preeminent art; and a bravura finale which sets the rousing march to words and to motion. Like the ABA form of the *Grand March*—appended in full at the end of this parleying—the poem modulates and resolves all change into the celebratory C major of its finale, and into a triadic harmony of personal, esthetic, and national influences.

4] *my window* The view here is that from B's study at 19 Warwick Crescent, where he moved in May 1862 and lived for twenty-five years. The same scene, wall, and creeper are described in the Prologue to *Pacchiarotto* (1876; see this edition, 13.135). The walled back garden is typical of a row house of the period.

17] *blackcap* The Blackcap (*Sylvia borin*) is a European warbler with a brown body and a glossy black crown. B's reference to his bird's brightness suggests that he means to describe the Great Tit (*Parus major*), which has a black cap and brilliant yellow underparts. The Great Tit behaves as B describes in ll. 27-29, and it has greenish-blue upper parts, as B alludes to in ll. 26-27 ("each wing/Greenly a-quiver"). The Blackcap is a dull-colored bird in both sexes.

27] *Greenly* Vigorously (*OED*).

29] *finch* Though not a true finch, the Great Tit is like finches in size and diet.

31-32] *wool . . . fence* In the country there would be sheep's wool caught on hedgerow fences.

33-35] *spoiled . . . new-suited* Appropriated by gardeners, taken as spoil (*spoiled*) for artful horticultural purposes, and then *new-suited* (pun) for the finch's nest. The little fable forecasts the spoiling and recasting of past musical achievements in the poem ahead.

37] *larch* Common name for *Larix*, a tree of the pine family which loses its leaves in winter. In spring it has red flowers (larch roses) which are followed by brown cones.

43-57] *relic . . . Newcastle* The word *relic* is the first of a series of puns or double entendres which pivot the anecdote of the bird into a working analogy for the central theme of the poem, the state of music in the late nineteenth century. The puns are *far-flyer* and *March* l. 45, *air* l. 50, *band* l. 52, and *Newcastle* l. 57. The *relic* is both rag and thought of Avison; memory is a *far-flyer* like the migratory bird; *March* is month and music as herald and processional for the past; the *air* of March is both tune and climate; the *band* is both community and musical ensemble; the old-world's *Newcastle* organist is the temporary refuge of B's nest-building memory.

55]   *pipe or wire*   Wind or string instruments.

66]   *novel modulation*   Frequent or unexpected shifts of key, associated with the music of post-classical periods and especially with the music of one of B's favorite composers, Richard Wagner, who was a master of chromaticism and *novel modulation*.

68-70]   *discord . . . concord*   A reference to the use of a dissonant note to enhance a resolution to the home key.

76]   *spurned*   Spurn: to strike or thrust with the foot (*OED*). Here a stronger word for "strode."

80]   *plucked the measure*   Kept time. A pun, as the next line shows.

81-84]   *John . . . bass*   A neighbor of the Bs in Camberwell, John Relfe (1763-c.1837) was a composer and writer on music theory who had been a musician in the court of George III and who taught the young B. In later years B told a friend, "I was studying the grammar of music when most children are learning the multiplication table" (*B's Youth*, 140). As the young B's teacher in theory and as author of two works regarded as important in their time, *The Principles of Harmony* (1817) and *Lucidus Ordo: Comprising an Analytical Course of Studies on the Several Branches of Musical Science; with a New Order of Thorough Bass Designation* (1819), he was a formative influence on B's musical knowledge and taste. It is the latter work to which these lines refer; thorough bass and figured bass are synonymous. The system of figured bass was a practice common to Bach and the baroque period, in which a single bass note with a numeral indicated the chord to be played with the melody line. It is a kind of shorthand and it required for realization a fluent technique and musical vocabulary. Relfe devised an alternative system of harmonic notation which was not adopted, and which in any case was an alternative to an art falling into disuse by the nineteenth century. The bass line in Avison's March, the full score of which is given at the end of the parleying, employs only the two main chords in the key of C, the tonic and dominant, and thus would need none of Relfe's *skill* in filling out. The passage suggests the emphasis in this parleying on traditional, even old-fashioned, values in musical structure and harmony, as exemplified in the music of Bach and Handel.

85-87]   *C . . . bar*   The key of C major employs the Greater Third in its tonic chord (four half-steps of the scale) rather than a minor third (three half-steps). The *March* is in three-quarter time, three *crochets* (quarter-notes) to a measure. Only in relatively modern times did a four-beat measure become standard for march music; marches were originally in either triple or duple time.

88]   *Tonic . . . Dominant*   See ll. 81-84n.

96]   *little book*   Avison's *An Essay on Musical Expression* (1752).

99-100]   *music-manufacture . . . shawms*   The composers named were all important in B's time. He knew and enjoyed their music. The faintly derogatory tone of *music-manufacture* suggests the greater technical brilliance of modern instrumentation and the virtuosity it enabled, beside the more limited baroque sound. Johannes *Brahms* (1833-97), Richard *Wagner* (1813-83), Antonin *Dvorak* (1841-1904), and Franz *Liszt* (1811-86) all wrote large orchestra pieces.

trumpets, shawms   Early versions of the modern trumpet and oboe used in the baroque period.

101-4]   *Handel . . . England*   The celebrated reputation of George Frederick *Handel* (1670-1747), whose successful vocal compositions were mainly oratorios rather than the Italian operas that he also wrote, was challenged by the opera composer Giovanni *Buononcini* (1670-1747), whom Handel had invited to London to build the reputation of his new Royal Academy of Music (1720). The continental rage for Italian opera in the eighteenth century was moderated in England to *fit laudation of the impartial few* for Buononcini, B says, yet it was felt. *We stand in England* may be an allusion to the custom of standing for the Hallelujah chorus of Handel's *Messiah* and to the lasting reverence for this work among the British—though here the reverence appears a token convention.

104-12]   *Fashion . . . organist*   These once celebrated names have all lapsed into obscurity. Francesco *Geminiani* (1687-1762) came to England in 1714. A great violin virtuoso as well as composer, he played at court with Handel as his accompanist. Avison studied with him and praises him in the *Essay*. John Christopher *Pepusch* (1667-1752) was an English composer born in Germany. His cantata *Alexis* was very popular, as were his selections and arrangements of music for John Gay's *The Beggar's Opera*. Pepusch took a D. Mus. at Oxford and was a founder of the Academy of Ancient Music. The formal attire of ranking musicians such as Handel, Bach and Pepusch included ornate wigs, in which they are invariably portrayed in illustrations. It is unknown which *Greenway* trilled *"Alexis,"* but it is likely that the allusion extends the idea of antiquated conventions and changing musical fashions evoked by the bushy wigs of eighteenth-century conductors (though in fact the modern conductor who stands before players and singers to direct them in performance was not known until the nineteenth century). Since another of the firmly established and popular conventions of eighteenth-century operatic performance was the casting of castrati in female roles, together with their often extreme license for virtuoso display such as long trills, probably *Greenway* was a castrato—again, like the other references in this passage, once celebrated, now sunk into oblivion.

127-29] *Hear . . . soul* Avison *tenders evidence* in the *Essay* that music speaks to the full range of emotions, refining and reconciling them. E.g., "[I]t is the peculiar Quality of Music to raise the sociable and happy Passions, and to subdue the contrary ones" (*Essay*, 5).

132-37] *"O Thou" . . . help* The famous baritone aria "To the Evening Star" in Wagner's *Tannhauser* is in a major key, and employs, albeit in a very understated way, the composer's characteristically innovative modulation in its harmony. This passage asks, "isn't it possible that an equally great aria might yet be written in a minor key without modulation and following a model set by Handel rather than Wagner?"

fatal Wagner Fatal in the sense of decisively influential, irrevocable.

138-39] *There . . . music* This bold unvarnished claim of the superiority of music over the other arts is followed by ten ll. of complex explication that seem calculated in their contrast, designed perhaps to embody in language the contrast between melodic theme and development in music. The claim that music is a form of higher truth sounds similar to the thinking of Walter Pater, who argued in *Studies in the History of the Renaissance* (1873) that "all art constantly aspires towards the condition of music" ("The School of Georgione"). Yet Pater's doctrine of art for art's sake is far from B's intention here.

148] *who . . . find* "Seek and ye shall find" (Matt. 7:7).

154] *enginery* Ingenious arts and machinery.

156-57] *stress of faculty* Exercise of its inherent and distinct power.

167] *operosity* Laboriousness (*OED*).

184] *emulate* Rival, spur on (*OED*).

212] *still* In the double sense of fixed, and lasting.

223] *nether-brooding* Bred in the deep underworld.

224-29] *Fleet . . . war* The speech is Helen of Troy's as she looks for her brothers Castor and Pollux among the Greeks in the siege of Troy, *Iliad* 3.235-44. As DeVane points out (*B's Parleyings*, 276 n. 74), it is likely that B took the example from Ruskin's chapter on the pathetic fallacy in *Modern Painters* (1856), where the speech is held up as an example of great pathos allied to high truth, especially the concluding lines, B's ll. 230-31, which in Ruskin's translation read, "So she spoke. But them, already, the life-giving earth possessed, there in Lacedaemon, in the dear fatherland." Ruskin writes, "The poet has to speak of the earth in sadness, but he will not let that sadness affect or change his thoughts of it. No: though Castor and Pollux be dead, yet the earth is our mother still, fruitful, life-giving" (III, ch. 12). B's copy of Volume

III of *Modern Painters,* now in the Morgan Library, is inscribed "Robert Browning, with John Ruskin's affectionate and respectful regards. January. 1856" (*Reconstruction,* A1983).

232-34] *Painter's . . . nothingness* Michelangelo's fresco of the creation of Eve on the ceiling of the Sistine Chapel on Rome. The theological doctrine that God created "ex nihilo," "out of nothing," is in contrast to art's ability to "produce change, not creation" (ll. 204-5). Thus Michelangelo in depicting the moment of creation represents the highest aspiration and achievement possible to art.

248] *wistful* Expectantly or yearningly eager, watchful, or intent (*OED*); here eager to know (wist).

249-76] *Could . . . invasion* The passage describes and documents, but does not lament, changes in musical styles and leaders over generations. In the contest between poetry, painting, and music for power to express the truth of soul, music is said to be both most successful and most transient, a paradox inherent in the nature of feeling and its mutability. B seems to have found this idea most clearly articulated in a biographical sketch of a sixteenth-century French Huguenot musician, Claude Le Jeune (c.1523-c. 1600), who was said to be a "Phoenix of musicians," but about whom was also written, "In Music, the Beau Idéal changes every thirty years" (*Esquisse biographique sur Claude Lejeune, surnommé le Phénix des musiciens, compositeur de la musique des rois Henri III et Henri IV* [Valenciennes,1845], an anonymous memoir in B's father's library). These epigraphs on Le Jeune struck B forcibly enough to generate almost the whole body of a letter to EBB 7 March 1846, a letter given over to music and musical examples. "For music, I made myself melancholy just now with some 'Concertos for the Harpsichord by Mr. Handel' brought home by my father the day before yesterday:—what were light, modern things once! Now I read not very long ago a french Memoir of 'Claude Le Jeune' called in his time the Prince of Musicians,—no, 'Phoenix'—the unapproachable wonder to all time. . that is, twenty years after his death about! and to this pamphlet was prefixed as motto this startling axiom—'In Music, the Beau Idéal changes every thirty years'—well,—is not that *true*? The *Idea,* mind, changes,—the general standard. . . . next hundred years, who will be the Rossini? who is no longer the Rossini even I remember—his early overtures are as purely Rococo as Cimarosa's or more . . . . the pity of it! Le Jeune, the Phoenix,—and Rossini who directed his letters to his mother as 'mother of the famous composer'—and Henry Lawes, and Dowland's Lute, ah me!" (Kintner, 523-24; *Correspondence,* 12.137-38).

253-55] *Radaminta . . . Rinaldo* Grand operas by Handel featuring scenes of passion and of pathos, both very popular in their day, both later neglected. *Rinaldo* (1711) was Handel's first London opera and was very successful, as was *Radamisto* (the correct title) after it in 1715.

257]   *spar*   A crystalline mineral often made into ornaments.

267]   *dawn-doomed phantoms*   Ghosts must vanish at first light, according to legend.

270-76]   *Gluck . . . invasion*   See *Sources* above. The sense of these lines is that the displacement of reputations among the great is inevitable, healthy, and non-fatal. As *Gluck* rivaled *Handel*, so *Mozart* outdid his teacher *Haydn*; so new stars will appear in the firmament. Christoph Willibald *Gluck* (1714-87), German-born composer whose operas were mainly performed in Paris, led a movement to reform the excesses of Italian opera and to restore dramatic truth to the operatic stage. Gluck knew Handel in London in 1745-46. Franz Joseph *Haydn* (1732-1809), Austrian composer, is best known for his symphonies and instrumental works. Wolfgang Amadeus *Mozart* (1756-91), also Austrian, is regarded as the master of late eighteenth-century opera, as well as of other musical genres, and as successor to Haydn. In these ll. and below the interest—especially to B himself—of less well-known or forgotten composers amid the rise and fall of exalted names is also implied—to wit, Avison.

274]   *flamboyant*   Flaming.

281-82]   *Relfe . . . pupil*   See ll. 81-84n.

290]   *reactives*   Reactivating agents, here musical devices unknown to the eighteenth century; see ll. 301-2.

302-3]   *turn . . . easy-going*   Render a simple melody shocking by the use of new harmonies.

304]   *Bach*   Johann Sebastian Bach (1685-1750), whose *Well-tempered Clavier* established equal temperament on keyboard instruments and made possible modulation among all the keys, although Bach's modulations were ordered and conservative by post-classical standards.

305]   *Hudl*   The German composer J. Hudl published a book on modulation in 1802. An enharmonic change is a shift from one key to another achieved by respelling the same chord with sharps or flats. This was not possible before the equal-tempered scale (see 304n.).

309-10, 315]   *Largo . . . Rubato / rhythm I break*   The nineteenth century was a great age of virtuoso performance, and B here mocks some of the excesses in tempo and distortions of rhythm indulged in by some performers of Romantic music. *Largo* is a very slow tempo; Handel's *Largo* from the opera *Xerxes* is one of his most frequently played pieces. *Rubato* means "robbing from the time value of one note to give to another"; it should be a sparing and subtle effect, not an obvious one.

312-13]   *Georgian . . . Grenadiers*   The term *Georgian* refers to the reigns of the eighteenth-century Georges (I, II, and III, 1714-1820) and is often applied to the classical Palladian architecture of the period. B here applies the order and symmetry associated with the *Georgian years* to Avison's March and its clockwork rhythm, *timed* to the *step precise* of the British *Grenadiers.* These were a company composed of the tallest, most imposing soldiers, who served as Guard of the Royal Household and were chosen for their handsome effect on parade.

314-18]   *score . . . Olympus*   If I press (*crowd*) the tempo and take liberties with the rhythm, the March becomes a theme for revolution. The *Titans* were the giant children of the first gods of Olympus, who overthrew their father.

322]   *three parts*   The harmony.

333]   *Purcell*   Henry Purcell (c. 1659-95) was a celebrated composer in his time whose reputation declined after his death, partly because of the unavailability of his work. In 1876, however, the Purcell Society was founded in London—an event of which B was certain to have been aware—with the purpose of reissuing his work in an authoritative edition.

335-38]   *C major . . . Third*   The key of A minor is the relative minor to C major, having the same key signature. The A minor tonic chord has a lowered or *Lesser Third.* B makes the traditional association of melancholy with the minor mode.

340]   *buying knowledge*   The penalty of mortality for tasting the fruit of the tree of knowledge (Gen. 3:19).

342]   *nescience absolute*   Ignorance which was never knowledge in the first place.

359]   *foremost . . . file*   (That which) is at the head of the marching parade (file).

361-62]   *Lift . . . immortal*   Avison as prototypical fallen and resurrected man.

372]   *garniture*   Dress, covering.

380]   *corolla-safeguard*   The petal envelope of a flower, here an opened one.

382]   *March-motive*   Both the tune of the march, as in a musical motif, and its seasonally-recurring purpose or meaning.

383-86]   *Sharps . . . trample*   Strange new harmonies played on early instruments will herald the march of cumulative, not revolutionary, progress into the future. An *ophicleide* is a bass brass instrument which in fact does not pre-date the nineteenth century. *Bombardon* was a name first given to an early type of oboe, later to a brass instrument.

388-89] *federated . . . Future* Human progress and British nationalism are allied in the image of an England extending around the globe, its progressive influence felt everywhere. The late nineteenth-century movement to establish a Federation of the Empire was intended to improve trade and defense of British power throughout the empire; it was defeated by Gladstone in 1893.

391-92] *sable-stoled . . . Tyburn* The somber procession of clergy that precedes the criminal to the place of execution. A *little-ease* was a dungeon in the Tower of London. *Tyburn* Hill, near what is now the Marble Arch at the NE corner of Hyde Park, was the site of the gallows where public hangings took place until 1783. The long *procession* from the Tower to Tyburn, a kind of parade inversely analogous to the march of progress l. 389, would have been on foot, with the prisoner in a cart.

394] *heading . . . hanging* The sentence which could be dealt to prisoners found guilty of a capital offense such as treason, given here in reverse order. The unhappy culprit was first hanged but cut down before he was dead, then disembowelled and quartered, then beheaded. The judge's phrasing of the sentence was "hanged, drawn, and quartered." A better contrast to the idea of political and intellectual progress could hardly be found.

395-96] *recusants . . . ago* Dissenters from the Church of England during the reign (1558-1603) of Elizabeth I were known as *recusants*. They were subject to stiff fines but not to capital punishment.

397] *Elizabethan plain-song* The phrase is misleading. Plain-song, also called Gregorian chant, is a name given to very early monophonic liturgical music of the Catholic and Eastern church. Although the chorale-style music of the Protestant service which developed in Elizabethan times was quite different from Gregorian chant, the musical notation was indeed similar, and both systems were altogether different from modern notation; see below ll. 399, 400-402 and nn.

399] *classic vengeance* By depriving it of rhythm; see below.

400-402] *Larges . . . Aside* Before modern musical notation was developed in the early seventeenth century, temporal values in music were indicated by a complex mensural notation without bar lines. *Larges*, *longs*, and *breves* were the three largest note values; they do not correspond to modern note values. In modern notation a *crochet* is a quarter note, a *quaver* an eighth note.

pertness Cleverness, skill, briskness. Eighteenth-century Baroque music was often highly embellished with runs and ornamentation, as in, for example, Handel's *Messiah*.

404] *Nor . . . day* Whether night or day.

407] *Preston Pans* There were two battles by this name, one at *Prestonpans* in Scotland fought in 1745 by Scots supporters of Prince Charles against the English, the other fought at *Preston* in Lancashire between Cromwell's army and the Royalist army in 1648, during the Civil War. The invocation at ll. 410-11 of "the famous Five" from this period argues that the reference here is to the latter.

409-12] *Parliament . . . Southwark* The *famous Five* were M.P.'s whom Charles I attempted to impeach and arrest in 1642. B's friend John Forster wrote a detailed account of this episode in *Arrest of the Five Members by Charles the First, 1641-42* (London, 1860), an inscribed copy of which was in B's library (*Reconstruction*, A983). Denzil *Hollis*, Sir Arthur Haselrig, William *Strode*, John *Hampden*, and John *Pym* fled the threat of arrest by seeking refuge in the safety zone of the City. When the king followed them there on 5 January, 1642, he found an angry mob facing him. In Forster's words, "The multitude pressed around his coach with confused shouts of Privilege of Parliament! Privilege of Parliament!" As in B's l. 409, *privilege* refers to the immunity from arrest claimed by Members of Parliament. The *Train Bands*, or trained bands of local militia were made up of the people of London and its suburbs. When the famous Five returned to Parliament on 10 January "Divers . . . of the borough of Southwark then came and offered the assistance of their Trained Bands . . . to be our guard at Westminster" (Forster, 349, quoting a contemporary account).

423-33] *Pym . . . Pym* Forster (see preceding n.) calls *Pym* "Beyond all question the most popular man in England at this time [1641-42]" (p. 39), for his ability to preserve order in the House of Commons, to defend its privileges, and to establish a parliamentary army as the Civil War loomed. Born in *Somerset* Pym was M.P. for the borough of *Tavistock*, and he was a hero at *Westminster*, the seat of Parliament.

426] *Strafford . . . Eliot* Pym and Sir Thomas Wentworth, Earl of *Strafford* (1593-1641), adviser to Charles I, were friends estranged by Strafford's loyalty to the king. B's historical tragedy *Strafford* tells this story and the events leading to Strafford's beheading; see this edition, 2.3. The Parliamentary leader Sir John *Eliot* (1592-1632) was imprisoned by King Charles in 1629 for resisting the dissolution of Parliament. He died in the Tower, of consumption.

FUST AND HIS FRIENDS

Sources and Backgrounds Johann Fust, or John Fust in B's "Epilogue," lived c.1400-1466 in Mainz, Germany, called Mayence here as in B's

French source, the *Biographie Universelle*. Fust was the patron and partner of Johannes Gutenberg for about five years, up to the production of the first book printed in Europe with movable types, the Gutenberg Bible, in 1455. Thereafter as a result of litigation and Fust's repossession of the printing house in payment of the money Gutenberg owed him, Fust became owner of Gutenberg's invention and printer of the first book inscribed with both the printer's name and the full date of publication. The book was a Psalter (book of psalms), in Latin, like the Gutenberg Bible. As a consequence of these circumstances, the popular belief that Fust was the first printer extended well into the nineteenth century. The *Biographie Universelle*, that stalwart of B's early reading and authoritative source for many of his poems, gives a benign cast to Fust's dealings with Gutenberg and full credit to Fust as co-inventor of the printing press, both judgments which have been reversed by historians.

One correction that was, however, made to popular belief about Fust by the *Biographie*, B chose not so much to ignore as to explore. "On a quelquefois confondu Fust avec Faust le Magicien," says the *Biographie* (16.204) ("There have been occasional confusions between Faust the magician and Fust."). The confusion is made very stubbornly by Fust's seven friends, who visit him fully expecting to find his soul possessed by the fiend. (Clyde D. Ryals speculates that the seven benighted friends "represent the nay-sayers of the seven preceding parleyings" (*Browning's Later Poetry* [Ithaca, NY, 1975], 224). The conflict between the friends' superstitious distrust of technical and scientific progress, and the poem's eventual reconciliation of religion and progress, science and religious truth, make up the drama of this little morality play, and make of it a fitting epilogue to the themes and structure of *Parleyings* as a whole.

As "Apollo and the Fates" foreshadows in the figure of Apollo and his "invention" of wine a proto-Christian plea for a "compensative law" of love in contrast to that of the cynical Fates, so Fust and his press predict a new beginning for the Word. Revelation and dissemination will go hand in hand, says Fust in his long millenial speech ll. 258-360, a speech linking history and progress; art, science, and religion; earthly good and heavenly hope—and the potential for abuse and evil in these as in all human experience. B's quest for truth in *Parleyings* ends with a clear assertion of the necessity of ambiguity that is as appropriate to the personal truth of the series as to its grand human themes. At the same time, in its emphasis on the mechanics of the *printed* word, the epilogue to *Parleyings* restores a balance between abstract conceptual truth and its practical demystified applications that is also true to B's career and character. As Allan C. Dooley details in his study of the interactive dynamics of author, publisher, and printer in the Victorian Age, B's close involvement in the production of his books reflected a respect for authorial control at every level that was typical of his vigorous pragmatism (*Author and Printer in Victorian England* [Charlottesville, Va., 1992], esp. Ch. 5). Fittingly, the epilogue to *Parleyings With Certain People of Importance in Their Day* reminds us of this balance.

Stage direction]   *Mayence, 1457*   The French word for Mainz, Germany; the year and presumably the day, 14 August 1457, printed in Fust's Psalter.

12]   *gossipry . . . sib* A proverbial phrase: friends and relations. The friends are probably all monks of various orders and status; see ll. 55, 114-15 and nn.

14]   *crib* Shut off.

17]   *roundly* Summarily, severely.

18]   *Divine* A monk.

22]   *Black Artsman* Evil magician, one who relied on spirits. White or natural magic could achieve results without supernatural means.

23-24]   *paying . . . Church* He bought his pardon from the Church, presumably with ill-gotten gains from his pact with Satan.

26-29]   *Fiend . . . Faust* An account from one of the early versions of the Faust legend collected in the *Faustbuch* (1587), translated as the *Faust Book* (1592), confirms the second friend's claim: seeking Faust, his students found that "all the hall lay besprinkled with blood, his brains cleaving to the wall: for the Devil had beaten him from one wall against another, in one corner lay his eyes, in another his teeth . . . . Lastly they came into the yard where they found his body lying on the horse dung, most monstrously torn, and fearful to behold, for his head and all his joints were dashed in pieces" (Philip Palmer and Robert More, *The Sources of the Faust Tradition* [New York, 1936], 230).

    Faust . . . Fust See *Sources* above.

32]   *Solomon . . . goads* "The words of the wise are as goads" (Eccles. 12:11). It is doubtful that Solomon, traditionally assumed to be the "Preacher" of Ecclesiastes, wrote that book.

35]   *palinodes* Recantations, here in the sense of last minute or deathbed confessions.

44-45]   *Devil . . . thee* Echo of 1 Pet. 5:8, "Be sober, be vigilant: because your adversary the devil, as a roaring lion walketh about seeking whom he may devour."

51]   *plie . . . corrugate* Do those pursed (*corrugate*) lips open to utter a plea? (*OED* lists *plie* as an alternate spelling of *plea*.)

52] *Lost . . . surmise* He is lost in his thoughts, not in traffic with the devil.

55] *Barnabite . . . advise* A *Barnabite* is a member of a minor Catholic order named for St. Barnabas. The Second Friend hushes the First Friend by implying that he is a member of an inferior and incompetent order; the First Friend returns the compliment in the same terms at l. 114.

57] *trucked* Bartered.

62] *Sir Belial* One of the names of Satan, used in the Bible (see 2 Cor. 6:15) and in Milton (see *Paradise Lost*, 1.490.

63] *Helen of Troy* Faust's affair with the beautiful Helen, whose abduction by Paris to Troy was the cause of the Trojan war, is treated in many versions of the Faust legend, but most extensively in Goethe's *Faust*, 2.3. She was conjured up for Faust by Satan. Fust points out that his mistress (*leman*) was procured in the ordinary way, by gold.

70] *leman* Helen of Troy; see l. 63n.

72] *guttler* Greedy eater.

74-75] *out . . . cluster* This feat is part of the Faustian lore in the *Book of Faust* (see ll. 26-29n.), and appears in Part I of Goethe's Faust.

84-85] *counting . . . disbursed* The sense of the gibe is that the wits of drunks are befuddled and easily conned: they count on their fingers, they spend freely without doing an accurate reckoning of the cost. A *guilder* is a coin of considerable value, much more than a *groat*, which according to Johnson's *Dictionary* is "a proverbial name for a small sum."

86] *skinker* Tapster.

90] *Rhenish . . . Raphal* An inexpensive local wine from the Rhine valley and a much finer French wine, St. Raphael.

101-3] *honours . . . peer* Goethe's Faust is given honors and gifts by the Emperor in Part II.

106] *vanities . . . sun* "Then I returned, and I saw vanity under the sun" (Eccles. 4:7).

108] *crapulosity* Intemperance, debauchery; the noun form is B's invention.

114] *Barnabites* At l. 55 the First Friend was the Barnabite; see n.

115] *Dominican* The Dominicans were a powerful and influential order in the Catholic Church. During the Inquisition they were under Papal instructions to discover and punish heresy, as the First Friend pretends to do here.

118] *Peter . . . partner* The Psalter published by Fust (see *Sources*, above) bore the names of himself and his son-in-law, Peter *Schoeffer*, who came from *Genesheim*, and who had also worked with Gutenberg.

121] *famulus* Private secretary to a magician or scholar.

134-35]   *unscreened . . . candle*   Unprotected by the Church. An excommunication from the Catholic Church ended by a *bell* being rung, a *book* closed, and a *candle* extinguished.

136]   *Balm . . . Gilead*   "Is there no balm in Gilead; is there no physician there?" (Jer. 8:22) *Gilead* is a mountainous part of Palestine E of the Jordan where healing balsam grows. Jeremiah asks why the Jews do not avail themselves of salvation when it is so near at hand.

139]   *pottle and punk*   Drink and prostitute.

151]   *Heureka*   The classical Greek form of "Eureka," "I have found it," attributed to Archimedes (see l. 190n).

153-54]   *hatched . . . cygnet*   Fust worries that his invention may turn out to be a tempter to vice rather than a source of inspiration and beauty for humanity. The *serpent* of Gen. 3:1-6, and the mythical and symbolic associations of the swan (*cygnet*) with poetry and music, seem to be the referents here.

157]   *discover*   Disclose.

162-85]   *that potent . . . ripe Latin*   The Latin in these lines is a pastiche and garble of a Latin exorcism against evil spirits drawn from the psalms. Exorcism was a rite closely restricted and regulated in the Catholic church, and the claims of the friends to knowing the formula are bragging and competitive rather than informed. The tags of Latin that they come up with resemble certain refrains in the Psalms, but are as meaningless in sequence as some of the lines in the rustics' version of "Pyramus and Thisbe" in *A Midsummer Night's Dream*, for example. The friends are pompous and ignorant busybodies with little knowledge of Latin; this is the comedy behind their clumsy attempts to reconstruct the rite of exorcism. That B has no correct model in mind is indicated when Fust, having consulted his printing press with all the Psalms definitively set there for his Psalter, produces the correct version but does not read it. B enjoys evoking the sonority of a dead language without its accompanying meaning in his progressive little tale forecasting the coming power of vernacular in the new print culture. We give translations of lines below, and possible sources in the Psalms.

166]   *Asmodeus . . . Hussite*   In Hebrew myth, *Asmodeus* was the offspring of Adam and the female demon Lilith. In the Book of Tobit he is frustrated by the smell of burning fish-heart and liver (ch. 6-8). *Hussites* were followers of Jan Hus (c. 1372-1415), a Czech reformer and follower of Wycliffe who was burned for his heresies. The Seventh Friend is name-dropping.

169-72]   *Ne . . . fulmina*   "Do not, being dust and ashes, bear yourself haughtily, lest lightning . . ." Cf. Psalms 103:14, "he remem-

bereth that we are dust"; and Psalms 104:4,6, "Man is like to vanity
. . . . Cast forth lightning, and scatter them: shoot out thine arrows,
and destroy them."

172]   *dorrs*   Fools.

173-75]   *Ne . . . mors*   "of the perfidious man the just fate are thun-
derbolt and hail and dread death."

176]   *Irati ne*   "Lest the angry."

181-84]   *Nos . . . spe*   "We, dust and ashes, trembling, groaning,
come to you, Lord. Give light, help, so that, pursuing holy things our
heart . . . hearts may be uplifted by hope." Cf. Psalms 22:1, "Why art
thou so far from helping me, and from the words of my roaring?" and
Psalms 141:1, "Lord, I cry unto thee."

186]   *Canon*   A clergyman belonging to the governing body of a
cathedral or collegiate church; a person of learning and authority.

187]   *sheepskin*   Parchment.

190]   *Pou sto*   Archimedes (c.287-212 B.C.), who discovered the prin-
ciple of the lever, said "Dos pou sto kai ton kosmon kineso": "Give me
a place to stand and I will move the world."

200]   *Archimedes*   See l. 190n. above.

203]   *initium to finis*   "First to last."

205]   *Black . . . gold*   Fust shows his sense of the superiority of
print to medieval illuminated manuscript.

206-8]   *ibis . . . peribis*   "You will go / You will return / You will die
in hell!"

211]   *Bamberg*   A town in SW Germany, possibly chosen here for its
association with a famous Bible printed there in 1460.

213]   *debentured*   A debenture is a legal acknowledgment of indebt-
edness; in this case, payment for service rendered by the devil.

214-15]   *dog's . . . fury*   The devil takes the shape of a black dog in
legend and in Goethe's *Faust*, Part 1.

216]   *lurcher*   A mixed-breed dog bred for catching poachers.

226]   *Myk*   The name of the Sixth Friend.

229]   *pelf*   Material profit; see ll. 186-87.

233]   *Thomas the Doubter*   The apostle who refused to accept the res-
urrection of Jesus without tangible proof (John 20:25).

240]   *criss-cross*   The cross strokes on Ts, for example.

243]   *Sub-Prior*   Assistant and secretary to the head of a Priory.

249]   *fulmen*   Thunderbolt.

251]   *seventy . . . seven*   "Jesus saith unto him, I say not unto thee,
Until seven times: but Until seventy times seven"—meaning
indefinitely. (Matt. 18:22)

257]   *tittle and jot*   A *tittle* is the smallest letter of the Hebrew alpha-
bet; a *jot* is a stroke or part of a letter. "Till heaven and earth pass, one
jot or one tittle shall in no wise pass from the law" (Matt. 5:18).

258]   *cur . . . quare*   The Latin means "why" and "wherefore," and
both are puns on cur-dog and quarry.

259]   *complot*   Plot together (archaic).

265]   *Arch-moment*   Peak moment, decisive moment.

272]   *Types*   The movable letters or type of the printing press.

274]   *gripes*   Grips.

285]   *word . . . began*   "In the beginning was the Word" (John 1:1).

299-302]   *Satan's . . . father*   "Ye are of your father, the devil, and
the lusts of your father ye will do . . . he is a liar, and the father of it"
(John 8:44). Satan is proverbially the Father of Lies.

310]   *lie-mark*   A pun on point of arrest, and untruth.

313]   *eyes horny*   Bleary-eyed, vision become opaque. Cornea, the
covering of the eyeball, means *horny* tissue.

329-55]   *goldsmith . . . chalice*   Gutenberg was a member of the
goldsmith's guild, but it is probable that B's analogy between the fine
engraving on the gold *chalice* and the technique of printing letters on
paper had a more immediate source in his own association between
truth, gold, alloy, and fine craftsmanship in *The Ring and the Book*. See
the first 31 ll. of that poem and nn. in Vol. 7 of this edition.

331]   *Tuscan artificer*   The people of ancient Etruria, later Tuscany,
mastered an art of finely embellishing gold jewelry, an art which was
later lost but retraced and imitated by the Castellani firm of jewelers in
Rome. The gold ring of *The Ring and the Book* was a Castellani one of
Etruscan design; this ring is now in the Balliol College library (A.N.
Kincaid, "The Ring and the Scholars," *BIS* 8 [1980], 151-60).

352-53]   *graving . . . cinders*   B develops a pun on grave / graving.

361-62]   *Schoeffer . . . Genesheim*   The same person; see l. 118n.

363-64]   *Plough . . . riddle*   "If ye had not plowed with my heifer, ye
had not found out my riddle" (Judg. 14:18). Samson's wife gave her
Philistine countrymen the secret of his strength.

368-69]   *rectius . . . im-per-ti-te*   "If you have known anything better,
impart it!" Horace, *Epistles* 1.6.67-68.

373]   *first . . . creation*   The unity of creation and the omniscience
of God are themes throughout the Bible. "For by him were all things
created, that are in heaven, and that are in earth, . . . all things were
created by him, and for him: And he is before all things, and by him all
things consist" (Col. 1:160).

379]   *finger*   The finger of God recurs in the Bible as an image of om-
niscience and sometimes of punishing power. For example, after the

plague of lice in Egypt, Pharoah was told, "This is the finger of God" (Exod. 8:19).

381] *Man, Microcosmos*   Made in the image of God, Gen. 1:26-27.

382] *thought . . . deed*   The phrase is part of the ritual of confession in the Roman Catholic Church.

385] *reed*   A paltry obstacle.

391-92] *height . . . depth*   "If I ascend up into heaven, thou art there; if I make my bed in hell, behold, thou art there" (Ps. 139:8).

415-16] *fee . . . hold*   Originally a reward (fee) from a feudal lord for service. Here, increased knowledge for the faithful.

418] *sapience*   Derogatory: would-be wisdom.

420] *Monks' . . . sunt*   To wish "May things always be as they are" is to live in a Fool's Paradise—the implied phrase behind *Monks' Paradise.* The dissemination of Martin Luther's teaching through the printing of the vernacular Bible will fuel the Reformation, as Fust suggests.

425] *asymptote*   A mathematical term for a line which approaches but does not touch a curved line, though if projected to infinity the two would meet.

441] *Heretics, Hussites*   See l. 166n.

456-57] *Beghard . . . Hussites*   Sects dissenting from the Catholic Church. The Waldenses were twelfth-century followers of the French Peter Valdes (Waldo). *Behards* were small religious communities originating in the Netherlands in the thirteenth century. *Jeronimites* or Hieronymites were the Hermits of St. Jerome who spread through Spain in the fourteenth and fifteenth centuries.

    Hussites   See l. 166n.

460] *Refined . . . fire*   "But who may abide the day of his coming? . . . for he is like a refiner's fire" (Mal. 3:3).

461] *opuscule*   A small opus or book.

468] *An . . . ans*   "Whether such and such is to be believed." The proposition is an exercise to elicit a rational defense of a religious principle, following Thomas Aquinas' classic method in the *Summa Theologica.* The Second Friend forecasts a time when challenge, not defense, will answer the proposition.

472] *With . . . began*   A contemptuous reference to Eve.

473] *idiom unpolished*   In Czech, which—like other vernacular languages—the Second Friend considers an uncivilized tongue.

474] *Swan*   Martin Luther. The reference is probably to the ancient legend that swans sing before they die. In leaving the world the Lutheran Bible, Luther both quenched the fire under heretics and quenched the power of the Roman Catholic Church. Luther greeted the printing press as his ally: "Printing is the last and also the greatest

gift of God. By it He wanted to have the cause of the true religion be-
come known and spread in all languages."

POEMS BY ELIZABETH BARRETT BROWNING (1887)

Prefatory Note]   The publication to which B was responding is *The Poeti-
cal Works of Elizabeth Barrett Browning, from 1826 to 1844,* (London: Ward,
Lock & Co., [1887]). The editor of this collection, which was unsanc-
tioned by B, was John Henry Ingram, who composed a memoir of EBB
as a preface to the volume. Ingram had begun attempting to get infor-
mation about EBB from B in the late 1870s. B's testy responses and re-
fusals are found in Hood (169, 188-89, 210-11, 257), and he character-
ized his continuing displeasure with Ingram and all others who wanted
to pry into EBB's private life in numerous letters to her brother George
(Landis and Freeman, 304-6, 308-9, 312-14, 324, 327-28). Ingram did
not take kindly to B's corrections in this note, and an exchange of let-
ters in the *Athenæum* followed. In 1888, Ingram expanded his "Memoir"
into the first book-length biography of EBB; B later said that this book
proved Ingram was "simply a literary *hack—bound* to get a livelihood by
scribbling" (Landis and Freeman, 327; see also S. Donaldson, *EBB: An
Annotated Bibliography . . . 1826-1990* [New York, 1993], items 1887:1,
1887:11, 1888:4, 1888:9, 1888:10, 1888:11).

The collection to which B added this note seems to have been put
together on short notice. Infuriated by Ingram's "shameful reprint" of
"all the juvenile and immature poems she was so anxious to suppress,"
B wrote in November 1887: "All I can think of doing is to bring out a
complete edition, in a cheaper form [than Ingram's] and add a few
notes, to give it distinction. This will keep the copyright in our hands
so far" (Landis and Freeman, 308-9). Whether or not this was the gene-
sis of the 1887 "little edition," as B called it (Hood, 278), B rushed his
corrective note to Smith, who inserted it into the new *Poems.* T. J. Wise
stated that not all copies of the 1887 *Poems* contained B's "Prefatory
Note," an assertion repeated in the British Museum Catalogue. The
note was, however, often reprinted in later editions on both sides of
the Atlantic.

POETICAL WORKS (1888-89)

Publication]   In the late autumn of 1887, B began to prepare the final
edition of his poems. Using a copy of the old six-volume collected edi-

tion (probably a late impression of the 1870 plates as corrected in 1875) and individual editions of his publications since 1868, he carefully corrected his texts again. (For more detailed treatments of the creation of the *Poetical Works* of 1888-89, see the Preface, Section III, and the articles cited therein.) By mid-January 1888 he was far enough along that Smith, Elder announced the "new and uniform edition" in the *Athenaeum*, and the first volume was published on 26 April. The rest of the sixteen volumes followed at roughly one-month intervals, the last appearing on 27 July 1889. The first eight volumes of this first impression bore the date 1888 on the title-page; from Volume IX (published 21 December 1888) onward the title-pages were dated 1889.

Smith, Elder ordered 3000 copies of each volume, but well before the last volume appeared, some of the earlier ones were sold out. As was his habit, B seized the opportunity of a second impression to make some minor corrections; he got through *The Ring and the Book* (Volume X) before leaving for Italy in August 1889. The corrections were made to the stereotype plates of the edition, and the second and later impressions from these plates (all dated 1889 on their title-pages) show that B's instructions were closely followed. The plates remained in use for many years, however, and some of the poet's corrections disappeared in late copies.

In 1894, five years after B's death, Smith, Elder added a seventeenth volume; it contained *Asolando*, two indices to the edition, and 153 pages of annotations that are close enough in style to the *Browning Cyclopedia* to suggest that Edward Berdoe was their compiler. F. G. Kenyon's assemblage of materials sold at Sotheby's in 1913, entitled *New Poems by Robert Browning and Elizabeth Barrett Browning*, was published in 1914 by Smith, Elder in a size and binding matching that of *The Poetical Works*, completing the set as it is sometimes found today.

Illustrations]   The engraved illustrations that grace several volumes of 1888-89 include the following:
Volume III: Beard's 1835 sketch of B. The original pen-and-ink drawing is in the National Portrait Gallery, London. A different engraving of the portrait appeared in *The New Spirit of the Age* (1844), a miscellany edited by R. H. Horne. Horne was a friend to both B and EBB, and both poets assisted him in his editorial work. The engraving of the Beard sketch was the first image of B that EBB ever saw; she discussed her unfavorable opinion of it in a letter to B during their courtship. Thus the picture, whatever its faults, had special standing with B in later years (Kintner, 306; the engraved image is reproduced in Kintner, 307).

Volume VII: Talfourd's 1859 portrait of B. The original chalk drawing by Field Talfourd (*Reconstruction*, G20) is now in the National Portrait Gallery, London. The image is reproduced (as are the others discussed here) in G. E. Wilson, *Robert Browning's Portraits, Photographs, and Other Likenesses* . . . (Waco, 1943).

Volume VIII: coin bearing the image of Pope Innocent XII. It is likely that B owned this coin, which pictures the speaker of Book X of *The Ring and the Book.* A silver Italian *scudo* of 1696 like that illustrated in 1888-89 went through the Browning sale in 1913 (*Reconstruction*, H648). The engraved image is reproduced in this edition (Vol. 7, [3]).

Volume X: drawing of Guido Franceschini. B owned this drawing of the speaker of Books V and XI of *The Ring and the Book*, which was said to have been done on the day of Guido's execution in 1698. The original (*Reconstruction*, H133) is now at Balliol College, Oxford.

Volume XVI: R. W. B. Browning's 1882 portrait of B. The original oil painting by B's son (*Reconstruction*, K33) is now in the Armstrong Browning Library, Baylor University; the image is reproduced as the frontispiece to Vol. 15 of this edition.

B's footnote]   Two matters in the note B placed at the beginning of Vol. 1 of 1888-89 require comment. First, his implication that *Pauline* (an "eyesore" endured for "twenty years") finally had a little light revision is misleading. When B decided on a sudden impulse in February, 1888 to rework *Pauline*, he created essentially a second version of that problematic poem (see the variant listings and notes in Vol. 1 of this edition).

Second, B's desire to maintain a chronological arrangement of his works, an aim fulfilled by the present edition, was not well met in 1888-89. Indeed it could not be, given B's own rearrangement of his poems under his several categories in 1863 (see the discussions of *Dramatic Lyrics*, *Dramatic Romances and Lyrics*, and *Men and Women* in Vols. 3-6 of this edition). Poetic and dramatic efforts of the 1830s, 40s, 50s, and 60s were freely mixed together in the first seven volumes of 1888-89; things are slightly more historically sound from *The Ring and the Book* onward, but *The Inn Album, Aristophanes' Apology, Pacchiarotto*, and other late works have wandered from their proper positions. And though such juxtapositions as that of *Aristophanes' Apology* and *The Agamemnon of Aeschylus* in Vol. 13 are intriguing, it is doubtful whether there was any principle of sequence operating beyond "the prescribed size of each volume."